Marxist Sociology in Action

Marxist Sociology in Action

A Sociological Critique of the Marxist Approach to Industrial Relations

J. A. BANKS

FABER AND FABER
London

First published in 1970
by Faber and Faber Limited
24 Russell Square London WC1
Printed in Great Britain by
Latimer Trend & Co Ltd Plymouth

ISBN 0 571 09418 X

CONTENTS

CONTENTS

Part One

THE MARXIST ANALYSIS

I

POINT OF DEPARTURE

Who reads Vilfredo Pareto today? Yet, in 1937 when Talcott Parsons first published *The Structure of Social Action*, he thought fit to base the greater part of his exposition on the writings of Pareto, Durkheim and Weber; and it seemed reasonable to him to agree with Sorokin that these three, and these three alone, were the most important of 'recent sociologists'.[1] Of an older generation only Alfred Marshall was thought to warrant a chapter to himself, and the work of Karl Marx was compressed into two small sections.[2] Since that time, however, *The Mind and Society* has largely disappeared from the reading lists of University courses in sociological theory, at least in Britain, and it is Marx rather than Pareto who now shares, with Durkheim and Weber, the central place in the curriculum. No one, that is to say, who set out to repeat Parsons' exercise by examining the major theoretical preoccupations of modern sociologists, could afford to ignore the marked revival of interest in the original work of Marx and Engels which has occurred over the past twenty years.

Such quickened attention no doubt has its source, at all events with some sociologists, in a desire to understand the frame of mind of the contemporary rulers of the U.S.S.R. and China. Just as Fascism was believed to be exemplified in all its simplicity in the doctrines of *The Mind and Society*, so it is thought that the Communist ideology is most readily apprehended through a careful scrutiny of its sacred books. After all, the education of

[1] Talcott Parsons, *The Structure of Social Action*, 2nd edition, Free Press, 1949, p. 14, n. 2.
[2] Ibid., pp. 107-10, 488-95.

Communist leaders and of those of their followers who seem destined to replace them in the last quarter of the twentieth century, has been permeated through and through with emphasis on the importance of the works of Marx and Engels, and of the commentaries on them produced by Lenin and other prominent figures. To follow along the lines of the same tradition would seem to be a reasonable course for those who wish quickly and economically to master a world outlook which might otherwise prove elusive. However, it is unlikely that a complete explanation of the sociological rediscovery of Marx will be found in methodologically dubious assumptions of this sort. Sociologists, of all people, are only too aware of the dangers of deriving attitudes of mind from a study of documents, divorced from the concrete social situations with which the readers of those documents, as well as their authors, have to deal. The works of Marx, Engels and Lenin can be no more than a very first, and a very rough, approximation to the ideology which dominates so much of the world at the present time. The decline in Fascism and the rise of Communism as systems of ideas, that is to say, can have but a small part to play in the substitution of Marx for Pareto as precursor to modern sociology.

A more valid explanation for this substitution arises, it would seem, from developments within the subject itself. In recent years sociologists have become dissatisfied with conceptualizations of the equilibrium variety, and have cast about for some other type of formulation which might further their comprehension of massive historical events. Impressed by the evident fact that all about them societies are currently experiencing rapid social change, they have become impatient with the dominant preoccupations of their more 'scientifically-minded' colleagues, especially in America, who seem content to postpone the understanding of how societies change until more has been learned of the minutiae of how they work. Structural-functional analysis in particular has been singled out for attack because of the slowness of its adherents to apply its conceptual apparatus to the more urgent problems of our time;[1] and in

[1] Ralf Dahrendorf, 'Toward a Theory of Social Conflict', *Journal of Conflict Resolution*, Vol. 11, 1958, pp. 170–83, reprinted in Amitai Etzioni and Ena Etzioni, eds. *Social Change: Sources, Patterns, and Consequences*, Basic Books 1964, pp. 98–111. Irving L. Horowitz, 'Consensus, Conflict and Co-opera-

turning away from the emphasis on societies as examples of 'going concerns', it is perhaps understandable why sociologists have turned to the Marxist rather to any of the other consistent systems of ideas, which have also been developed to account for historical periods, both of comparative quiescence and of revolutionary upheaval. Neither the 'evolutionary gradualism' of L. T. Hobhouse nor the 'challenge-and-response-cyclism' of Arnold Toynbee seems to possess the same kind of predictive power as the 'scientific historicism' of Marx and Lenin; and this is also true of the serial succession of 'foxes' and 'lions' in Pareto's scheme of history. Max Weber's historical and comparative work, linking culture, especially religious belief, and economics together with a multi-factor account of social change, has been seen by some sociologists as a viable alternative to Marxism; but even Weber was profoundly influenced by Marx and indeed has been claimed to have become a sociologist in consequence of 'a long and intense dialogue with the ghost of Karl Marx'[1]; so that the sociologist who makes use of him is obliged to consider what there is about his approach in this respect which makes it different from any of the other revisions of the Marxist conception of history.

Nevertheless, while the reasons for a revival of interest in Marxism seem obvious enough, what is not so clear is why contemporary sociologists have taken this step in a largely scholastic, rather than in a scientific manner. Marx's own contribution, to be sure—to say nothing of his disciples—has not always been quite so free from ambiguity as it might have been, so that some conceptional discussion is inevitable in any attempt to make use of it. But why should a sociologist believe that textual criticism exhausts his part in the matter? Indeed, to ascertain meticulously what Marx really meant is of peripheral scientific value to anyone. Or again, since Marx died in 1883, empirical data have accumulated which raise serious doubts about the

tion: a Sociological Inventory', *Social Forces*, Vol. 41, 1962—3, pp. 177–88. Lewis A. Coser, 'Karl Marx and Contemporary Sociology' in his *Continuities in the Study of Social Conflict*, Free Press, 1967, pp. 140–3, 147–51.

[1] A. Salomon, 'German Sociology' in Georges Gurvitch and W. E. Moore, *Twentieth Century Sociology*, Philosophical Library, 1945, p. 596. For detailed examination of this claim see Irving M. Zeitlin, *Ideology and the Development of Sociological Theory*, Prentice-Hall, 1968, Ch. 11, *passim*.

validity of some of the propositions which Marx himself seemed to believe were deducible from the more general principles of his system. But why should it be thought that this necessarily implies that the whole system should be jettisoned? Or alternatively, why regard it as so sacrosanct that the uncomfortable facts must be denied or explained away? If sociologists were genuinely concerned to employ Marx's contribution scientifically, they would surely be busy amending its body of propositions to take account of incompatible data, and hence be seeking to build a more satisfactory set of hypotheses to account for social change.

The history of the last twenty years, it would appear, has presented the sorry spectacle that, in the confrontation of sociology with Marxism, ideological issues have come to dominate what purports to be a serious scientific discussion; and instead of treating the ideas of Marx, Engels, Lenin and others, as so many hypotheses, open to modification as knowledge advances, sociologists have allowed themselves to become involved in a political controversy, dividing along the lines of commitment to, or hostility against, a dogma. While this is not the place to consider why this has occurred, nor to examine the extent to which Marx himself was largely responsible for establishing the ideological mode of approach to his work, it is important to recognise what has in fact happened in order to contrast it with an alternative procedure, more consonant with theory construction in scientific disciplines generally.

Such an alternative takes its point of departure from the assertion that a genuine theory is properly to be conceived as 'a deductive system in which observable consequences logically follow from the conjunction of observed facts with the set of fundamental hypotheses of the system'.[1] To the degree that this is understood, it should be clear that the investigation of Marx's ideas should have taken the form first of identifying the set of hypotheses which constitutes his system of thinking and then of specifying the consequences which are to be observed. Thereafter, in so far as some of the observations actually made would presumably have differed from what had been logically predicted, some amendment would have been made to the

---

[1] Richard B. Braithwaite, *Scientific Explanation, a Study of the Function of Theory, Probability and Law in Science*, Harper Torchbooks, 1960, p. 22.

system of hypotheses in its original form. By this time, eighty years after the death of Marx, it is to be expected that the 'theory' would have been modified beyond all recognition, even if the name of Marx were still attached to it in his honour, as a great pioneer, just as the name of Darwin is still associated with evolutionary theories in biology.

Of course, it is a permanent feature of the theoretical development of any science that the process of amending hypotheses is carried on in an atmosphere of debate. Because hypotheses are usually linked together in an explanatory system, any single one which is contradicted by evidence may nearly always be retained if the supporting hypotheses are amended,[1] but since this involves an element of personal judgement about which procedure to follow, scholars will differ over the kind of modifications which should be made. For this reason, it is likely that, in addition to the ideological overtones of sacrilege which have always accompanied what is usually referred to as 'revisionism' amongst Marxists, there have also occurred genuine differences of opinion over the scientific implications of proposals to revise. The problem facing the sociologist who is genuinely concerned to make proper scientific use of the great mass of Marxist and anti-Marxist literature, is how to distinguish between what is at best little more than ideology and what is valid discussion of the implications of discordant facts.

Moreover, it seems incontrovertible that truly scientific debates over Marxism have their origin in the undoubtedly impressive intellectual structure which Marx himself employed in his analysis, ranging from generalisations about social behaviour, largely independent of historical epoch, to those which were understood to be strictly relative to a given place and time. This means that the scientifically-minded sociologist has always to decide where to lay the emphasis in any bid to improve. For example, what kind of revision to the Marxist analysis is he to make to take account of the evidence that the course of real wages in Britain since the end of the nineteenth century has not corresponded with the prediction that as capitalism develops poverty increases? One amendment might replace the purely economic basis of class conflict by one of the other

---

[1] Ibid., pp. 19–20.

features of industrial employment, considered by Marx to be an ingredient in the development of class consciousness amongst the proletariat. Real wages may rise, so runs the argument, but workers become mere automata, fitting like cogs into a machine over which they have no control, and it is this progressive alienation from the processes of production which intensifies class conflict over time. However, the sociologist who accepts this amendment should recognize that it comprises, not merely a revision of the Marxist conception of industrial relations under capitalism, but a modification of the general Marxist notion of social change as applied to all periods of history. The emphasis is now laid, that is to say, on psychological rather than on economic deprivation as the root cause of revolutionary upheaval. A less drastic alternative might therefore be preferred which would leave untouched the basic notion of economic conflict between those who rule and those who are subject to that rule, and hence to amend the special hypotheses which Marx developed in his analysis of capitalism. From this point of view, a rise in real wages in a single country may be accounted for in terms of the conflict being translated from the national to the international sphere as capitalism turns imperialistic. The workers at home, that is to say, benefit from the exploitation of those abroad. Thus, two very different modifications of the Marxist system of ideas may be proposed to meet the case of a single set of data running contrary to what may be deduced from the original and unmodified system. It is for this reason that the sociologist who is concerned to test Marxism empirically, needs to examine it conceptually in order to know what any form of amendment implies.

In what follows an attempt is made to outline these two levels of generality in more detail for the purpose of developing predictions about the behaviour, and attitude of mind, of the participants in what are usually referred to as industrial relations. This means that the special Marxist notions of feudalism, slavery, and so forth, are ignored. Of course, it is recognised that careful empirical investigation of the implications of such notions might lead, in the long run, to such a modification of the general Marxist notion of social change that the special notion of capitalism, and with it the even more specific Marxist notion of collective bargaining under capitalism, might be seriously affected. But, until such time as sociologists undertake the necessary scientific labour which is required for dealing precisely with more remote historical data, it will suffice to concentrate on those aspects of the Marxist system which for the present purpose seem most directly relevant to the understanding of industrial relations today.

Proceeding, therefore, in logical order from the most general to the least, the next chapter begins by clarifying the processes which Marx believed to be characteristic of social change in all periods of history. These constitute the broadest social hypotheses in the Marxist system. The next step is to introduce the special conditions which distinguish one epoch from another, or in the present instance, which characterize the single epoch, capitalism. This is the task of Chapter Three. At this point, the Marxist system is still some way from the empirical evidence. Hence, a further step is necessary, the conversion of the processes of social change under capitalism into recognizable relationships between broad classes of people—employers and employees—as these demonstrate themselves in organized movements, such as trade unions. This is attempted in Chapter Four. As will be seen later, this does not exhaust the process of clarification, since the empirical verification or falsification of hypotheses reached at this level still requires their conversion into propositions which are, at least in principle, open to such empirical test. This means that many other deductions from the Marxist system of ideas, such as the relationship between husband and wife under capitalism, must perforce be ignored; but it cannot be too often repeated that genuine scientific research is never applied in a single instance to the whole of a theoretical apparatus. The work of validation proceeds piecemeal.

Sociologists will, of course, be aware that the Marxist approach to industrial relations, or to social change generally for that matter, is not confined to intellectual appreciation merely. It comprises also an evaluative assessment of what is and what may be, and a vigorous programme for action. Taking Marx's eleventh 'thesis' on Fuerbach as a kind of categorical imperative, his followers have set out, not simply to understand the world but to change it, and they have pointed to the successes of the Communist Parties of the world as support for the truth of their position.[1] If Marx was correct, they seem to have implied, this is precisely what we should have expected to happen. Doubtless it is true that active Marxists have regularly underestimated the logical complexities hidden behind the language of Marx's second 'thesis'—that men must prove the truth of their thinking in practice—and they have regularly committed the logical fallacy of affirming the consequent, assuming that because Communist revolutions have occurred, Marx must have been correct. Indeed, they have been so sure of their position that they have swept aside as irrelevant and derisive any proffer of alternative hypotheses to account for the rise of Communists to power and for the subsequent dictatorship of the 'proletariat' in those countries where this has happened. Nevertheless, the sociologist should notice that this propensity to preserve the predictive power of the dogma intact, while scientifically suspect, has had the empirical consequence that Communists have been inspired to follow a policy of militant activism amongst trade unionists and in the field of industrial relations generally. Such a programme of action may quite legitimately be termed 'the Marxist approach to industrial relations.' It is perhaps hardly necessary to add that although the empirical fact behind this meaning of the expression is an essential part of any investigation into the validity of the Marxist intellectual position, it is of itself not what is referred to by the sub-title of this study. The intention, here, is unreservedly to draw attention to the possible contribution of Marxist thinking to the development of truly scientific theory in sociology. The presumption of the author is that these chapters will be read with this intention in mind.

[1] See, for example, Otto V. Kuusinen, ed. *Fundamentals of Marxism Leninism*, Foreign Languages Publishing House, 1961, pp. 18–19, 181, etc.

2

SOCIAL CHANGE

According to Engels' assessment of the work of his colleague, Marx was responsible for 'two great discoveries, the materialist conception of history and the revelation of the secret of capitalist production by means of surplus labour'.[1] As will become apparent later, the second of these discoveries needs special interpretation since the term 'surplus labour' was used by Marx in connection with all periods of history and not with his own times merely. Nevertheless, as compared with the relatively little he had to write about other types of society, the three large volumes of *Capital* bear witness to their author's deep absorption with the mechanisms of capitalism, so that there is justification for separating out Marx's analysis of that system for special mention. At the same time, because this analysis of capitalism depends in part on logical deductions from the more general Marxist notion of social change, consideration of its nature may reasonably be postponed in order that the materialist conception of history—'doubtless one of the greatest individual achievements of sociology to this day'[2]—may first be outlined and discussed.

Of course, it is true to say that in his more philosophical moments Marx regarded his conception of history as derivative from an even more general notion of the material nature of the universe. He held that everything, human and non-human,

---

[1] Frederick Engels, *Herr Eugen Dühring's Revolution in Science*, translated by E. Burns, Lawrence and Wishart, 1936, p. 33.

[2] Joseph A. Schumpeter, *Capitalism, Socialism, and Democracy*, Allen and Unwin, 1943, p. 10.

animate and inanimate, demonstrated the same broad features of successive development, and he castigated as defective what he called 'the abstract materialism of natural science, a materialism that excluded history and its processes'.[1] For present purposes, however, it is not necessary to consider the truth or falsity of the Marxist 'dialectic of nature'. Indeed, detailed consideration of the general Marxist notion of social change is required only to the extent that it makes plain what is to be understood by the special Marxist notion of industrial relations under capitalism; for, there is in strict logic no reason why the rest of the Marxist intellectual system could not be false while its application to the contemporary industrial scene provided an explanation which was true. Marx and Engels might be wildly wrong about nature; the materialist conception of history might not satisfactorily account for what happened in Ancient Greece; but what is left of their ideas, modified to limit the field of empirical data to be covered by them, may still be of value to the sociologist concerned with industrial affairs in Britain at the present time.

What is important to note from this point of view is that Marx thought of history as consisting of 'so many epochs in the progress of the economic formation of society'.[2] The notion, that is to say, is linear rather than cyclical, and the movement through time is considered to be marked by ever-growing emancipation on the part of mankind from the constraints of the environment, by ever-increasing human control over it. This movement, to be sure, is not to be thought of as proceeding at a steady pace. There are periods of slow and periods of rapid change, and the latter are especially important because they are to be understood as indicating the advent of progression to a new epoch, to a further level of development. Hence the 'Asiatic, ancient, feudal, and modern bourgeois' epochs listed by Marx differ from one another in terms of some marked features of economic and social life, and transition from one

[1] Karl Marx, *Capital, a Critical Analysis of Capitalist Production*, Vol. I, translated from the third German edition by S. Moore and E. Aveling, and edited by F. Engels, Foreign Languages Publishing House, Moscow, 1959, p. 372, n. 3.
[2] Karl Marx, *A Contribution to the Critique of Political Economy*, translated from the second German edition by N. I. Stone, Kerr, 1904, p. 13.

epoch to the next is held to be accompanied by impressive events in human history.[1]

This should not be taken to imply that Marx believed every epoch to be completely different from the rest. Although each is held to have its dominant characteristics, there survive within it aspects of previous stages; and, similarly, even before the events occur which indicate that the period of transition has arrived, there appear in each epoch aspects of the one to come. Of course, this idea is of some importance in the application of Marxist thinking to industrial relations, since it implies that there will be parts of the economy which are ahead of, and parts which are behind the main level of development in an epoch; and Marx himself had, in this connection, some further things to say on the extent to which the proletariat in more advanced sections of the economy, and in the more advanced countries of the world, assumed the leadership of the working-class movement.[2] This is a point to which it will be necessary to return later. For present purposes what is much more significant about the Marxist conception of development is not that it makes room for irregularities and unevenness, but that the transition from stage to stage is always thought to occur during a period of social and political upheaval, a period of revolution.

Perhaps there is no term in the whole Marxist battery which has given rise to so much violent controversy as the term

[1] George Plekhanov, in his *Fundamental Problems of Marxism*, edited by D. Ryazanov, 1928, translated by E. and C. Paul, Lawrence, n.d., asserted that there was 'reason to believe' that Marx changed his mind, after reading Morgan's *Ancient Society* (1877), and concluded that 'the logic of development of China, or of ancient Egypt, did not lead to the appearance of the classical method of production'. Plekhanov, p. 50. Karl Wittfogel's comment on this point, (*Oriental Despotism*, Yale University Press, 1967, p. 416, note d.), that 'Plekhanov's efforts to correct Marx on this point . . . sought to remove an obstacle that was not there', arose from his conviction that Marx did not view 'progress' as 'actual historical development' but as a measure of the degree of freedom which was enjoyed in these societies, i.e. the difference between them was in terms of a classificatory not a historical scheme. It is not the task of this book to consider this issue in detail but Wittfogel's position should be noted as relevant to the consideration of empirical data in Chapters 10 and 15, especially pp. 142 and 228 below.

[2] Karl Marx and Frederick Engels, *The German Ideology*, Parts I and III edited by R. Pascal, Lawrence and Wishart, 1938, pp. 58 and 73-4.

'revolution'.[1] At its crudest it may be taken to express a tauto-
logy. A revolution is known to have taken place, that is to say,
because the social system at a given point in time is recognized
to be very different from what it was in the previous 'pre-
revolutionary' era. On the other hand, Marx's personal and
intense preoccupation with political issues suggests that he himself saw the transition as taking place through definite political
struggle. In this sense it may be asserted that although economic
changes were held by him to provide the mainspring of action,
human history remained essentially political history. Not until
the new economic relationships had demonstrated their potency
by prompting the 'successful' overthrow of one political regime
and its replacement by another, committed to a very different
economic programme, might it be said that a new historical
epoch has arrived. Yet it does not follow from this that political
struggle in every epoch must inevitably involve civil war or any
large-scale bloodshed. Within the formulation of the general
Marxist conception of history, there is room for many different
kinds of actions which will lead to the political changes which
Marx held to correspond with the transition from one economic
stage to the next.

The term 'revolution' in this context therefore should be
understood as a theoretical term[2] and should not necessarily
be confused with the empirical term 'revolution', which refers to
any violent and drawn-out attempts to over-throw a ruling
group, whether the revolutionaries are associated with a radically
different economic policy or not. From the Marxist point of
view, riots and revolts, *coups* and *putsches*, some of them failures,
some of them successes in the eyes of those who participate in
them, will occur long before the change from one historical
period to another takes place. What is important is not that
power changes hands, but that the social system which the new
regime regards as legitimate and which it will use force, if

---

[1] George D. H. Cole, *A History of Socialist Thought*, Vol. 3, Part 2, Mac-
Millan, 1956, Ch. 28. Charles Wright Mills, the *Marxists*, Dell, 1962, Ch. 8,
reproduces useful quotations on the subject from Kautsky, Bernstein and
Luxemburg.

[2] Theoretical terms have indirect meaning only. They are to be understood solely in terms of the hypothetical or theoretical system in which they
are used and will be misleading if employed in a different context. See
Braithwaite, op. cit., Ch. 3.

necessary, to maintain, differs structurally from the social system which the previous regime struggled unsuccessfully to protect. Hence any kind of political activity, violent or non-violent, which is designed to result in, or—whether designed or not —actually results in such structural change is, for Marx, 'revolutionary'. Even the *Communist Manifesto*, for example, put forward the winning of 'the battle of democracy' as the first step in the revolution leading from capitalism to socialism.[1]

It is a corollary to this idea that not every political struggle will lead immediately to a successful overthrow of the existing system. There is likely, indeed, to be a fairly long period of 'false-starts' before the revolutionary period properly begins and the change from one historical epoch to another takes place. This occurs, Marx believed, because for some time men find themselves in conflict without quite understanding why they should be. The political struggles of the pre-revolutionary periods, that is to say, are taken to indicate the growing awareness on the part of those engaged in them that there is no way out of the conflict save the destruction of the old order and the creation of the new; and this awareness is to a smaller or greater extent a recognition of what the struggle is about. Towards the end of an epoch political conflict gradually comes to be seen in its true nature as a struggle for power between social classes, which previously were in conflict over economic issues without necessarily realising that such conflict is an inevitable outcome of the structure of society.[2]

Some individuals indeed, even at this late hour, suffer from 'false' class consciousness, believing themselves to have different class interests from what is in fact the case, although generally speaking, one consequence of the political struggles towards the end of an epoch is that people come to learn the true nature of the economic conflicts in which they are engaged. The Marxist conception of history also implies that because the whole process is progressive, each successive revolutionary phase contains not only growing consciousness of the political

[1] Karl Marx and Frederick Engels, *Selected Works in Two Volumes*, Foreign Languages Publishing House, Moscow, and Lawrence and Wishart, 1950, Vol. 1, p. 50.
[2] Karl Marx, *The Poverty of Philosophy*, Foreign Languages Publishing House, Moscow, and Lawrence and Wishart, n.d. (1955?), p. 137.

and economic class structure of that epoch, but accumulated understanding of the process itself. The kind of knowledge about political economy, for example, which had been denied to the Greeks was an open book to the capitalist bourgeoisie;[1] and Marx believed that in his time it was possible for the proletariat to gain an understanding of the general nature of history. The revolutionary overthrow of capitalism, he thought, would lead to a classless society because in the process of conducting the struggle the proletariat would 'succeed in ridding itself of all the muck of ages and become fitted to found society anew'.[2]

Of course, it is a logical outcome of the general Marxist notion of social change that this knowledge would be obtained at some point in human history. Because the underlying idea is of a progressive sequence of epochs, it allows for new forms of thinking and behaviour at different points in the process. Hence, although in point of fact there is nothing in his more general notion of history which makes it possible to decide in which epoch real understanding of the nature of social life would appear, Marx was convinced that there were certain features of capitalism which made it inevitable that the class consciousness of the proletariat might be said to be 'the ideology to end all ideologies'.[3] Nevertheless it should be clearly understood that even for the revolutionary period marking the transition from capitalism to the next epoch, the driving force behind change is to be sought for not in sociological sophistication, but in man's growing control over his material and social environment. Whatever knowledge of society was possessed by human beings at any period of time was determined, Marx believed, by the kind of experiences of economic and social relationships which they had. This is the meaning behind his epigrammatic assertion, 'it is not the consciousness of men that determines their existence, but on the contrary, their social existence that determines their consciousness'.[4]

The problem of seeking to understand the processes of social

[1] Marx, *Contribution to the Critique*, op. cit., pp. 300–1.
[2] Marx and Engels, *The German Ideology*, op. cit., p. 69.
[3] Alfred G. Meyer, *Marxism, the Unity of Theory and Practice*, Harvard University Press, 1954, p. 96.
[4] Marx, *Contribution to the Critique*, op. cit., p. 11.

change becomes, accordingly, that of accounting for those modifications which occur in this social existence. Or, more precisely, since Marx regarded this as dependent upon the economic structure of society—('the real foundation, on which rise legal and political superstructures and to which correspond definite forms of social consciousness')—explanation of massive historical events is to be sought for in economic change. By asserting that 'the mode of production in material life determines the general character of the social, political and spiritual processes of life' he intended deliberately to draw attention to the importance of changes in that 'mode of production' as the driving force behind history; and the mode of production itself was held to consist of 'the existing relations of production' especially in so far as they are influenced by 'the material forces of production in society'.[1]

If, then, it is accepted that for Marx 'all struggles within the State, the struggle between democracy, aristocracy and monarchy, the struggle for the franchise, etc., are merely the illusory forms in which the real struggles of the different classes are fought out amongst one another',[2] it is to 'the relations of production' that the sociologist must turn if he would discover the basis of class conflict; and it is 'the material forces of production' which he must examine if he would learn how class conflict eventually becomes translated into revolution. Both refer to theoretical concepts, comprehensible only by virtue of their place in the Marxist deductive system, and because Marx and Engels were not concerned to work out their ideas in a formal logical framework, both expressions have presented difficulties to later commentators. Meyer, for example, sees difficulties in the expression, 'the forces of production',[3] while Plamenatz is perplexed by 'relations of production'.[4] Perhaps the most obvious line to take is to argue that since for Marx all production takes place in a social context,[5] the expression 'relations of production' as used by him in the Preface to the

[1] Ibid., pp. 11 and 12.
[2] Marx and Engels, *The German Ideology*, op. cit., p. 23.
[3] Meyer, op. cit., pp. 17–18.
[4] John Plamenatz, *German Marxism and Russian Communism*, Longmans, Green, 1954, pp. 21–8, 35, 51–2, 59, 67–8, 70, 108–9. See also the second thoughts in his *Man and Society*, Longmans, Vol. 2, 1963, pp. 279–83.
[5] Marx, *Contribution to the Critique*, op. cit., pp. 265–8.

Contribution ot the Critique of Political Economy in 1859 represented no significant change in thought from the way in which in 1847 he had described production as co-operation. Similarly, the expression 'material forces of production' of 1859 might be taken as equivalent to the 'means of production' and 'instruments' which in 1847 were held to determine everything else.[1]

Indeed, in this first attempt by Marx to meet the charge that up to that time he had nowhere analysed 'the economic relations which constitute the material foundation of the present class struggles and national struggles',[2] there is a great deal of support for the view that he was a technological determinist, but even in *Wage Labour and Capital* there are passages which will not bear out this interpretation and the whole of the emphasis in the Marxist notion of social change on the over-riding significance of the class struggle, suggests that amongst all those relations which exist between producers in a co-operative system, certain of them—the class relations—are more important historically speaking, than the rest. The alternative approach,[3] therefore, which is favoured here, is to interpret 'relations of production' in a rather more restricted sense than is implied by *Wage Labour and Capital*, the sense which appears to be contained in the assertion that 'at a certain stage of their development, the material forces of production come in conflict with the existing relations of production, or—what is but a legal expression for the same thing—with the property relations within which they had been at work before. From forms of development of the forces of production these relations turn into their fetters. Then comes the period of social revolution. . . .'[4]

Such an interpretation, to be sure, in spite of Marx's repeated reference to the private ownership of the means of production, should not be taken to mean that empirically speaking the conflicting classes are to be identified simply in terms of property ownership, or even in terms of ownership of the means

[1] Karl Marx, *Wage Labour and Capital*, reprinted in Marx and Engels, *Selected Works*, op. cit., Vol. 1, pp. 83–4. This, incidentally, is the interpretation favoured by Harry B. Acton in his *The Illusion of the Epoch; Marxism-Leninism as a Philosophical Creed*, Cohen and West, 1955, pp. 137–8 and 159–68.

[2] Marx, *Wage Labour and Capital*, op. cit., p. 74.

[3] Kuusinen, op. cit., pp. 146–8. Meyer, op. cit., pp. 19–20.

[4] Marx, *Contribution to the Critique*, op. cit., p. 12.

of production. On the contrary, according to Marx, property relations are 'nothing but a metaphysical or juristic illusion' except in so far as they are seen in terms of the underlying class relations—the relations of production.[1] Hence, the 'history of all hitherto existing society', the 'history of class struggles', the history of 'freeman and slave, patrician and plebeian, lord and serf, guildmaster and journeyman, in a word, oppressor and oppressed,' is to be seen not simply as a history of conflict between property owners and the propertyless, as such, but as an inevitable consequence of the division of society along the lines of a relationship in which the products of one class are appropriated, at least in part, by the other. In brief, however exploitation is achieved, whether through force or through socially approved methods of legal justification, the distinction between social classes is to be drawn along the lines of the manner in which the products of labour are distributed.

Indeed, for the purpose of making this distinction clear, Marx differentiated between 'necessary labour', the labour which a man must undertake in order to continue to exist and to rear his progeny, and 'surplus labour', the labour which he undertakes for some other person and his progeny; and he concluded, 'the essential difference between the various economic forms of society, between, for instance, a society based on slave-labour and one based on wage-labour, lies only in the mode in which this surplus-labour is in each case extracted from the actual producer, the labourer'.[2] Clearly, this conception makes more sense of the notion of class conflict than reference to mere property ownership as such, since for any given amount of the products of labour, the more that is appropriated as surplus labour, the less there remains to meet the needs of the labourer, and vice versa. Hence, from the point of view of this conception, economic conflict is inherent in the relationship between the labourer and whoever in fact is able to direct his activities.

This meaning of the expression 'relations of production'

[1] Marx, letter to P. V. Annenkov, 28th December 1846, reprinted in Marx and Engels, *Selected Works*, op. cit., Vol. 2, p. 404.
[2] Marx, *Capital*, op. cit., Vol. 1, p. 217. See also Karl Marx, *Wages, Price and Profit*, reprinted in Marx and Engels, *Selected Works*, op. cit., Vol. 1, p. 389.

implies also that all the relationships which labourers have *with other labourers* in a co-operative system must be seen as part of the 'material forces of production'. There is no special difficulty about this, unless the term, 'material' is interpreted in a rigidly non-human, non-animate,—that is non-Marxist—fashion. Labour for Marx was a material activity, and the division of labour and the co-operation which is a corollary of such a division was, for him, a material, productive force.[1] Hence, if he was a technological determinist, it was in a very unusual sense of the term, 'technological'; for he saw a reciprocal relationship at work between developments in the instruments of production and developments in the division of labour. 'That is why,' he wrote, 'every big mechanical invention is followed by a greater division of labour, and each increase in the division of labour gives rise in turn to new mechanical inventions'.[2] Capitalism's most outstanding achievement in this sphere, the creation of the factory system, was a case in point. 'So soon as the different operations of a labour-process are disconnected the one from the other, and each fractional operation acquires in the hands of the detail labourer a suitable and peculiar form, alterations become necessary in the implements that previously served more than one purpose. . . . The manufacturing period simplifies, improves and multiplies the implements of labour, by adapting them to the exclusively special functions of each detail labourer. It thus creates at the same time one of the material conditions of the existence of machinery, which consists of a combination of simple instruments'.[3] Unless the term 'technology' is understood to cover, not only 'tools' and 'machines' and the knowledge of how to use them, but also the economic, social and psychological techniques which are employed in the production of goods and in the appropriation of surplus labour by the ruling class, the idea that Marx 'undertook to base all the major developments of history and economic life upon technological change'[4] is in-

[1] Marx, *Capital*, op. cit., Vol. I, p. 386.
[2] Marx, *The Poverty of Philosophy*, op. cit., p. 156.
[3] Marx, *Capital*, op. cit., Vol. I, pp. 341-2.
[4] S. C. Gilfillan, 'Social Implications of Technical Advance', *Current Sociology*, Vol. I, no. 4, 1953, p. 193. The looser formulations of Engels might however be open to this objection. See, for example, his *Anti-Dühring*, op. cit., pp. 303-5.

correct. He was an economic determinist, as this expression is usually understood, not a technological one.

It is nevertheless true that the use of the term, 'determinist' in this context is likely to be misunderstood; and indeed there has been a regular trend in discussion over the Marxist system of ideas to interpret it as equivalent to the belief that human beings are no more than puppets, incapable of exercising their wills in the face of the inexorable succession of events. From this point of view, Marx's own active, propagandist and political career, to say nothing of the efforts of so many of his followers, would appear to be yet another instance of the inconsistency of prophets and millenarians. The alternative can only be to think of 'determinism' as in some sense divorced from its companion term, 'free-will', and as compatible with the clear conviction that social change can be brought about, consciously, by individuals who understand the nature of social change and who have scientific knowledge of the workings of society. This is the position of those who like Marx himself are convinced that the body of concepts to which he gave his name is scientific; and it is justified on the ground that the understanding which comes from science, far from being enervating, is in fact liberating. Just as knowledge of the laws of nature, deemed in the nineteenth century to be deterministic, enables men to act in new ways by controlling their natural environment in a fashion not open to their predecessors, so it is believed that a knowledge of the processes of social change will provide mankind with powers which will realise, not thwart, the human will. Science, from this alternative point of view, is said to break with the past. 'It escapes from the iron circle of habit, instinct, the endless repetition of old methods, the iron determinism of an external nature that we do not understand'.[1]

At the same time, such knowledge as science can give does not mean that men become free to act in any way they choose. They can achieve results solely within the framework of constraints set by an environment which can only be controlled in

[1] John Lewis, *Marxism and the Open Mind*, Routledge & Kegan Paul, 1957, p. 36. The whole of this chapter on 'Historical Inevitability' may be read with profit in this context. See also Meyer, op. cit., pp. 3-11, and Alexander D. Lindsay, *Karl Marx's Capital, an Introductory Essay*, Oxford University Press, 1925, Ch. 2.

terms of instruments created out of it. In the social sphere this is the meaning of the expression that 'men make their own history; but they do not make it just as they please'. The historical emphasis in the Marxist analysis means that 'they do not make it under circumstances chosen by themselves, but under circumstances directly encountered, given and transmitted from the past'.[1] Hence, in spite of the obviously contradictory assertions in *Capital* about 'tendencies working with iron necessity towards inevitable results'[2]—a heritage of nineteenth-century terminology about the nature of science—'economic determinism' must be interpreted as a statement of what these circumstances entail, namely that change can be brought about only through the mechanism of class conflict intensified by the constant stream of technical and economic devices which men invent. It is important to emphasize this last point because of the danger in the formulation of the materialist conception of history which Marx produced for the Preface to the *Critique of Political Economy*, in 1859, that *all* ideas are to be regarded as 'reflections' of economic activity. Labour, indeed, held a very special meaning for him, as a process which distinguished man from animals. 'A spider', he wrote, 'conducts operations that resemble those of a weaver, and a bee puts to shame many an architect in the construction of her cells. But what distinguishes the worst architect from the best bees is this, that he raises his structure in imagination before he erects it in reality. At the end of every labour-process, we get a result that already existed in the imagination of the labourer at its commencement'.[3] Ideas, in this sense, clearly operate as a driving force behind human action and as an impelling force behind social change inasmuch as they may be converted as a matter of fact into new, and more efficient, ways of producing goods. What Marx had in mind, apparently, was a continuous process of interaction between ideas and their manifestation in human attempts to control the environment. Men are constantly on the search for something new. They succeed to the extent that their ideas are consonant with the nature of the materials, human and

[1] Karl Marx, *The Eighteenth Brumaire of Louis Bonaparte*, in Marx and Engels, *Selected Works*, op. cit., Vol. I, p. 225.
[2] Marx, *Capital*, op. cit., Preface to Vol. 1, p. 8.
[3] Ibid., p. 178.

non-human, animate and inanimate, which they employ for the purpose. Marx was quite aware, of course, that men also have fantasies, illusions, visions, dreams, but these he regarded as ineffective to bring about social change, except to the degree that some part of them corresponds to what is in fact the case.

The form taken by the general Marxist notion of social change, which has emerged from this account, should by now be reasonably clear. Historical epochs, at least for the period which is relevant for understanding industrial relations in contemporary Britain, are distinguished one from another most clearly by the different ways in which surplus labour is extorted. When an epoch opens, this relationship of exploitation between the classes is a liberating one. It leads to the development of new and more efficient ways of producing goods, to new social relationships, and to new ideas in philosophy, religion, art and politics. But, thought Marx, there comes a time when this no longer holds. The technological and economic forms which the class relationships have created, together with the drive towards technical and economic invention which they have released, 'come into conflict' with those relations.

How this occurs is not explained in the general notion of social change, other than in the language of the Hegelian metaphysic, 'turned right side up again';[1] although it does seem clear that one of the features which Marx had in mind was the fact that towards the end of an epoch, experiments in economic organization emerge which depend upon a different method for appropriating surplus labour than that which dominates the epoch. Thus, formally free wage-labourers employed by embryonic capitalists appear under feudalism,[2] and a classless system of factory production, the co-operative factories,[3] under capitalism. At the same time, class conflict between labourers and those who extort surplus labour from them is intensified as a result of this other 'conflict' between the relations of production and the forces of production. To begin with, such class conflict is economic in form—a clash of economic interests—but it

[1] Marx, 'Afterword to the Second German Edition', *Capital*, op. cit., Vol. 1, p. 20.
[2] Ibid., Vol. I, p. 715.
[3] Karl Marx, 'Inaugural Address of the Working Men's International Association' in Marx and Engels, *Selected Works*, op. cit., Vol. I, pp. 347–8

gradually becomes shifted to the political arena as those involved in the conflict, especially the subject class, develop class consciousness. This leads them to realise that the solution to their difficulties lies in adopting the new system of productive relationships which already exists in their midst. Both serfs and capitalists, that is to say, have an interest in the revolutionary overthrow of feudalism. Both the industrial proletariat and the workers in co-operative enterprises have an interest in the revolutionary destruction of capitalism. What will be put in its place will depend on the stage of history reached by mankind, at the time of revolution.

From the point of view of contemporary sociology all this implies that it is impossible empirically to test the validity of the Marxist hypotheses about the processes of social change without first taking into consideration the special form which each epoch is said to have. This consists essentially of identifying the social classes of the epoch in accordance with the particular type of surplus labour which characterises the economic system of the time. It also entails an examination of the nature of the progressive development in the material forces of production, relevant to that epoch, so that the point at which they become 'fettered' by the relations of production is made plain. In the present context this means that the *special* Marxist notion of capitalism is to be understood only in terms of the application of the *general* Marxist notion of social change to a system of production by legally free wage labourers employed by the owners of capital for profit. What this means in detail is the subject of the next two chapters.

3

CAPITALISM

That the identification of surplus labour under capitalism constituted an intellectual problem of some magnitude was recognized, if not indeed accentuated by Marx, and he pointed in particular to the marked contrast between feudalism and other economic systems in this respect. Since on the feudal manor the organization of the serf's labour was divided into 'labour-time for himself and enforced labour-time for his feudal lord'[1] the distinction between necessary and surplus labour was obvious; and the conflict between the two classes, presumably, could be analysed in terms of attempts by the lords to encroach upon the serfs' own labour-time and of the resistance of such serfs to an increase in the amount of enforced labour extorted from them. Both slavery and the system of wage labour, on the other hand, blurred and confused the distinction, the former because it gave the impression that the labour of the slave was all 'given away for nothing' and the latter because 'on the basis of the wages system even the unpaid labour seems to be *paid* labour.'[2]

It is accordingly one of the major tasks of *Capital* to distinguish between necessary and surplus labour under capitalism as forms of paid and unpaid labour, and to examine the ways in which the conversion of all transactions into monetary terms creates the illusion that the capitalist, as capitalist, performs a function in production quite distinct from the contribution he

[1] Karl Marx, *Capital*, Vol. III, Foreign Languages Publishing House, Moscow, 1960, p. 770.
[2] Marx, *Wages, Price and Profit*, op. cit., p. 389. Italics in the original. See also *Capital*, op. cit., Vol. I, pp. 539–40.

might otherwise make in 'the work of directing, superintending, and adjusting' the co-operative efforts of his employees.[1] For present purposes it does not seem necessary to go into the details of the price mechanism as analyzed by Marx.[2] On the other hand, it is important to notice that in *Capital* he introduced two further theoretical terms into his battery in order to make his general explanatory scheme more readily adaptable to the special intricacies of capitalism. These are the terms, 'absolute' and 'relative', as applied to different ways in which surplus labour may be increased. Of course, both these terms and the ideas behind them could be employed for the analysis of serfdom and slavery, and as a matter of fact Marx made passing reference to these systems when using the terms to examine capitalism, but it was in the study of this last type of society that he made most use of them, demonstrating that their separate impacts on class conflict had rather different consequences.

The concepts themselves are not difficult to understand, provided that Marx's division of a day's labour into necessary and surplus, analytically distinct, parts is comprehended. What Marx had in mind here was the notion that at any moment of history, with the techniques of production and the instruments of labour available at that time, it is reasonable to assume that a fixed and determinable amount of work on the part of the labourer is all that is required to produce sufficient goods for his own needs and to ensure that further labourers with his skill and capacity are produced to replace him when his working days are through.[3] Granted that it is reasonable to assume this, it seems equally reasonable to assume that exploitation may be increased in at least two ways. Either the total amount of time a labourer works may be extended, so that a larger proportion of his time is devoted to the production of goods for his employer, or new techniques and tools may be introduced which reduce the amount of time he takes to produce his means of subsistence so that more time remains to be devoted to surplus labour. In either case the share of the total product going to the exploiter is increased.

---

[1] Marx, *Capital*, op. cit., Vol. 1, pp. 330–2.
[2] For a recent discussion see F. Seton, 'The "Transformation" Problem', *Review of Economic Studies*, Vol. 24, 1956–7, pp. 149–60.
[3] Marx, *Wage Labour and Capital*, op. cit., p. 82.

Surplus labour increased by the former of these two devices
—'the prolongation of the working day'—Marx called 'absolute'
and by the latter—'the curtailment of the necessary labour-
time'— he called, 'relative'.[1] While there are slaves to be easily
obtained, he exclaimed, it is a maxim of slave management, in
slave-importing countries, that the most effective economy is
that which takes out of the human chattel in the shortest space
of time the utmost amount of exertion it is capable of putting
forth'.[2] In this sense an increase in absolute surplus labour was
the obvious device which exploiters made use of when the
occasion afforded, and while there was a surplus population
readily available in the form of 'primitive and physically
uncorrupted elements from the country' it was a maxim of
early factory management to be 'reckless of the health or
length of life of the labourer'.[3] Thus the working day was seen
to contain 'the full twenty-four hours, with the deduction of
the few hours of repose without which labour-power absolutely
refuses its services again'.[4] Nevertheless, by the time *Capital*
was written a limit had been set to the working day, and this
was seen by Marx as the outcome of 'centuries of struggle
between capitalist and labourer.'[5]

During the first four centuries of the capitalist era this struggle
took the form of attempts by capitalist employers to prolong
the working day by statute and compulsion. So long as the
labourers had some alternative source of livelihood, as under
the domestic system of manufacture, the force of economic conditions was insufficient to allow of anything but a slow and
gradual prolongation of the working day.[6] At the end of the
eighteenth century, however, with 'the birth of machinism and
modern industry' there took place 'a violent encroachment
like that of an avalanche in its intensity and extent. All bounds
of morals and nature, age and sex, day and night, were broken
down'; but, 'as soon as the working class, stirred at first by the
noise and turmoil of the new system of production, recovered,

---

[1] Marx, *Capital*, op. cit., Vol. i, p. 315.
[2] Ibid., p. 266.
[3] Ibid., pp. 269–70.
[4] Ibid., p. 264.
[5] Ibid., p. 270.
[6] Ibid., pp. 271–7.

in some measure, its senses, its resistance began.'[1] Capitalism had entered its revolutionary phase.

The immediate outcome of the struggle was the passing of a series of Factory Acts by the English parliament and the establishment of a corps of factory inspectors to ensure that the Acts were implemented. These had the unintended and unanticipated consequence of causing employers to divert their attention from absolute to relative surplus labour and hence to accelerate the industrial revolution which was already proceeding 'spontaneously'. As Marx put it, 'the compulsory regulation of the working day as regards its length, pauses, beginning and end, the system of relays of children, the exclusion of all children under a certain age, etc., necessitate on the one hand more machinery and the substitution of steam as a motive power in the place of muscles. On the other hand, in order to make up for the loss of time, an expansion occurs of the means of production used in common, of the furnaces, buildings, etc., in one word, greater concentration of the means of production and a correspondingly greater concourse of people'.[2]

The general extension of factory legislation, that is to say, 'hastens on the general conversion of numerous isolated small industries into a few combined industries carried on upon a large scale; it therefore accelerates the concentration of capital and the exclusive predominance of the factory system. It destroys both the ancient and the transitional forms, behind which the dominion of capital is still in part concealed, and replaces them by direct and open sway of capital; but thereby it also generalises the direct opposition to this sway. While in each individual workshop it enforces uniformity, regularity, order, and economy, it increases by the immense spur which the limitation and regulation of the working day give to technical improvement, the anarchy and the catastrophes of capitalist production as a whole, the intensity of labour, and the competition of machinery with the labourer. By the destruction of petty and domestic industries it destroys the last resort of the 'redundant population,' and with it the sole remaining safety-valve of the whole social mechanism. By maintaining the material conditions, and the combination on a social scale of the processes of production, it

[1] Ibid., p. 278.
[2] Ibid., pp. 474-5.

matures the contradictions and antagonisms of the capitalist form of production, and thereby provides, along with the elements for the formation of a new society, the forces for exploding the old one'.[1]

The implications of these passages about the conflict over absolute surplus labour, and the successful attempt to limit the working day by legislation should not be misunderstood. Marx does not seem to have believed that it was this conflict which provided the greatest impetus to the revolutionary overthrow of the capitalist order. Parliamentary legislation to limit or reduce the hours of labour was most effective in this respect, only because it forced capitalists to intensify their demand for more relative surplus labour. It hastened their downfall only to the extent that they were able to increase the productivity of the labour they employed, especially in those branches of industry which supplied the necessaries of life or the means of production for such necessaries. Intensification of class conflict to the point of political revolution occurred, he seems to have thought, through the mechanism of successful attempts by capitalists to reduce the proportion of his labour time which the labourer spends on necessary labour. Through technical and organizational advances capitalism develops the seeds of its own destruction.

Historically, Marx traced the process by which the capitalists raised the productivity of the labouring class as passing through a number of stages. He began with co-operation, the organizational technique whereby, irrespective of their tools, the workmen could be induced to produce more without extra effort or longer hours of work. Closely linked with co-operation he put the division of labour and the consequent development of new tools and equipment as work became specialized. The next step was the development of a factory system of production. This was an important step, because it increased 'the social productive power of labour', and created 'new conditions for the lordship of capital over labour',[2] as well as leading on to increased invention of new and more powerful machinery. It is at this point that the extortion of relative surplus labour added an impetus to the extortion of absolute surplus labour, since machinery 'becomes in the hands of capital the most powerful

---

[1] Ibid., p. 503.   [2] Ibid., p. 364.

means, in those industries first invaded by it, for lenghtening the working day beyond all bounds set by human nature'.[1] It also 'produces, partly by opening out to the capitalist new strata of the working class previously inaccessible to him, partly by setting free the labourers it surplants, a surplus working population, which is compelled to submit to the dictation of capital'.[2] Because the machines were themselves produced by labourers, Marx concluded that 'the labouring population therefore produced, along with the accumulation of capital produced by it, the means by which itself is made relatively superfluous, is turned into a relative surplus population; and it does this to an always increasing extent'.[3] This surplus population, which Marx called the 'industrial reserve army' represents a threat to the level of living of those who have not as yet been displaced by machinery. Hence 'the higher the productiveness of labour, the greater is the pressure of the labourers on the means of employment, the more precarious, therefore, becomes their condition of existence. . . . Accumulation of wealth at one pole is, therefore, at the same time accumulation of misery, agony of toil, slavery, ignorance, brutality, mental degradation, at the opposite pole, i.e. on the side of the class that produces its own product in the form of capital.'[4]

The doctrine of increasing misery for the working class under capitalism, it has often been pointed out, has been a source of considerable embarrassment to convinced Marxists. The facts do not fit the prediction. As time has gone by the material lot of the working class has undoubtedly improved, even if to this day the facts are sometimes denied for Britain and the U.S.A.[5] Perhaps more commonly Marxists are inclined to follow the line taken by Kuczynski in his detailed study of labour conditions in the nineteenth and twentieth centuries. This is to argue

---

[1] Ibid., p. 403.
[2] Ibid., pp. 407–8.
[3] Ibid., p. 631.
[4] Ibid., p. 645.
[5] Recently S. P. Figurnov has apparently made this point in his *Real Wages and the Raising of Material Welfare of the Working People in the U.S.S.R.* (in Russian), 1960. See the discussion in A. Nove, 'A Study of Soviet Wages' in *British Journal of Industrial Relations*, Vol. I, No. 1, February 1963, p. 71. See also the references given in E. Mandel, *Traité d'Economie Marxiste* (Treatise on Marxist Economics), Julliard, 1962, Vol. 1, p. 179, footnote.

that 'while the absolute living conditions of the English worker had improved for about twenty years at the expense of workers employed abroad by English capital, and while they have remained about stable for perhaps thirty years more, or declined relatively little during this period, the relative position of the English worker has deteriorated continuously and very considerably'.[1] The problem at issue is how to reconcile what has happened with Marx's own references to increasing misery, by which he undoubtedly meant 'physical impoverishment, and not psychological dissatisfaction'.[2]

Of course, it is possible to find passages in *Capital* which support the assertion that Marx was really talking about relative misery, after all; but equally there are passages, like the one about polarisation, quoted above, which cannot be interpreted in this fashion.[3] Both positions, indeed, seem to have been held by Marx, even in his later years, and it is likely that this was so because underlying his conception of revolutionary class consciousness was a theoretical psychological difficulty which he had not satisfactorily clarified and hence not been able to solve. In his Hegelian days he had believed that the proletariat would become the liberating class *par excellence* because it had 'radical chains'. It was, he wrote, 'a class in civil society which is not a class of civil society, a class which is the dissolution of all classes, a sphere of society which has a universal character because its sufferings are universal, and which does not claim a *particular redress* because the wrong which is done to it is not a *particular wrong* but a *wrong in general*'. Such a class suffered 'a *total loss* of humanity' and could 'only redeem itself by a total *redemption* of humanity'.[4] Marx, in those days, des-

---

[1] Jurgen Kuczynski, *Labour Conditions in Western Europe 1820 to 1935*, Lawrence and Wishart, 1937, p. 68. Notice, however, Geiger's point on German experience at least, that Kuczynski does not take into account welfare provisions that have improved the relative position of the working class. Theodor Geiger, *Die Klassengesellschaft im Schmelztiegel* (Class Society in the Melting Pot), Kiepenheuer, 1949, p. 64.

[2] Mandel M. Bober, *Karl Marx's Interpretation of History*, Harvard University Press, 1950, pp. 218–19.

[3] See the examples quoted in Bober, op. cit., pp. 214–20. Mills, op. cit., pp. 67–70.

[4] Karl Marx, 'Contribution to the Critique of Hegel's Philosophy of Right', translated and edited by Thomas B. Bottomore in his *Karl Marx, Early Writings*, Watts, 1963, p. 58.

cribed this loss of humanity in terms of *conditions* of society 'in which man is an abased, enslaved, abandoned, contemptible being';[1] and class consciousness, leading to *'popular revolution and the emancipation of a particular class* of civil society', was conceived by him in terms of the recognition that another class stood in the way of the achievement of humanity by the subject class.[2]

It does not seem unreasonable to claim that in one sense Marx never fully abandoned this idea, since his notion that the political revolutions at the end of the capitalist epoch would lead to a classless society appears to have depended essentially on it.[3] But, having committed himself to the argument that a *growth* in class consciousness depended on consequences arising from the intensification of the tension between the material forces of production and the relations of production, he was logically obliged to show how 'fetters' on the material forces of production could become converted into a loss of humanity; and it apparently did not seem reasonable to him to assert that a total loss of humanity was compatible with a rise in the level of living. Hence he sought to provide the mechanism for the growth of class consciousness in an inevitable decline in the amount of goods and services received by some members of the working class, on the one hand, and in the invidious comparison between the level of living of the better off among them and that of the capitalists, on the other; and he provided a mechanism in the form of falling rates of profit, which he asserted forced capitalists into recurring crises.[4]

Of course, he also believed that changes were occurring in the mode of production itself which made workers increasingly into automata, but it can hardly be claimed as Sowell has done that this was for Marx a 'fundamental deprivation which cannot be remedied by higher wages',[5] if by 'higher wages' is

[1] Ibid., Bottomore, p. 52.

[2] Ibid., pp. 55–6.

[3] See Marx and Engels, *The German Ideology*, op. cit., pp. 68–78.

[4] For a modern discussion of this point see P. A. Samuelson, 'Wages and interest: a Modern Dissection of Marxian Economic Models', *The American Economic Review*, Vol. 47, 1957, pp. 884–912, and H. D. Dickinson, 'The Falling Rate of Profit in Marxian Economics', *Review of Economic Studies*, Vol. 24, 1956–7, pp. 120–30.

[5] T. Sowell, 'Marx's "Increasing Misery" Doctrine', *The American Economic Review*, Vol. 1, No. 1, March 1960, p. 119.

meant an ever-increasing and permanent rise in the level of living; for, the chief argument of *Capital* is that under capitalism the inevitable growth of the industrial reserve army not only increased the amount of casual labour and sheer pauperism in the community, it also threatened the security and lowered the rates of wages of the regular employed. 'This is the absolute general law of capitalist accumulation'.[1] The development of technology might thus be responsible for the dehumanization of labour, but of itself it does not appear to have been regarded by Marx as a likely source of the growth of class consciousness. Indeed, hostility to machinery was seen by him as revolutionary only when it was linked with the recognition that machines are destructive of the workers' means of livelihood.[2] By the time that Marx came to write *Capital* alienation had largely given place to exploitation as the mechanism whereby the political events leading to the overthrow of capitalism would be achieved,[3] although in other respects the 'old' Marx still gave as much emphasis to the concept of alienation as had the 'young' Marx.[4]

This interpretation of alienation, to be sure, depends upon the prior assumption that in his early days Marx had all along 'been searching for the way in which the human being was robbed of his potential'.[5] In the *German Ideology*, however, there is another use of the term, *Entfremdung*,[6] which while not contradictory to the concept of the total loss of humanity, nevertheless has different implications. Central to this usage is the idea that the social system 'which arises through the co-opera-tion of different individuals as it is determined within the divi-sion of labour, appears to these individuals, since their co-opera-tion is not voluntary but natural, not as their own united power but as an alien force existing outside them, of the origin and end of which they are ignorant, which they thus cannot control and

---

[1] Marx, *Capital*, op. cit., Vol. 1, p. 644. This sentence is in italics in the original. See also Marx, *Wage Labour and Capital*, op. cit., p. 96.
[2] Marx, *Capital*, op. cit., Vol. 1, p. 430.
[3] See Daniel Bell, *The End of Ideology*, Collier Books, 1961, p. 367.
[4] See the discussion in Irving M. Zeitlin, *Marxism: a Re-examination*, Van Nostrand, 1967, pp. 45 et seq.
[5] Bell, op. cit., p. 361. See also George Lichtheim, *Marxism, an Historical and Critical Study*, Routledge & Kegan Paul, 1961, p. 43.
[6] For a discussion of Marx's terminology, see Zeitlin, *Marxism*, op. cit., p. 45, and his *Ideology*, op. cit., p. 86.

which on the contrary passes through a peculiar series of phases and stages independent of the will and the action of man, nay even being the prime governor of these.'[1] From this point of view, the dehumanization of labour, as demonstrated in the monotony of semi-skilled and unskilled work in mass production industries, is of less importance *per se* than the general sense of being at the mercy of forces over which no one, not even the capitalists, can exert a controlling influence. It is in this sense that economic crisis may be said to stand central to Marx's analysis,[2] in addition to their direct significance in helping to create class consciousness through causing pauperization. 'The ultimate reason for all real crises,' wrote Marx, 'always remains the poverty and restricted consumption of the masses as opposed to the drive of capitalist production to develop the productive forces as though only the absolute consuming power of society constituted their limit.'[3] Crises might thus also lead to the development of class consciousness on the part of the working class in a desperate attempt to put an end to the insecurity in their lives which periodic booms and slumps create.

Hence, one way out of the problem set by the factual contradiction to the increasing misery doctrine would seem to lie in a revision of the Marxist analysis of crises, particularly in the form of the assumption that developments of technology *necessarily* lead to unemployment under capitalism. Can Marx's ideas about wage and employment determination be employed, that is to say, 'to disprove Marx's increasing misery prediction'? It has been claimed that they can, on the ground that Marx did not 'prove that the demand for labour forthcoming from mechanization *via* capital accumulation is insufficient to compensate for the labour displaced by mechanization'.[4] It may also be claimed

[1] Marx and Engels, *German Ideology* op. cit., p. 24. See also the discussion of this point by Rudolf Schlesinger in a review of two books in *Soviet Studies*, Vol. 10, 1958–9, pp. 410–11.

[2] See, for example, Marx, *Capital*, op. cit., Vol. III, Ch. 15, *passim*. Note that in *The Communist Manifesto* the failure of capitalists to control crises was given as an indication of the conflict between 'modern productive forces' and 'modern conditions of production'. Marx and Engels, *Selected Works*, op. cit., Vol. 1, p. 38.

[3] Marx, *Capital*, op. cit., Vol. III, pp. 472–3.

[4] F. M. Gottheill, 'Increasing Misery of the Proletariat: An Analysis of Marx's Wage and Employment Theory', *The Canadian Journal of Economics*

that it is possible to show that just as there came a time, even under capitalism, when a limit was set to the prolongation of the working day, so a limit was set to the extent of unemployment and pauperism in a community, albeit at a later date. Just as factory legislation was seen by Marx to be 'not all the product of Parliamentary fancy' but to have 'developed gradually out of circumstances as natural laws of the modern mode of production . . . the result of a long struggle of classes',[1] so the development of what is now called 'the Welfare State' may be seen to be the result of the same struggle. Provided that, in the process of elaborating this argument, the essential ingredients of the Marxist general notion of social change are maintained —the development of conflict between the material forces of production and the existing relations of production, the growth of class consciousness, and the revolutionary overthrow of the ruling class—it should still be possible to develop hypotheses for testing the special Marxist notion of capitalism empirically, instead of abandoning it altogether because of the weakness of the increasing misery prediction.

How would such hypotheses be framed? Presumably, in British experience, Workmen's compensation, Minimum Wage legislation, the Trade Board Acts, the National Insurance legislation, nationalization of certain industries, and latterly the employment of fiscal measures by the State apparatus to keep the trade cycle in check, are the late nineteenth and twentieth century answer to the tendency of capitalism to develop an ever-growing industrial reserve army, casual labour and pauperism. Such measures prevent the occurrence of the 'misery, oppression, slavery, degradation, exploitation' of the working class which was the inevitable accompaniment of polarization as Marx himself saw it,[2] but they can only do so, if the Marxist notion is still to hold, by forcing the capitalist to seek to increase his relative surplus labour by some other device. Just as the Factory Acts, by setting a limit to the length of the working day, hastened the process whereby the larger capitalists

and Political Science, Vol. 28, No. 1, February 1962, p. 111. See also Plamenatz, *German Marxism*, op. cit., Ch. 6.

[1] Marx, *Capital*, op. cit., Vol. I, p. 283.
[2] Ibid., p. 763.

of that period drove smaller capitalists out of business, so these later examples of State intervention would continue the process. The 'centralization of the means of production' and the 'socialization of labour' which Marx saw as an inherent development of capitalist organization would be speeded up by these developments and the revolutionary period ushered in by the very measures which were intended, in some sense, to prevent it.

Marx had already sketched the outline of two aspects of the development of capitalism, which, it seems reasonable to suppose, would be accelerated by this process. On the one hand, the possibility had always been open to capitalists to increase their share of surplus labour by finding foreign markets for their products and for cheaper sources of raw materials;[1] and, on the other, the device of the joint stock company divorced ownership of capital as such from a 'function in the actual process of reproduction'[2] and hence placed more total capital at the disposal of the entrepreneur who thereby could increase his own relative share of the surplus labour controlled by it. Pressure on the capitalist to raise wages and employment at home could be met, for a time at least, by increasing the export of products, and latterly, of capital[3] to mechanize industry and agriculture abroad. At the same time, the intensification of what has been called 'the corporate revolution', monopolization, and cartelization,[4] would make it possible for some capitalists to benefit at the expense of others whose relative share of surplus labour would fall. Thus capitalism would become world-wide, imperialist capitalism, to use Lenin's term, and it would speed up the polarization process in one sense by reducing drastically the number of capitalists with genuine control over industry. Private ownership of the means of production would, in effect, be replaced by a social form of ownership, and the transition to the socialist society, already foreshadowed in the social organization of production under the factory system, would be vastly assisted by the development of the social organization of its control.

[1] Marx, *Capital*, op. cit., Vol. 3, pp. 232–4.
[2] Ibid., p. 427, 'reproduction' here refers to the reproduction of capital.
[3] Vladimir I. Lenin, *Imperialism, the Highest Stage of Capitalism*, in Vladimir I. Lenin, *Collected Works*, Vol. 22, Progress Publishers, 1964, Ch. 4.
[4] Ibid., Ch. 1.

Capitalism

What is not so clear is how this relates to the conflict between the material forces of production and the class system. Empirically it is not at all difficult to show that technical developments are sometimes not exploited beyond the inventor's prototype at this later stage of capitalism.[1] Presumably rather than meet the demand for higher wages by increasing mechanization, which would create unemployment and arouse trade union hostility, employers seek an easier way out, exploiting surplus labour elsewhere in the world or forming combines and cartels to drive their relatively less efficient competitors out of business. Presumably, too, there is a limit to this process and the state eventually steps in with nationalization and other programmes of economic control to meet the gaps in home production and technical development which capitalists do not believe it profitable to fill. The question at issue is how the growth of class consciousness can become accelerated at this stage by such developments, since the whole of the trend away from increasing misery might be thought to be working in the opposite direction, leading a whole section of the working class in Lenin's words, to be '*bribed* out of imperialist superprofits and converted into *watchdogs* of capitalism and *corrupters* of the labour movement'.[2] Undoubtedly the Marxist interpretation of capitalism has to find room for the so-called *embourgeoisement* or 'bourgeoisification' of the working class, in so far as this is exemplified in the acquisition of 'material possessions, which bring it approximately to the level that the middle class was previously at, and that the lower-middle class is now'; and even perhaps in the adoption of 'new norms, values and standards which are middle class',[3] but it is still open to question whether such developments, difficult as they are to interpret, add up to the empirical falsification of the Marxist interpretation of history.

Contemporary Britain, that is to say, may be seen as an

---

[1] Evgenii Varga and L. Mendelsohn, eds., *New Data for V. I. Lenin's Imperialism, the Highest Stage of Capitalism*, Lawrence and Wishart, n.d. (1939?), pp. 245-51.

[2] Vladimir I. Lenin, *Imperialism and the Split in Socialism*; Lenin, *Collected Works*, Vol. 23, Progress Publishers, 1964, p. 110. Italics in the original.

[3] D. Lockwood, 'The "New Working Class"', *Archives Européennes de Sociologie*, Vol. 1, no. 2, 1960, p. 25.

openly stratified society; but this does not make it incompatible with the notion of polarization without pauperization, provided that such stratification is understood to be measured by differences of income and in styles of life, rather than in terms of degrees of economic power involving decisions about the exploitation of labour resources. Contemporary Britain, too, may be seen as the setting for a 'convergence' of working-class and middle-class consciousness towards what has been termed 'instrumental collectivism', demonstrated by 'the continuing strength of trade union organizations, and the growth especially of white-collar unionism, which cannot easily be accommodated into the conception of *embourgeoisement* as this has been developed so far.'[1] It is an important feature of the Marxist interpretation of the revolutionary overthrow of capitalist society that in his political writings Marx emphasized the part to be played in the class struggle by organizations— trade unions, political parties, international working-men's associations. The growth of class consciousness might be said to be measured by an extension of the membership of such bodies to an ever-growing proportion of the population, always provided, of course, that in their aims and in their activities, they continued to work towards the overthrow of the capitalist ruling class and to the creating of a classless society.[2] The Marxist interpretation of industrial relations under capitalism, in brief, is incomplete without an examination of the part to be played in historical developments by the trade unions.

[1] J. H. Goldthorpe and D. Lockwood, 'Affluence and the British Class Structure', *The Sociological Review*, Vol. 11, no. 2, July 1963, p. 152. Italics in the original.

[2] In the Middle Ages, similarly, it was the organization of burghers in different towns against 'the landed nobility to save their skins' that created class consciousness in the *bourgeoisie*. Marx and Engels, *The German Ideology*, op. cit., p. 48.

4

TRADE UNIONISM

In view of the many thousands of words he wrote about capitalism, it is surprising that Marx never undertook any detailed analysis of the place of trade unions in such a society, or of the part they would play in the transition to socialism. Nevertheless, it is commonly understood that there underlies his work 'the idea that the trade unions are schools of solidarity, schools of socialism.'[1] In his earlier theoretical formulations his view seems clear enough. 'Large-scale industry', he wrote, 'concentrates in one place a crowd of people unknown to one another. Competition divides their interests. But the maintenance of wages, this common interest which they have against their boss, unites them in a common thought of resistance—*combination*.' In the course of time such organizations of working men meet ever-increasing resistance from their employers who 'in their turn unite for the purpose of repression'. Hence the workers are gradually forced from their original position. 'The maintenance of the association becomes more necessary to them than that of wages. . . . Once it has reached this point, association takes on a political character'.[2] The school of trade unionism, it might be said, teaches them the lesson of the materialist conception of history. They become self-conscious about the class struggle. The interests they are now defending are class interests.[3]

Over the years, however, Marx became disturbed by the

[1] Aleksander Lozovsky, *Marx and Trade Unions*, Lawrence, 1935, p. 15.

[2] Marx, *The Poverty of Philosophy*, op. cit., pp. 194–5. See also Lozovsky, op. cit., p. 28.

[3] Marx, *Poverty of Philosophy*, op. cit., p. 195.

failure, of the English trade union leaders especially,[1] to develop the kind of revolutionary class consciousness demanded by his theory, and he began to work towards another view of trade unionism which allowed for the possibility that the lessons of history were not always learned. 'Trade Unions work well as centres of resistance against the encroachments of capital', he told the General Council of the International Working Men's Association in 1865, 'They fail generally from limiting themselves to a guerilla war against the effects of the existing system, instead of simultaneously trying to change it'.[2] What he now began to see was a much clearer distinction between an economic and a political movement, between 'the attempt in a particular factory or even in a particular trade to force a shorter working day out of individual capitalists by strikes, etc.' and 'the movement to force through an eight-hour, etc. law'; but he still believed that the latter activity grew everywhere out of the former.[3] The working class, that is to say, was thought to be 'always increasing in numbers, and disciplined, united, organised by the very mechanism of the process of capitalist production itself'.[4]

Of course, Marx had always given a special role to Communists as 'practically, the most advanced, and resolute section of the working-class parties in every country', and, theoretically as 'clearly understanding the line of march, the conditions, and the ultimate general results of the movement as a whole'.[5] Nevertheless, it was left to Lenin to work out the implication of this notion of the 'vanguard of the working class' for the conversion of economic movements into political ones. The point at issue was the extent to which trade unionists would come spontaneously to appreciate their position in the historical process or would develop only trade-union consciousness, which Lenin otherwise regarded as 'the ideological enslave-

[1] Lozovsky, op. cit., pp. 59–60. See also Vladimir I. Lenin, *Karl Marx*, in Lenin, *Collected Works*, Vol. 21, Progress Publications, 1964, p. 76.

[2] Marx, *Wages, Price and Profit*, op. cit., p. 405.

[3] Letter to F. Bolte, 23rd November 1871, Karl Marx and Frederick Engels, *Selected Correspondence*, Foreign Languages Publishing House, n.d., p. 328.

[4] Marx, *Capital*, op. cit., Vol. I, p. 763.

[5] Marx and Engels, *The Communist Manifesto*, op. cit., p. 44.

ment of the workers by the *bourgeoisie*'.[1] At this later point in the history of modern society the disciple differed from the master in regarding political action by trade unionists as not necessarily revolutionary, because it could be designed 'to secure from the government measures for alleviating the distress to which their condition gives rise', without being intended to 'abolish that condition' and to 'remove the subjections of labour to capital'.[2]

Indeed, in this debate with those Marxists who still held that class consciousness was inevitable and spontaneous in the working class, Lenin asserted categorically that it must be brought to the trade unions from without. 'The history of all countries', he wrote, 'shows that the working class, exclusively by its own effort, is able to develop only trade union consciousness, i.e., the conviction that it is necessary to combine in unions, fight the employers and strive to compel the government to pass necessary labour legislation, etc. The theory of Socialism, however, grew out of the philosophic, historical and economic theories elaborated by educated representatives of the propertied classes, the intellectuals'.[3] From this point of view, the transition from an economic to a political movement, in Marx's sense, could occur through the intervention of an intellectual leadership, rising rarely, if at all, from the working class itself, and consisting largely, if not wholly, of members of the *bourgeois* intelligentsia, like Marx and Engels, who threw in their lot with the masses.[4]

It is at this point that it becomes necessary to consider a

[1] Vladimir I. Lenin, *What is to be Done?* in Lenin, *Collected Works*, Vol. 5, Foreign Languages Publishing House, 1961, p. 384.

[2] Ibid., p. 387.

[3] Ibid., p. 375.

[4] See Thomas T. Hammond, *Lenin on Trade Unions and Revolution, 1893–1917*, Columbia University Press, 1957, *passim*. These intellectuals were, presumably, those who in the words of the *Communist Manifesto* had 'raised themselves to the level of comprehending theoretically the historical movement as a whole', Marx and Engels, *Selected Works*, op. cit., Vol. 1, p. 42. Compare the statement by Marx and Engels in a 'Circular Letter' of September 1879, that they could not 'co-operate with people who openly state the workers are too uneducated to emancipate themselves and must be freed from above by philanthropic big bourgeois and petty bourgeois. The emancipation of the working classes must be conquered by the working classes themselves.' Marx and Engels, *Selected Correspondence*, op. cit., p. 395.

question of crucial significance for the Marxist notion of industrial relations. If revolution is primarily an idea promulgated by intellectuals, and if, as a matter of fact, trade unions are sometimes attracted and sometimes repelled by the attempts of intellectuals to persuade them to take a revolutionary attitude, what is the Marxist 'explanation' for the relative successes and failures of intellectuals to develop such class consciousness on the part of the working class? The increasing misery doctrine had the point at least of implying that, as polarization developed, the workers would turn in their misery to whoever seemed to have a workable solution to their condition; and one writer has developed this idea into a non-Marxist account running along cyclical lines. Revolutionary activity by the working class, that is to say, has been said to decrease and increase with booms and slumps on the one hand, and with government tolerance and repression of trade unionism, on the other.[1] Since, however, such an interpretation involves the conclusion that revolution may be postponed indefinitely through economic and political reforms under capitalism, it must be regarded as an alternative to the Marxist hypothesis rather than an amendment. Granted that economic and political reforms certainly occur under capitalism, some other interpretation must be found for the degree of influence wielded by intellectuals, if the notion is to be maintained that the transition from capitalism to a fresh epoch in human history is inevitable.

Lenin, it must be admitted, never provided this account. In some of his writings, it is true, he argued the case for reforms under capitalism as tending to aid the movement toward revolution in certain circumstances, but these all appear to be located further back in the historical process than the imperialist phase of capitalism; for, they either apply to the achievement of political reforms, such as the extension of freedom of the press, and the legalization of political parties which make agitation public and hence increase class consciousness; or they refer to a level of living on the part of the working class which

[1] Selig Perlman, *A Theory of the Labour Movement*, MacMillan, 1928, pp. 36–49 (the Russian Revolution) and pp. 105–28 (the German Revolution). Perlman's 'theory' was that the basis of working-class consciousness arose from fear of scarcity of opportunity, ibid., pp. 6 and 242.

is so low, as under the early factory system, that individual workers have insufficient moral and mental energy to practise heroism, self-denial, and devotion to the cause.[1] But for later stages of capitalism Lenin argued more characteristically that economic and political reforms, far from encouraging revolutionary fervour, positively hindered it, partly by destroying the unity of the working class and partly by giving the workers an apparently vested interest in the continuation of capitalism.[2] At no time did he appear to have realised that for such stages to mark a transition from capitalism to the next social system a great deal is left to be explained, and in this sense it may well be true that at bottom he still held to the increasing-misery doctrine. Reforms under capitalism might be possible, but they were temporary only. In the long run the system was certain to collapse by driving the workers to revolt.[3]

The problem at issue, then, resolves itself into yet another example of the confusion over the term 'revolution' which was referred to above.[4] If the increasing-misery doctrine is abandoned, the notion that the transition from capitalism to the next epoch in human history will necessarily be catastrophic must also be abandoned, at least within the framework of single societies. Lenin's difficulty, understandable perhaps in the Russian context, was that he saw violent overthrow of the political order as an essential ingredient of class consciousness, and the task of his highly disciplined Communist Party was to nerve trade unionists, among others, to a genuine conviction that the Russian political machine must be smashed. He held, after all, that the state was 'an apparatus of physical coercion, an apparatus of violence' and its capacity for coercion was increased with every development in the technology of weapon construction which corresponded to the general technology of an epoch.[5] Yet, it is not a necessary feature of the Marxist notion of social change that revolutions must proceed in this fashion, and Marx himself appears to have believed that the more

[1] Hammond, op. cit., pp. 111–13.
[2] Ibid., pp. 106–11.
[3] Ibid., pp. 96–103.
[4] See above, pp. 22–4.
[5] Vladimir I. Lenin, *The State*, *1919*, in Lenin, *Collected Works*, Progress Publishers, Vol. 29, 1965, p. 478.

capitalism developed, the easier it would be to achieve the transition to a socialist society. 'The transformation of scattered private property, arising from individual labour, into capitalist private property is', he wrote, 'naturally, a process incomparably more protracted, violent, and difficult, than the transformation of capitalistic private property, already resting on socialised production, into socialised property. In the former case, we had the expropriation of the mass of the people by a few usurpers; in the latter we have the expropriation of a few usurpers by the mass of the people'.[1]

Trade unionists, then, play their part in the historical process by organizing successfully for economic reforms which reduce the number of capitalists facing them, but they need not intend to achieve this, nor need they be aware that it is a consequence of their action. Strikes which result in a shorter working week or in an increase in wages which the employer finds difficult to pass on to the consumer, may not be designed to cause him to search for new ways of maintaining his share of surplus labour by forcing less efficient or less ruthless competitors out of business, but insofar as this occurs, polarization without pauperisation is intensified. Political agitation which leads to an extension of the Factory Acts, or to measures to prevent destitution or unemployment, may equally be carried on without the further understanding that an accompanying result is the amassing of the control of more and more capital in fewer and fewer hands. Such trade union activities, economic and political, are not revolutionary in the class-conscious sense of that term, unless they are informed by the clear understanding that a new social system, structurally different from capitalism, is the inevitable outcome.

It should be emphasized that *as a political movement* trade unionism must have this sense of the inevitability of history, if it is to qualify for the adjective, 'revolutionary', in the Marxist sense. Mere desire for an end of exploitation, or even yearning for a classless society, is not enough. Millenarian movements are after all not confined to the capitalist epoch. Nor is a sense of unity with other trade unionists sufficient for the revolutionary consciousness, although it may be necessary for the kind of

[1] Marx, *Capital*, op. cit., Vol. i, p. 764.

political activity which is required to bring about revolutionary change. What is essential is that trade unionists should have a worked-out programme for economic and political action which is manifestly designed to replace capitalist control of economic enterprise by a system of control by public servants, responsible to the community and rewarded for their services by the community. A classless society, in this sense, is one in which there is no class permitted to retain surplus labour for itself. Insofar as there is a difference between what a worker produces and what he actually receives, it is not allocated to any *one* section of the community, but is employed for the development and maintenance of services of communal benefit—schools, hospitals, cultural centres and so on—all designed to improve the quality of life and hence in a sense also part of the cost of producing and maintaining the labour force. Insofar as class consciousness amongst trade unionists exists, it will take the form of economic and political agitation to change the power structure of economic life in this general direction.

It should be clear that, as a matter of empirical fact, trade union leaders and trade union members often carry on economic and political struggles without this further end in view. It should also be clear that one of the tasks of those intellectuals, who, in Lenin's sense, form the revolutionary leadership of the working class, will be to demonstrate to trade unionists that their achievements are precarious and indeed that they can achieve even better results for themselves and their fellows by following the more radical programme. If the Marxist notion of the transition from capitalism to the next epoch is valid, moreover, it should also be true that intellectuals will succeed in this the more the employers in a given industry embark upon policies to make their businesses big; for, according to Marx, the 'class movement of the proletariat' would be led by the 'proletarians created by big industry' who would 'carry the whole mass along with them'.[1] They will also succeed the more that capitalists, seeking to avoid the political crises associated in their minds with technological unemployment, engage in internecine warfare amongst themselves, in the form of cutthroat competition, take-over-bids, and so forth, rather than

---

[1] Marx and Engels, *The German Ideology*, op. cit., p. 58.

embark upon technical, economic and social improvement to increase productivity. More obviously, they will succeed wherever capitalists take the alternative route and seek to minimise the effect upon themselves of massive developments in productivity, such as are associated with the term, 'automation', by bringing strong pressure to bear on the trade unions, 'either to practise wage restraint in a voluntary manner, or to be restricted in their bargaining possibilities in the legal right to strike'.[1] The degree of tension between the material focus of production and the existing relations of production, that is to say, must be retained if the analysis is to remain basically Marxist; and it is this tension which provides the conditions for the success of the revolutionary leaders of the working class to induce their followers to adopt a Marxist class-conscious approach to its historical task.

At the economic level, therefore, the Marxist approach to collective bargaining, or to industrial relations generally, consists in emphasizing that the industrial scene is marked by bodies of capitalists and workers, sometimes unorganized, sometimes highly organized, struggling together to maintain their relative positions in the power system whereby the products of necessary and surplus labour are distributed between the two classes. It is converted to the political level whenever either side to the struggle seeks to influence the state machinery to intercede on its behalf. It becomes genuinely revolutionary when the workers' organizations, be they trade unions, be they political parties, seek to use the state machine to abolish altogether the capitalist's power to extort surplus labour; and this is possible, historically speaking, once it can be demonstrated that co-operative production on a classless basis is possible. The special Marxist notion of capitalism provides a rider to the more general conception of history at this point, that is to say, by providing a clue to the conviction that the history of class struggles will come to an end with the downfall of capitalism.

---

[1] E. Mandel, 'The Economics of Neo-Capitalism' in Ralph Miliband and John Saville, eds., *The Socialist Register, 1964*, Merlin Press, 1964, p. 63. Mandel instances the 'Taft-Hartley law in the U.S.A., French anti-strike laws; big financial penalties imposed upon "wild-cat strikes" in many Western European countries; attempts to impose an "Anti-strike law" in Belgium' in support of this last point.

The various types of co-operative society, gas and water socialism, experiments in municipal and state enterprise may all be read as 'proof' of the assertion that large-scale, complex industrial organization can be run effectively under the control of men, who do not form a class apart from the workers by virtue of their power to extort surplus labour from them. The crowning achievement of capitalist society is that it makes possible the knowledge of how this can be done, largely by dissociating the administration and management of industry from its financial control. The revolutionary, class-conscious member of the proletariat is he who sets out to extend this process by placing such financial control in the hands of the community, or its representatives.

For present purposes it does not matter very much if Marx was a little too sanguine about this. Even though there may already be emerging a new system of society in which those who control industry form a ruling class, extorting surplus labour by some device different from that used by capitalists *per se*, the Marxist account of industrial relations under capitalism might still be largely valid. Provided that all the endeavours of workers in their organizations—whether they are motivated by trade-union consciousness only, or by Marxist revolutionary class consciousness—tend towards the conversion of capitalist enterprise into state, municipal or co-operative enterprise, they will be playing the part in history which the Marxist interpretation asserts they will play. The real test of this interpretation is whether it is falsified or supported by fact, and not whether a classless society in a Marxist, or other sense, is possible. Hence, the task of the sociologist who wishes to make genuine scientific use of the Marxist intellectual apparatus for sociological purposes, is to find ways of converting this form of analysis of the relationships between capitalist employers and their employees into testable propositions about the behaviour of members of identifiable trade unions employed by identifiable business organizations. The remainder of this study is devoted to an outline of how this may be done.

Part Two

EMPIRICAL ASSESSMENT

5

METHOD OF PROCEDURE

Fundamental to the sociological critique of Marxism, as it has been developed in these pages, is the assumption that its theoretical apparatus is, or should be, open to examination by means of the methods of empirical enquiry. The fact, however, that the Marxist set of hypotheses has so far not been subjected to rigorous testing in this fashion opens up the logical possibility that there is some feature of them which precludes such verification. It has, for example, been argued that one of the reasons why the subject has been ignored by empirically-minded sociologists largely everywheı e is because 'it is incapable of arithmetization, of scaling and scheduling, of interviewing and of providing research projects with precise and neat conclusions'.[1] In so far as contemporary sociology is conceived to depend upon such techniques this assertion might well go far towards an explanation, since no substantial empirical survey of the last decade or so, employing quantitative methods, has been designed to confirm or refute the Marxist system of ideas.

Certainly, it can hardly be denied that the hypotheses, discussed in Part One above, do not lend themselves readily to arithmetization. In considering the relatively simple issue of technology alone, for example, the problems of measurement are formidable. How is a social scientist to decide upon a unit to indicate, say, the level of mechanization achieved by an industry, or even by a firm within an industry? Such an apparently obvious ratio as the horse-power capacity per worker is open to quite serious objections. 'A delicate mechanism

[1] D. G. MacRae, 'Social Stratification: A Trend Report', *Current Sociology*, Vol. 2, 1953–4, p. 16.

designed for a specific job such as a cigarette making and boxing machine involves in its production high expenditure of money and man-power, but in its operation may not use much horse-power. On the other hand, a rough and inexpensive steam hammer or crane may use up a very high horse-power'.[1] The interpretation of data of this kind and their appplication for the purpose in mind constitute pitfalls to be overcome in all sociological research attempting to relate social and technical facts.

Nevertheless, the recognition that such research is inordinately difficult is not at all the same thing as assuming it to be impossible; and at the present stage in the evolution of scientific sociology there does not seem to be any good reason why use should not be made of admittedly very crude approximations in measurement for the purpose of testing propositions derived from the Marxist conceptual framework. It is surely not altogether irrelevant, for instance, that 'in so far as horse-power per worker measures intensity of investment the *greater* an *industry's* investment, the larger the prevailing size of plants'.[2] Later sociologists, with more ingenious and rigorous techniques of measurement at their disposal, may be able to reverse, or seriously modify, such a relationship between level of technological advance and scale of operations; but for the time being crude generalizations of this order will suffice to begin the more critically sociological appraisal of Marxism.

The deliberately tentative nature of the present approach may, moreover, be further justified by the fact that the Marxist analysis of social phenomena is essentially developmental; and the necessary sociological, as compared with historical, techniques for the study of movement from one stage to the next are rudimentary in the extreme. Indeed, so complicated are the problems involved that sociologists are reluctant to turn their professional attention towards their resolution, and it has been claimed with some truth that 'the study of social change has become something of a part-time concern in recent years'.[3]

---

[1] Philip Sargant Florence, *Investment, Location, and Size of Plant*, Cambridge University Press, 1948, p. 93.

[2] Ibid., p. 109, italics in the original.

[3] A. Boskoff, 'Social Change: Major Problems in the Emergence of Theoretical and Research Foci' in Howard Becker and Alvin Boskoff, *Modern Sociological Theory*, Dryden Press, 1957, p. 261.

For present purposes, therefore, it is not to be expected that much assistance will be forthcoming from the stock of current, sociologically tested, empirical knowledge. Although 'ultimately, the power of sociology rests in its accumulation of provable and applicable ideas, not merely of facts',[1] it is notorious that none of the landmarks in the journey from the origins of scientific sociology in 1897 to its chronicling in 1963 was commemorative of an empirical study into change over time, even remotely applicable to the Marxist system of ideas. This means that much of the present discussion will perforce be conducted by reference to data more familiarly those of the historian than of the sociologist, although empirical surveys of contemporary industrial relations, carried through without detailed references to changes over time, will be made use of wherever their findings appear relevant.

It is pertinent to enquire why what have now become the more traditional sociological techniques should not have been applied instead to this problem. In part the answer has already been given. Because the Marxist analysis is developmental it is difficult to envisage what a large scale enquiry for this purpose would look like, if it were to employ sampling techniques and a body of interviewers armed with questionnaires, interview schedules, attitude scales and all the other 'instruments' which sociologists employ in the study of current problems. The resources required for such a method to be applied to a single national population, or even to the members of a single trade union, were the aim to study them over a sufficiently long enough period of time, would seem to be colossal, and clearly beyond the reach of a solitary scholar. At the same time, to cut the research down to manageable size would of necessity entail its application to a limited set of hypotheses, more strictly investigated doubtless, but of less immediate value to the appraisal of the Marxist system, understood in its wider theoretical implications.

The aim of the present study, that is to say, is to begin rather than to complete the sociological critique of the Marxist approach to industrial relations. It will use whatever knowledge there is to point up problems for later research, without making

[1] John Madge, *The Origins of Scientific Sociology*, Tavistock Publications, 1963, p. 1.

other than the most tentative steps towards their solution. Nevertheless, the intention throughout will be to aspire to the soundest criteria of modern sociological enquiry, and the fact that so much of the data to be employed will not have been accumulated by sociologists raises the question, crucial indeed to the further use of historical material for sociological purposes, of what special methodological issues are involved in work of this kind. Far too often sociologists who would never dream of conducting a survey except in the most methodologically precise and meticulous way, are careless and slipshod to the extreme when making use of references to the past prepared by other scholars about whose methods they know next to nothing. There is a kind of trained incapacity here which those who seek to develop the study of social change, should take very special steps to avoid.

Perhaps the point in question is best made clear by reference to the two tasks which sociologists of a philosophical turn of mind regard as essential to be tackled if their discipline is to flourish. These are (1) how is it possible for sociologists to be objective? and (2) how is it possible for them to be precise? Without doubt these two tasks are rather more logically complex than much of contemporary discussion would seem to allow, but fortunately, this is not a preoccupation of the present enquiry; for it is not the objectivity and precision of sociology *per se* which are of immediate concern but the relation of these *desiderata* to the use the sociologist may make of other people's data. Hence the questions always to be considered in what follows are (1) how objective was such-and-such a historian, chronicler, biographer, keeper of the records, and so on? (2) how precise are the details which his account preserves? Of course, these are questions which can only be answered in principle, not in detail, and the present author does not pretend even to have answered them to his own satisfaction, before applying the data to the task in hand. The whole point of raising them here is not to give the present critique an air of spurious punctiliousness but, it is hoped, to indicate some of the ways in which a more scrupulous attack on some aspect or other of the Marxist approach to the study of industrial relations, might be mounted.

One aspect of the problem should be noted at the outset. The objectivity of the present author is not an issue of much significance. Since in what follows the references will always be given to the sources from which the material was derived, the dissatisfied reader may always pursue his own researches into the same and other sources, as a check on bias arising from the personal idiosyncrasies of a particular individual. Broadly speaking, this is also true of the objectivity of secondary sources used by the author, where the documents and other artefacts used by that secondary source compiler are extant and publicly available. Precision, however, is altogether another matter. In assembling this critique the author proceeded with the conviction that he had taken pains to get his material as complete and accurate as possible. To that extent the work may, of course, be checked for omissions arising from ignorance and for errors arising from fatigue and from the failure to take trouble. But, inasmuch as most of the original data were collected for very different purposes in the past, there must always be a doubt about the degree to which the facts of the case approximate to what has been recorded and handed down to posterity.

Indeed, it may well be that this very uncertainty is one of the reasons why so many sociologists today prefer to collect their data *ab initio*. At least they can satisfy themselves about the degree of precision involved. To the extent, too, that they describe their methods and techniques in detail future generations will have a better basis for judging how precise these reports are than is the case with most of the material available from the past. What they fail to see, however, is that on such a criterion of precision most empirical data become a closed book to the student of social change, and will always remain so until so much data is accumulated on sound sociological principles that the problem disappears. The alternative to postponing research into historical issues to the point at which contemporary sociology becomes history, is to face the question of precision in history on its own terms, admitting that some inference is inevitable and some controversy about rival interpretation unavoidable. This makes the results of such research necessarily tentative; but is this not in any case an essential feature of the scientific adventure? In this respect, just as the first part of this study may be read as what Marx means to one sociologist,[1] so the remainder may be read as that same sociologist's understanding of the meaning of the sources.

The Marxist approach to social change, to be sure, is sometimes held to be incapable of testing, because of its holist tendency, in the sense that it views all human history in the same way as it views society, 'as a social universe, an all-embracing system in which everything is related to everything else'.[2] Marx and Engels, indeed, said as much, asserting that their conception of historical materialism depended on the ability of men 'to expound the real process of production, starting out from the simple material production of life, and to comprehend the form of intercourse connected with this and created by this (i.e. civil society in its various stages), as the basis of all history; further, to show it in its action as State; and so, from this starting-point, to explain the whole mass of different theoretical products and forms of consciousness, religion, philosophy, ethics, etc., etc., and trace their origins and growth, by which means, of course, the whole thing can be shown in its totality (and therefore, too, the reciprocal action on these various sides on one another)'.[3] Now, if this means, as it certainly appears to mean, that the aim of Marxist methodology is to study a totality consisting of all the properties, qualities or aspects of a social system as it changes over time, laying a special emphasis on all the relations holding between its constituent parts, the task becomes not merely colossal but impossible. No student could describe a whole, concrete social system in this sense 'since in every such case it would always be easy to point out aspects which have been neglected; aspects that may nevertheless be most important in some context or other'.[4]

The alternative is to take the term, 'whole', to denote 'certain special properties or aspects of the thing in question, namely those which make it appear an organized structure rather than a 'mere heap' '.[5] This is, broadly, the approach to Marxism

[1] Meyer, *Marxism*, op. cit., p. xvii, 'every work on Marx should really be entitled *What Marx Means to Me*'. Italics in the original.

[2] Ibid., p. 18.

[3] Marx and Engels, *The German Ideology*, op. cit., pp. 28-9.

[4] Karl Popper, *The Poverty of Historicism*, Routledge Paperback, 1961, p. 79.

[5] Ibid., p. 76.

made by this study; and the author, accordingly, rejects as invalid to the proper scientific treatment of Marxism any interpretation of the data which refers to wholes in any other sense than this. Thus, examination of the degree of class consciousness demonstrated by the *working class* at any given point in time has been carried out here by reference to data about behaviour of individual persons and of identifiable collectivities, such as specific trade unions and political parties, denoted by their proper names. Only when evidence can be provided of the existence of relationships between such persons and collectivities of the nature, that they behave as though they thought of themselves as *parts* of a larger unity, has it been taken as permissible to write about the working class *as a whole*. In all other cases of its appearance, therefore, the term should be assumed to refer to a simple aggregate of manual workers and to collectivities of manual workers.

Similarly, in dealing with the relations between employers and employees in an industry, interpretation of their behaviour by reference to 'the industrial system of Great Britain', or to 'the structure of world markets', has been thought necessary only when evidence is available about the influence of such larger wholes on the relationship in question. As will become clear, on very many issues the author has not been able to discover information in support of assertions about such wider influences; and although it cannot be assumed that lack of evidence implies a lack of connection, the onus of proof is on those who would assert that the whole about which there is doubt *must* exist because the Marxist set of hypotheses entails that it should. Proof of validity, that is to say, depends upon the production of incontrovertible evidence; and where the present study has not presented it, the correct logical procedure for the controversialist is to point out sources which have been overlooked or data which have been missed. Mere assertion is not enough. Verification and falsification proceed in scientific enquiry through manipulation of facts as hard as, or harder than those employed by the authority to be attacked.

This understood, the programme of investigation to be followed should now become clear. Scrutiny of the Marxist approach to the study of industrial relations has been made on the basis of a temporal framework, using historical data, largely from secondary sources. It has also been comparative, across industries, firms, trade unions, political parties, and so forth, although the focus of attention in the first instance has been on a single English industry, and indeed on a single trade union within that industry. Broadening out from this basis has followed according to the exigencies of deduction from the juxtaposition of the Marxist hypotheses with relevant empirical fact. That this is not the only possible mode of procedure should be apparent from everything that has been said so far and will not be repeated. What is more important is to emphasize that, throughout, the search has been for negative instances, for examples of human behaviour which may legitimately be taken to falsify one or other of the hypotheses in question. To this extent Popper's characterization of 'the empirical method' has been taken as axiomatic. namely, 'its manner of exposing to falsification, in every conceivable way, the system to be tested'.[1] All that is necessary to add is that what is meant by legitimate falsification to the present author is not simple rejection but the replacement of a less satisfactory hypothesis by one which is more easily accommodated to the demands of intransigent fact. It is in this sense that the work has been designed as a contribution to the development of scientific sociology; and it is in this sense that it should be judged.

---

[1] Karl Popper, *The Logic of Scientific Discovery*, Hutchinson, 1959, p. 42.

6

TRADE UNION SOLIDARITY

The Marxist system of ideas, as analyzed in Part One of this book, emphasizes that technical and organizational developments intensify class conflict and hence lead to revolutionary upheaval.[1] It also emphasizes that the impact of these developments is not uniform throughout a society and in particular that the leadership of the working class is to be found amongst the more advanced sections of the economy.[2] These emphases on the 'material forces' of production as a crucial factor in social change lead logically to the scrutiny of the relevant indicators of such forces as the first step in empirical investigation. Differences in class consciousness generally, in political affiliation, in trade-union militancy should, if the hypotheses hold, be subject to explanation in terms of the technical achievement obtaining in one industry compared with another, in terms of difference in their scale of operations, in terms of differences in the degree of centralization of ownership and control, and so forth. Unfortunately, as has already been pointed out, the problem of measurements for these 'factors' has not yet been solved, so that in consequence it is not possible to proceed according to the obvious requirements of strict logic, especially since the process of validation requires reference to data at different points in time. For example, it was not until 1945 that any thorough analysis was made of the nature of concentration in British industry,[3] and this was a pioneer effort based on

---

[1] See above, pp. 24–32.
[2] See above, p. 21.
[3] H. Leak and A. Maizels, 'The Structure of British Industry', *Journal of the Royal Statistical Society*, Vol. 108, 1945, pp. 142–99.

data published as a result of the Census of Production, carried out in 1935. The next comparison over time is with the data of the Trades and Sub-Trades of the Census of Production in 1951,[1] and no detailed comparisons with a later period have appeared since. Quite apart from the obvious lacuna in information for the period before 1935, therefore, it is clearly of limited value to look at 1935 and 1951 alone as indicating a trend over time. Some other first approach to the problem must be employed.

The procedure followed here—and it is admitted that almost any other procedure might have been followed instead—is to decide on a single industry, the steel industry, and to use this for the purpose of indicating the kinds of issues which arise, when the Marxist approach is taken towards industrial relations in a community. The general justification for this position is that the set of hypotheses which constitute the Marxist analysis is so constructed that they form a logically coherent system which may be studied from any starting point; but there is a more specific justification for starting from this particular point, namely, that at first sight, this industry satisfies many of the conditions which are required to be satisfied if the Marxist system is to be adequately tested.

The steel industry is an old industry in Britain. Iron-making was carried on by the Celts in about 450 B.C.[2] and the manufacture of steel at about the same time or perhaps a century or two later.[3] One authority, it is true, claims that 'from the earliest period of which we have exact information iron making in this country has been conducted on capitalistic lines—capitalistic not only in that the workers are dependent upon an employer for their raw materials and markets, but also in that they are brought together in a 'works', are paid wages, and perform their duties under conditions not dissimilar to those of almost any large industry of modern times'.[4] This clearly raises

---

[1] Richard Evely and Ian M. D. Little, *Concentration in British Industry*, Cambridge University Press, 1960, *passim*.

[2] Hans R. Schubert, *History of the British Iron and Steel Industry from C. 450 B.C. to A.D. 1775*, Routledge and Kegan Paul, 1957, p. 4.

[3] Ibid., p. 29.

[4] Thomas S. Ashton, *Iron and Steel in the Industrial Revolution*, 3rd edition, Manchester University Press, 1963, p. 1.

problems for the study of the Marxist analysis of feudalism—and, incidentally, Weber's attempt to tie back the origins of capitalist enterprise to the Protestant ethic—but it does not appear of much significance here, since the issue in question is the development of industrial relations in the steel industry over the past hundred years or so. The points to notice are that the steel industry is *at least* as old as capitalism itself and that, therefore, developments which might in the case of relatively new industries, such as motor-car manufacture, be attributed to copying the achievements of established industries, are much less likely to have occurred in this case.

The steel industry is also a highly mechanized industry, that is, in so far as the horse-power capacity per worker may be taken in this instance as an indicator of mechanization. In Britain in 1935 it ranked second in order of magnitude and in 1951 within the top four industries, measured by this ratio. In the U.S.A. on both occasions it ranked within the top five.[1] Such mechanization is employed typically in large plants, as these were defined by Florence in 1948, namely that 50 per cent or more of the total number of people employed in the industry were in establishments of 1,000 workers or more.[2] In 1951 the actual figure for iron and steel, melting and rolling was 68.1 per cent—fifth in order of this magnitude.[3] Of course, relatively large-scale industrial units were common in the iron and steel industry 'long before these had appeared—apart from exceptional cases—in the textile and other trades' in the early days of the Industrial Revolution.[4] Richard Crawshay, for example, owned six iron furnaces in 1803 and employed over 2,000 men at one plant alone.[5] Contemporary data on scale, that is to say, should not be loosely read as also implying growth. Nevertheless, the general point is clear enough; the iron and steel industry exhibits those kind of technical characteristics which justify its treatment as in the vanguard of the development of the material forces of production in the Marxist sense, as com-

---

[1] Philip S. Florence, *Post-War Investment, Location and Size of Plant*, Cambridge University Press, 1962, Appendix C, p. 51.
[2] Florence, *Investment*, op. cit., Table IIc, p. 17.
[3] Florence, *Post-War Investment*, op. cit., Appendix A, p. 35.
[4] Ashton, op. cit., p. 7.
[5] Ibid., p. 96.

pared with the general level of our own and previous times; and this implies that the iron and steel proletariat should be amongst the leaders of the working-class movement.[1]

It is, therefore, of some importance to notice that evidence of trade union organisation amongst this section of the proletariat is very meagre indeed for the eighteenth century and is confined in any case to the fringes of the industry. No information has come down to us about combinations of smelters, founders and forgemen.[2] Crawshay's puddlers at Cyfartha are recorded as going on strike on threat of a reduction of wages in July 1816[3], but there is no indication that a permanent organisation existed amongst them and blame seems to have been attached instead to *Calvinistic* Methodists whose doctrines were said to be 'influential and dangerous'.[4] On the other hand, ironfounders are listed by the Webbs amongst those who in 1819 were prosecuted 'nominally for leaving their work unfinished, but really for the crime of combination',[5] and the Friendly Society of Ironfounders which had over seventy branches and more than 7,000 members in the middle of the nineteenth century, was formed in 1805,[6] although the foundation of John Kane's Associated Iron and Steel Workers of Great Britain in 1862 is usually taken as the beginning of the national movement of iron and steel workers as they are organised today.[7]

Marx himself appears never to have noticed this peculiarity of the workers in the Iron and Steel industry, which in the light of his anticipation of revolution as early as 1848, surely requires explanation. No matter how we interpret the part played by this section of the proletariat in the events *after 1862*, it seems abundantly clear that it was not in the vanguard of the creation

[1] See above, pp. 21 and 53.

[2] Ashton, op. cit., p. 206.

[3] Arthur Aspinall, ed., *The Early English Trade Unions, Documents from the Home Office Papers in the Public Record Office*, Batchworth Press, 1949, p. 220.

[4] Ibid., p. 231.

[5] Sidney and Beatrice Webb, *The History of Trade Unionism*, 2nd edition, Workers' Educational Association, 1912, p. 69.

[6] Sidney and Beatrice Webb, *Industrial Democracy*, Longmans Green, 1911, p. 112, n. 1. James C. Carr and W. Taplin, *History of the British Steel Industry*, Blackwell, 1962, pp. 14–15. Alan Birch, *The Economic History of the British Iron and Steel Industry*, Cass, 1967, dates this as 1809, p. 248.

[7] Arthur Pugh, *Men of Steel by One of Them*, Iron and Steel Trades Confederation, 1951, pp. 32 et seq.

of those institutions which are said to typify the emergence of a self-conscious working class between 1790 and 1830.[1] For all that iron and steelworkers may have been encouraged by 'the very novelty and rapidity of the social change which engulfed them . . . to think in terms of an entirely changed society, based on their experience and ideas as opposed to their oppressors',[2] they do not seem to have flocked to join in with the textile, clothing, building and pottery workers who figure so prominently in the annals of the 'general' union movements of the 1830's.[3] Nor, unlike the cotton workers, did they hasten to subscribe to the Chartist Land Plan in the 1840's.[4] Indeed, their support for Chartism generally seems to have been confined to South Wales, where some workers at Cyfartha and Dowlais are known to have been sacked for being Chartists in 1842.[5]

Thus, there is much to be said for the view that the iron and steel workers of that time stood apart from the revolutionary class consciousness of the 'labouring poor' because it was 'utopian' rather than 'scientific' in the Marxist sense. In so far as it is true that before 1848 working class militancy was characteristic of 'the skilled craftsmen, independent artisans, small-scale domestic workers and others who lived and worked substantially as they had done before the Industrial Revolution, but under far greater pressure',[6] it is likely that such pressure was lacking in this rapidly expanding industry; and hence, those kind of disturbances which led to millenarianism, as was the case on the fringes of textiles, [7] did not appear amongst iron

[1] Edward P. Thompson, *The Making of the English Working Class*, Gollancz, 1963, pp. 193–204. For the alternative view, that there was no such unified, self-conscious, working class at this time, see R. Currie and R. M. Hartwell, 'The Making of the English Working Class', *Economic History Review*, 2nd Series, Vol. 18, 1965, pp. 633–43.

[2] Eric J. Hobsbawm, *The Age of Revolution, Europe, 1789–1848*, Weidenfeld and Nicholson, 1962, p. 209. Hobsbawm argues that class consciousness was born of such novelty early in the century.

[3] S. and B. Webb, *History of Trade Unionism*, op. cit., Ch. 3. George D. H. Cole, *Attempts at General Union*, MacMillan, 1953, *passim*.

[4] J. MacAskill, 'The Chartist Land Plan' in Asa Briggs, ed., *Chartist Studies*, MacMillan, 1960, p. 317.

[5] D. Williams, 'Chartism in Wales' in A. Briggs, ed., op. cit., p. 244.

[6] Hobsbawm, op. cit., p. 213.

[7] Neil J. Smelser, *Social Change in the Industrial Revolution*, Routledge and Kegan Paul, 1959, Ch. 10.

and steel workers. The process whereby they might work their way forward through trade-union consciousness and political consciousness to revolutionary class consciousness, rather than being telescoped into the years between the first modern expansion of the industry and 1848, seems to have begun effectively in what Marx contemptuously referred to as 'the period of corruption' after 1848,[1] and appears to have run in parallel with technical and organisational developments on the employers' side.

In this respect, it should be understood, Marx himself misinterpreted what was going on, not because the facts necessarily contradicted predictions made from his set of hypotheses, but because he was politically too eager for capitalism to be overthrown in his lifetime to be patient with the slowness of the processes of change. Paradoxically, indeed, the evidence that Marx made no reference at all to the iron and steel industry,[2] may be read as indicating that the kind of organisation which was emerging in that industry, was more in accord with what the first four chapters of this book might lead one to expect, than otherwise. The iron and steel unions of his later years were combinations of the better paid sections of the working class.[3] It was not poverty caused by low wages, nor destitution caused by unemployment, which led them into industrial action, but on the contrary the difficulties of their employers, faced by growing competition from abroad.[4] It is also important to notice, although this is not so easily accommodated in the

[1] Karl Marx, letter to W. Liebknecht, 11th February 1878, reprinted in Karl Marx and Frederick Engels, *On Britain*, Foreign Languages Publishing House, 1953, p. 509.

[2] Engels noted that one of the greatest efforts of the Industrial Revolution was the expansion of the iron industry, but neither he nor Marx followed the point through. Frederick Engels, *The Condition of the Working-Class in England* (1944), republished in Marx and Engels, *On Britain*, op. cit., p. 46. Lenin, on the other hand, asserted that 'in Russia—as probably in other capitalist countries—the metal workers represent the vanguard of the proletariat'. They are 'the best paid, the most class conscious and best educated proletarians'. Vladimir I. Lenin, 'Lecture on the 1905 Revolution', 9th January 1917, published in his *Collected Works*, Progress Publications, Vol. 23, 1964, pp. 240–1.

[3] For details, see Carr and Taplin, op. cit., p. 146.

[4] Ibid., Chapters 3 and 4, Duncan L. Burn, *The Economic History of Steelmaking 1867–1939*, Cambridge University Press, 1940, Chs. 1 and 2.

Marxist framework, that their combination was set in the context of challenge to their position coming from the less privileged workers in their own industry. Thus, the puddlers, shinglers, furnacemen, rollers, and other millmen of the National Amalgamated Association of Ironmen were 'very largely' contractors paid on tonnage rates, who employed underhands to whom they paid day rates.[1] These latter were entitled to join the Association 'at half the contribution. But this afforded them no trade union protection, since they could take no active part in its proceedings, (and) could not be elected on its executive'.[2] The iron and steel unions began, that is to say, very much as organisations of sectional interests among the working class and only slowly moved towards a more united front.

Indeed, the passing of the old contract system is illuminating in this respect. In 1886, when the British Steel Smelters' Union was formed, what Hobsbawm has called, 'co-exploitation',[3] was still very general in the steel trade, just as it was in the iron trade. The new union, under the leadership of John Hodge, was implacably opposed to the system from the start, whereas the Ironmen's union, soon to become the Associated Iron and Steel Workers of Great Britain,[4] was its main advocate. The difference between them, it is said, 'arose from the contrast between the two systems of organizing production. In both iron and steel the contractors were paid by the ton; but whereas in iron the contractor was the leading man in each process, employing the less-skilled day-wage man, in steel he ran a whole melting shop, which normally contained a number of furnaces each with its complement of leading and subordinate hands, all of whom were paid day wages. In the forges and rolling mills he might contract for one, two or three mills, each

[1] Hugh A. Clegg, A. Fox and A. F. Thompson, *A History of British Trade Unions since 1889*, Clarendon Press, Vol. 1, 1964, p. 22.

[2] Pugh, op. cit., p. 157.

[3] Eric J. Hobsbawm, 'The Labour Aristocracy in Nineteenth Century Britain' in his *Labouring Men: Studies in the History of Labour*, Weidenfeld and Nicolson, 1964, p. 298. The contract system 'made many members of the labour aristocracy into co-employers of their mates, and their unskilled workers'. See also Reinhard Bendix, *Work and Authority in Industry*, Wiley, 1956, pp. 53–5.

[4] Pugh, op. cit., pp. 67–71.

with its team of workers. The steel unions—for this applies also
to the Associated Society of Millmen—were at first composed
almost entirely of day-wage men with a direct interest in
abolishing the contract system. They thus started life with a
radical egalitarian approach which contrasted sharply with the
aristocratic conservatism of the Iron workers'.[1] This last sentence
should, of course, not be read too carelessly. At the turn of the
century first hand melters in thirteen important British steelworks earned an average £7 6s od per week, while third hands
averaged £3 11s 6d[2]—a ratio of 2.28 : 1. The point to notice
is that the abolition of the contract system meant a loss of income
to the contractor, who became a tonnage man along with the
rest of the men, previously on day wages, while their incomes
were increased, sometimes by as much as 30—40 per cent.[3]
Moreover, and this was the main line of attack in John Hodge's
method of negotiation, the firm also benefited by an increase in
ouput.[4] The termination of the system, that is to say, was to the
advantage of both the employers and most employees, but for
reasons that are not at all clear it was, as Burn has put it, 'a
long time a-dying, and succumbed piecemeal'.[5]

In this connection it is important to emphasize that there was
no head-on clash between the unions for twenty years, for all
that they were opposed in principle. The secretary of the
Associated Iron and Steel Workers protested, it is true, at some
'poaching' of its members by Hodge's union in 1904,[6] but it was
not until 1909 that the issue came out into the open, and it is
significant that the events which precipitated the crisis were
related to organisational developments within the industry.
In that year John Summers and Sons, who were one of the
principal galvanized sheet makers in the country, decided to
lay down a steel plant for the purpose of making their own
steel bars on the spot. James Cox's Associated Iron and Steel
Workers' Union already organised the sheet mill contractors,

[1] Clegg, Fox and Thompson, op. cit., p. 205.
[2] Burn, op. cit., p. 142, n. 2.
[3] Carr and Taplin, op. cit., p. 141.
[4] John Hodge, *Workman's Cottage to Windsor Castle*, Low, Marston, 1938,
pp. 83–6.
[5] Burn, op. cit., p. 142, n. 3.
[6] Pugh, op. cit., p. 78.

but the new steel plant was organised by Hodge's Steel Smelters. In Pugh's words, the day men in the old mill 'could hardly fail to note the difference between their own position and that of their fellow workmen in the various departments of the steel works'. About a hundred of them, accordingly, joined Hodge's union, but were refused admission to a branch meeting on the ground that the tonnage men did not want to be 'swamped' by day-wage men. They staged an unsuccessful strike which nevertheless prompted the firm to put pressure on Cox's union to allow the day men to join, but 'within a few weeks of the branch being formed the contractors began a process of intimidation and coercion. Promotion was refused to men who by experience and seniority were entitled to it, and strangers brought in to fill vacancies. Men active in the new branch were discharged on one pretext or the other'. There then followed fourteen months of conflict, strikes, counter-strikes and attempts by the firm to employ blackleg labour. An abortive attempt at enquiry by the Trades Union Congress led to the withdrawal of Hodge's union from that body. Separate agreements with the two unions were signed by the firm and, although the upshot was the acceptance of the principle that both unions had the right to organise workers in the plant, the contract system was abolished. The underhands in the sheet mills took advantage of the agreement to negotiate direct employment with the firm on a tonnage or piece-work basis.[1]

This instance has been dealt with in some detail because it illustrates the point that trade union solidarity is not an automatic response to technical and organisational developments within an industry. To some degree these developments may result in conflicts of interest between different groups of workers which divert their attention away from working-class solidarity against the class of capitalist employers. Such conflicts of interest show themselves in inter-union struggles which have to be reduced to a minimum if revolutionary class consciousness is to flourish. In this case only a short period of time elapsed—six years—before the two unions were able

---

[1] Ibid., pp. 157–65. The accounts in Carr and Taplin, op. cit., pp. 282–4, and Clegg, Fox and Thompson, op. cit., pp. 447–8, are based on Pugh's admittedly confused account. Differences between them and that of the text above are largely differences in emphasis.

effectively to discuss amalgamation, forming along with the National Steel Workers' Association, Engineering and Labour League, a federated organization, the Iron and Steel Trades Confederation. This was, indeed, the prelude to a wholesale closing of the ranks in the steel industry, paralleling amalgamation and association on the employers' side.[1] Yet, for neither the workers nor the employers was there ever achieved the kind of unity in organisation which the Marxist hypothesizing seems to require. In 1951 there were still 282 'business units' engaged in melting and rolling in Britain, 24 in the manufacture of coke, 21 manufacturing steel sheets, and 35 producing iron,[2] although of course, some firms were counted more than once if they were engaged in more than one of these trades. There were, similarly, for iron and steel alone 17 separate trade unions.[3] Hence, although throughout its history the British Steel Smelters' Union had proclaimed itself in favour of what is usually referred to as industrial unionism, eighty years of industrial struggle has still left much to be achieved. The principle that 'in a well-defined industry such as iron and steel all workers engaged and necessary to the process of production, whatever their particular occupation, should as a matter of sound trade union practice be in the same organisation',[4] remains an ideal not an actuality; and this raises the question of whether the failure to achieve organizational unity needs to be explained if the Marxist approach to industrial relations is to stand.

In the *Manifesto of the Communist Party* there is a passage which is indicative of Marx's thinking on this point and of one aspect of his alienation thesis. 'Owing to the extensive use of machinery and to division of labour', he and Engels wrote, 'the work of the proletarians has lost all individual character, and, consequently, all charm for the workmen. He becomes an appendage of the machine, and it is only the most simple, most monotonous, and most easily acquired knack, that is required of him. . . . The less the skill and exertion of strength implied in manual labour, in other words, the more modern industry becomes developed,

[1] Burn, op. cit., pp. 370–82, 438–9.
[2] Eveley and Little, op. cit., Tables 3 and 4, pp. 54–8.
[3] Anglo-American Council on Productivity, Productivity Team Report, *Iron and Steel*, June 1952, p. 129.
[4] Pugh, op. cit., p. 20.

the more is the labour of men superseded by women. Differences of age and sex have no longer any distinctive social validity for the working class. All are instruments of labour'.[1] What Marx seems to have had in mind was a continuing historical process from craftsmanship to factory production with its 'tendency to equalize and reduce to one and the same level every kind of work that has to be done by the minders of the machines'. With the exception of 'a numerically unimportant class of persons, whose occupation it is to look after the whole of the machinery and repair it from time to time; such as engineers, mechanics, joiners, etc.',[2] that is to say, he seems to have thought that the direction of technical development was towards a situation where jobs would become so lacking in skill, so undifferentiated, that workers would become readily inter-changeable.[3] In these circumstances trade union solidarity would be enhanced. Separate unions for interchangeable occupations would cease to exist, and presumably industrial unionism, at least, would be a logical step in the process.

It should be emphasized that this is an inference, not a para-phrase of Marx's position. There are not enough detailed statements about trade unions in his writings to justify the categorical assertion that in fact he held this view, or for that matter, any other. Nevertheless, if his system of ideas is to be tested, inferences of this kind have to be made. The point is that technological and organisational developments in an industry must be held to be basic, if the Marxist approach is to be preserved, and from what he wrote on the matter the pre-ceding paragraph would seem to be a reasonable inference. Hence, the passing of the contract system may be interpreted in this light. During the years in which it was in decline 'the qualities required in a workman were being changed by the ad-vance of labour-saving plants. Nervous energy, as Marx put it, was taking the place of muscular energy, and though for most steelworkers' jobs, the men needed some training—often short —a rapidly decreasing number required either great strength or handicraft skill. Parallel with the decreasing importance of these qualities, the value of order and discipline grew. The

---

[1] Marx and Engels, *Selected Works*, op. cit., Vol. 1, p. 39.
[2] Marx, *Capital*, op. cit., Vol. 1, p. 420.
[3] Marx, *Wage, Labour and Capital*, op. cit., p. 95.

satisfactory working of a plant depended increasingly on the orderly performance of mechanical functions by a defined number of men'.[1] Collective endeavour, that is to say, became the key to productivity; and the demonstration that increased output could be achieved by paying tonnage rates to the melters would seem to be a possibly logical consequence of the development of steel technology.

This, however, does not satisfactorily account for the persistence of more than one trade union on the production side of a contemporary steelworks. When discussions were begun between the British Steel Smelters' Union and the Dockers' Union in 1861, for example, the latter resisted the moves which led eventually to the establishment of the Iron and Steel Trades Federation on the ground that this 'must mean . . . the "lopping off" of that section of the membership connected with the industry'.[2] While John Hodge had been campaigning against the contract system, and his union members had been resisting the request of the day workers employed by the contractors to join their union, Ben Tillett's union had been recruiting these underhands as general labourers to its ranks; and it successfully maintained them as a section of the Dockers' Union throughout the period of consolidation and amalgamation in the steel industry, during and immediately after the First World War. Nor is it the case that the simple division into wage labourers and tonnage labourers is what distinguishes the unions today. Although it is to a large extent the case that the Dockers' Union—now, of course, the Transport and General Workers' Union—organizes steelmen on finishing, packing and transport jobs not subject to tonnage rates, and the Iron and Steel Trades Confederation[3] organizes the men in melting and rolling work paid on a tonnage basis, no clear and permanent lines are drawn between the two types of jobs. At the margin,

[1] Burn, op. cit., p. 145. He gives no source for the reference to Marx.

[2] Pugh, op. cit., p. 256.

[3] For the purpose of this analysis it seems reasonable to use this name throughout. The meticulous, however, will be aware that the I.S.T.C. is the negotiating body and that another union, established at the same time by the same combining unions, deals with administrative matters. This is the British Iron, Steel and Kindred Trades Association; but it is not strictly speaking a different union from the I.S.T.C. in the sense that the T. and G.W.U. or the National Union of Blastfurnacemen is.

so to speak, the demarcation lines between unions are constantly shifting and workers employed at a steelplant experience being moved from one union to another many times in the course of their working lives.

Or again, the case of coke oven workers and blast-furnacemen is even more clearly illustrative of the point. There is a union, the National Union of Blastfurnacemen, Ore Miners, Coke Workers and Kindred Trades, which in general covers such employees in a modern, integrated steelplant. But in some firms the coke oven workers are organized by the I.S.T.C.; and in Scotland, this union is also responsible for the blast-furnace workers. Technical changes, especially when they involve backward integration, in the steel industry are in consequence inevitably accompanied by inter-union negotiations to decide which union is going to organize the men in the new, or changed jobs.[1] Clearly these are events in the field of industrial relations which would not occur if there were in fact a single industrial union to cater for all these workers, and they raise the question of whether, in spite of Marx's prediction about occupational homogeneity as the inevitable consequence of contemporary technological developments, occupational heterogeneity might not in fact have persisted, if not increased over time, giving workers in different occupations some kind of vested interest in maintaining their distinctiveness in spite of employment in a single industry. As opposed to Marx, for example, the growth of large-scale production has resulted in the proportion of the production workers in a single large steelworks falling from 82 per cent in 1925 to 65 per cent in 1953,[2] while the proportion of skilled craftsmen rose from about 7 per cent to 11 per cent,[3] forming a not insignificantly numerical working force at that time. Such workers, employed in maintaining the furnaces and machines, comprise fitters, turners, machinists, smiths, organized by the Amalgamated Engineering Union; electricians, organized by the Electrical Trades Union; welders, burners, platers, organized by the United Society of Boilermakers;

---

[1] William H. Scott, *et al.*, *Technical Change and Industrial Relations: A Study of the Relations between Technical Change and the Social Structure of a Large Steel Works*, Liverpool University Press, 1956, pp. 139–49.

[2] Ibid., Table 2, p. 44.

[3] Ibid., p. 153.

moulders, coremakers, organized by the Amalgamated Union of Foundryworkers, joiners, carpenters, organized by the Amalgamated Society of Woodworkers; and bricksetters, organized by the Amalgamated Union of Building Trade Workers.[1] The skills they use are not readily interchangeable, and their persistence raises questions which are not readily solved by reference to the Marxist analysis of industrial relations.

The nature of this argument should not be misunderstood. The truth, or falsity, of the Marxist system of explanatory hypotheses is not necessarily being challenged here; for, it might be the case that in spite of the perpetuation of multi-unionism in the British steel industry, there is sufficient unity of purpose for the unions to present for the most part a united front against their employers, sufficient to serve as evidence of class consciousness in their midst. Thus, all the craft unions listed above, with the exception of the Amalgamated Union of Building Trade Workers, are members of the National Joint Trade Union Craftsmen's Iron and Steel Committee, set up in 1947 to deal with common problems of craftsmen in the industry and to serve as 'national machinery of negotiation, providing for the ventilation of questions at all levels;'[2] and it could be the case that a united front might exist without there being formal machinery of negotiation established for the purpose. The argument, therefore, is not that data such as the continued existence of many trade unions in a single industry disprove the Marxist analysis, but rather that further examination of the question is needed before their significance can be properly appreciated. It might be that multi-unionism is an irrelevancy, although in this case the student of industrial relations might feel an explanation is nevertheless called for and be impatient of Marxism for failing to supply it. He might, indeed, look elsewhere for an explanation and, having found one, also discover that this provides a satisfactory account of all the other aspects of industrial relations covered by the Marxist approach. In such an event he would be justified in regarding the latter as an inference from an even more general theory, irrespective of its power to account for social changes elsewhere in society or

[1] Ibid., p. 154.
[2] *National Joint Trade Union of Craftsmen's Iron and Steel Committee Handbook, 1949*, Preface.

in other epochs. To the extent that the aim of science is to widen the coverage of explanatory theories, the social scientist may well expect the Marxist set of hypotheses to be replaced at some time by a broader theory of industrial relations. This is a possibility that must always be borne in mind.

For example, noting that 'the unfinished concluding section of Karl Marx's *Kapital* was evidently intended to deal with the problem of the class unity of the proletariat, which he held existed in spite of the high degree of qualitative differentiation',[1] Max Weber introduced what could prove to be a radical departure from the position of Marx in this respect. Regarding social classes as formed of 'groups of people who, from the standpoint of specific interests, have the same economic position', he asserted that 'ownership or nonownership of material goods, or possession of definite skills constitutes a class situation'.[2] The distinction between the two types of class determination is important because elsewhere Weber distinguished between 'property classes' and 'primarily market-determined income classes', claiming that the latter were especially prevalent in modern times'.[3] For all, therefore, that he referred to property ownership and 'lack of property' as the basic categories of all class situations,[4] he nevertheless gave a very prominent place to 'skills', arguing that 'only persons who are completely unskilled, without property and dependent on employment without regular occupation, are in a strictly identical class status'.[5] This implies that the market situation of the trade unionist, as determined not only by his lack of property but also, and perhaps even more so, by his possession or non-possession of a relatively scarce skill, could prove to be the important differentiating factor *within* the propertyless classes, leading to forms of trade union organization and con-

[1] Max Weber, *The Theory of Social and Economic Organisation*, trans. by A. R. Henderson and T. Parsons, Hodge, 1947, p. 179. The reference is to *Capital*, Vol. 3, Ch. 52.

[2] M. Weber, *The Religion of India*, trans. by H. H. Gerth and D. Martindale, Free Press, 1958, p. 39. See also *From Max Weber; Essays on Sociology*, trans. by H. H. Gerth and C. W. Mills, Kegan Paul, Trench, Trubrer, 1947, p. 405.

[3] *From Max Weber*, op. cit., p. 301.

[4] Ibid., p. 182.

[5] Weber, *Theory*, op. cit., p. 390.

sciousness distinct from, and even distinctive of, working-class unity.

The impact of the market situation had, indeed, already been given prominence by the Webbs, who described the ideology of 'the right to a trade' and the device of restricting as a 'vested interest' which workers organized to retain. 'To men dependent for daily existence on continuous employment, the protection of their means of livelihood from confiscation or encroachment appears as fundamental a basis of social order as it does to the owners of land. What both parties claim is security and continuity of lifelihood—the maintenance of the 'established expectation' which is the 'conditions precedent' of civilized life'.[1] Of course, they were aware that not all trade unions in their day adopted the device—'a few trades still making the strict Limitation of Apprentices and the Exclusion of Illegal Men a leading feature of their policy, whilst others throw their trades absolutely open to all comers'[2]—and they noted that the fraction which operated apprenticeship regulations was dwindling; but these were 'notwithstanding a strong trade union feeling in favour' of such regulations.[3] The persistence of this feeling in the face of technical changes and other events leading to encroachments on the right to a trade is what has to be explained.

As against Weber it should be emphasized that 'skill' in some objective sense is not the issue of significance. Trade unions do not provide their own training for apprentices. This is provided by firms. Nor are the unions much concerned with the adequacy of the training. The employers' endorsement of the apprentice's indentures is all they require in order to issue the skilled 'ticket' which entitles a worker to the wage rate of craftsmen.[4] As the Webbs themselves pointed out, such a device of restricting entry does not necessarily mean that quality of entrants is high.[5] Indeed, the stipulation that an apprenticeship must last for five years and what has been called 'the unions' obsession

---

[1] S. and B. Webb, *Industrial Democracy*, op. cit., p. 566.
[2] Ibid., p. 561.
[3] Ibid., p. 476.
[4] Kate Liepmann, *Apprenticeship: an Enquiry into its Adequacy under Modern Conditions*, Routledge and Kegan Paul, 1960, p. 140.
[5] S. and B. Webb, *Industrial Democracy*, op. cit., pp. 705–6.

with the age of twenty-one, at which every training must end'[1] restrict both the entry of older men and that of grammar-school boys, except where the latter leave school early, before their education is complete, in order to enter a 'skilled' trade.[2] Clearly, a union's power to control entry in such a fashion, whenever it results in a shortage of such ticket holders becomes a very good reason for its members to resist amalgamation with other, not so powerful, unions. In this sense, wage-differentials produced by differences in the market situation for different kinds of labour are themselves, in part at least, influenced by trade union action.

Such an approach towards an alternative explanation might also serve to accommodate other intractable facts which do not fit easily into the Marxist scheme, such as the part actually played by trade union leaders in the development of revolutionary class consciousness. Towards the end of his life Marx complained that the English working class had allowed its direction to pass 'completely into the hands of the venal trade-union leaders and professional agitators',[3] and Engels similarly referred to the petty 'jealousies of the particular trades, which become intensified in the hands and heads of the leaders to the point of direct hostility and underhand struggle'.[4] Apparently the argument here is that unity of purpose in the form of trade union solidarity is undermined because of the vested interests of the leadership. In terms of the simple pauperization thesis this could only be a temporary phenomenon, but once the Marxist hypotheses about polarization and pauperization are separated, as in Chapter III above, the argument is changed. Because contemporary society is a stratified society, movement up the inside of the trade union power structure involves also an advance up the income hierarchy. Trade union leaders, especially in America, have nowadays 'the income and prestige of a member of the upper-middle class'.[5] They have many personal

---

[1] Gertrude Williams, *Recruitment to Skilled Trades*, Routledge and Kegan Paul, 1957, p. 179. See also Liepmann, op. cit., pp. 157–8.

[2] Olive Banks, *Parity and Prestige in English Secondary Education*, Routledge and Kegan Paul, 1955, p. 194.

[3] Karl Marx, Letter to W. Liebknecht, 11th February 1878, reprinted in Marx and Engels, *On Britain*, op. cit., p. 509.

[4] F. Engels, letter to F. A. Sorge, 19th April 1890, ibid., p. 525.

[5] Seymour M. Lipset, M. A. Trow and J. S. Coleman, *Union Democracy*,

reasons for wanting to stay in office, and they will resist democratic interference in their activities by the membership, including no doubt any demand for amalgamation which could
result in the disappearance of their jobs. Regarding such
authority as a very good example of his 'iron law' of oligarchy,
Michels pointed out that by the turn of the century the right to
strike had passed in this way from the rank-and-file to the
leadership, on the tactical ground, that the latter knew better
than the former 'the conditions of the labour market thoughout
the country'.[1] In this respect there is much to be said for the
view that 'the labour leader organizes and sells wage workers
to the highest bidder on the best terms available. He is a jobber
of labour power. He accepts the general conditions of labour
under capitalism and then, as a contracting agent operating
within that system, he higgles and bargains over wages, hours,
and working conditions for the members of his union'.[2]

To the extent that this is true, it is to be expected that trade
union leaders will occasionally be at serious odds with some
sections of the membership, especially in those cases where the
union is composed of workers not in identical situations with
respect to the demand for their labour. Thus the General
Executive Council of the Transport and General Workers'
Union and its secretary, Ernest Bevin, in spite of a special
interest in the dockers, so failed to carry their London members
with them in an agreement over a staggered reduction of
wages in 1922 that a few thousand dockers left the union and
joined a rival organization which became the National Amalgamated Stevedors, Lightermen, Watermen and Dockers'
Union.[3] The T. and G.W.U. also experienced similar trouble
with London busmen in 1938 when an unofficial strike led to
the formation of the National Passenger Workers' Union;[4]

The Free Press, 1956, p. 10. For data on Britain see P. Jenkins, 'Unions:
What Makes The Leaders Tick?', *New Society*, 18th October 1962, pp. 9–10.
[1] Robert Michels, *Political Parties*, Dover Publications, 1959 (trans. by
Eden and Cedar Paul, 1915), pp. 143–5.
[2] Charles W. Mills, *The New Men of Power*, Harcourt, Brace, 1948, p. 6.
[3] Victor L. Allen, *Trade Union Leadership*, Longmans Green, 1957, pp.
58–9.
[4] Hugh A. Clegg, *Labour Relations in London Transport*, Blackwell, 1950,
Ch. 4.

and a minority of workers in the Tailors' and Government Workers' Union seceded in a like fashion in 1929 to form the United Clothing Workers' Union.[1] The explanation for such breakaway movements has been sought for partly in terms of the size and complexity of the parent unions and partly in terms of their heterogeneous membership. 'Unless their varied and sometimes conflicting needs and interests are met they eventually revolt. Secessions occur because members believe they should have greater power to control those decisions which affect them and because they lack this power within their union'.[2] The leadership, that is to say, may be faced with hostility arising from differences in interests within the union which it fails to reconcile. Of course, it may be argued that such conflicts are *really* the product of a clash between trade union consciousness and genuine class consciousness in the Marxist sense, but if this is maintained it must necessarily be shown which of the two outlooks is revolutionary, and how a particular group which is opposed to the rest has come to develop such contrary views. As in all such matters of verification, sheer assertion is not enough.

At this point the analysis has moved a long way from the examination of unity amongst steelworkers considered as an example of how such verification might proceed; and there is a danger that a digression on an alternative approach towards the explanation of an apparently minor discrepancy might usurp the place of the major concern. For this reason consideration of the analysis of industrial relations in Weberian, market-situation terms will be postponed and the chapter drawn to a close. The main theme has been that trade union solidarity in an industry in the vanguard of technical and organizational progress has not resulted in a single 'industrial' union but in multi-unionism. That this is not an inevitable consequence of

[1] Shirley W. Lerner, *Breakaway Unions and the Small Trade Union*, Allen and Unwin, 1961, Ch. 3.

[2] Ibid., p. 190. The origin of the National Union of Blastfurnacemen has been accounted for in these terms, i.e. as a kind of breakaway union from Kane's Ironmen in the period 1871–5. The Cleveland blastfurnacemen believed that they were 'deserted' by Kane's union and this convinced them that 'they must have a separate and strong union of their own'. Jack Owen, *Ironmen: A Short Story of the History of the Union from 1878 to 1953*, National Union of Blastfurnacemen, n.d. (1953?), pp. 10–11.

technical development, moreover, is borne out by the fact that in the American steel industry the opposite prevails. There are no separate craft unions. Process, service and maintenance workers are all organized by the United Steelworkers of America.[1] The fact that there are differences in the union organization within the same industries in different countries is another discrepancy which does not fit easily into the Marxist scheme. Nevertheless it does not make good scientific sense to reject the scheme outright at this stage merely because a number of points of contention have arisen. The dynamic structure of the Marxist conception of social change requires that at least an attempt be made to discover whether, in spite of the reservations which such awkward facts raise, the trend from union organization towards revolutionary class consciousness might nevertheless have occurred. Until this is done the correct significance of multi-unionism in Britain, in so far as the Marxist scheme of analysis is concerned, will not be properly understood, and it is towards a further elucidation of this problem that the study now turns.

[1] Anglo-American Council on Productivity, *Iron and Steel*, op. cit., pp. 75–6.

7

UNION MILITANCY

'Strikes', wrote the Webbs, 'are as old as history itself', and they cited 'the revolt, 1490 B.C., of the Hebrew brickmakers in Egypt against being required to make bricks without straw' as 'a curious precedent for the strike of the Stalybridge cotton-spinners, A.D. 1892, against the supply of bad material for their work'.[1] The point of this quotation is to support the argument that the record of a strike, as such, is not a reliable pointer to the existence of 'a continuous association of wage-earners for the purpose of maintaining or improving the conditions of their employment', which is what the Webbs understood a trade union to be.[2] Strikes in the past have occurred without there being a trade union already in existence to organise the strikers and to marshal their energies; and even in a period of history when trade union organization is the norm, strikes may occur without benefit of such organizations. The charwomen at the Burtonwood air-base, for example, who went on strike for several weeks in 1955, have been instanced as a case in point.[3] Hence, the incidence of strikes in an industry is not necessarily a very good measure of the degree of militancy displayed by the unions in that industry, for all that it may be indicative of industrial unrest there. Some other way of estimating the extent

---

[1] S. and B. Webb, *The History of Trade Unionism*, op. cit., p. 2. See also the examples given in Kenneth G. J. C. Knowles, *Strikes: A Study in Industrial Conflict*, Blackwell, 1952, pp. 1–2. Knowles uses them to support his much weaker argument that strikes are 'almost as old as work itself'.

[2] S. and B. Webb, *History*, op. cit., p. 1.

[3] Herbert A. Turner, *Trade Union Growth, Structure and Policy*, Allen and Unwin, 1962, p. 87.

of union solidarity, in so far as this is shown in collective action against employers, must be used if the issues raised towards the end of the previous chapter are to be explored in these terms.

Of course, this should not be read to imply that strike statistics should be ignored as altogether misleading. After all, Marx himself regarded strikes as significant. He thought that they always indicated that the workers on strike were engaged in some kind of collective struggle against their employers, and that they might indeed serve as a source of revolutionary class consciousness in the sense that strikers might learn from such experiences how the economic system really worked.[1] But just as Marx, and Lenin after him, drew a distinction between economic and political action as demonstrating different levels of revolutionary awareness, so they regarded a strike carried on by an established trade union as a more effective instrument for promoting social change on the economic front than a spontaneous outburst of working-class indignation. There are, that is to say, strikes and strikes; and the difference between them can only be understood in Marxist terms by the degree to which the drive behind them is informed by revolutionary class consciousness, or where this is lacking, by their relative effectiveness in producing revolutionary change.

There are, in consequence, many technical problems to be overcome if the employment of strike statistics for present purposes is to be fruitful. The published British figures, for example, do not differentiate trade union members from non-members in the number of workers recorded as having been involved in strikes or lockouts; nor do they usually distinguish unofficial from official strikes. Even the classification of industries is crude. Only seven industrial groups are identified in the annual statistics, and the figures for the iron and steel industry, of special interest here, are included in the compendious group of metal, engineering, ship-building, etc.[2] Moreover, many disputes between workers and their employers are not included in the figures at all. In Britain a stoppage of work is 'notifiable' only if it involves ten or more persons and lasts for at least one day or shift. Shorter stoppages which are, therefore, not recorded may nevertheless represent a not inconsiderable part

---

[1] Lozovsky, op. cit., Ch. 8.
[2] Knowles, op. cit., 'Statistical Appendix', *passim*.

of the procedure of negotiation and dispute in a situation of general conflict.[1] At the same time, the task of recording such disputes and those which are resolved without strike action is considerable, so that it hardly becomes possible to supplement the lack of official data by private research. In one colliery alone, for example, where 166 disputes passed through the conciliatory machinery in a period of eight months between November, 1957 and June 1958, the relevant information was obtained only through discussions once a week with two under-managers and the colliery manager, supplemented by less frequent consultations with the full-time union officers.[2] Obviously, to extend such a technique of investigation even to cover a whole industry, to say nothing of a comparison of industries, would demand research resources beyond the command of most, if not all, contemporary sociological organizations.

It is in the light of these considerations that it is necessary to interpret the assertion about the iron and steel industry that from the point of view of industrial peace, this has been one of the model industries of Great Britain.[3] Not since the occasion of the strike at John Summers and Sons, described in the last chapter,[4] have there been any major disputes within the industry, and it is usually considered to be the least prone to strikes of all what are called 'metal' industries.[5] The official union position on strikes was indeed forcibly expressed by a former general secretary of the I.S.T.C. in a special preface which he wrote for the union history in 1951. 'We believe in the peaceful settlement of differences, we believed in it fifty years ago when in the climate of trade union opinion at that time it was almost heresy to do so. We never believed there was anything attractive about a strike, it being at best an ugly and painful necessity. As the records show, however, when the behaviour of an employer left no alternative but the strike, it

---

[1] William H. Scott, *et al.*, *Coal and Conflict*, Liverpool University Press, 1963, Ch. 4. Royal Commission on Trade Unions and Employers' Associations, 1965–8, *Report*, H.M.S.O., 1968, pp. 19–20.

[2] Ibid., p. 122.

[3] Ian G. Sharp, *Industrial Conciliation and Arbitration in Great Britain*, Allen and Unwin, 1950, p. 58.

[4] See above, pp. 74–5.

[5] Knowles, op. cit., p. 172.

was never shirked, but we never sought a fight under those conditions'.[1] How then, if at all, has the union been able to maintain a militant policy without recourse to strikes?

The answer to this question must be seen against the background of the device of establishing joint conciliatory organizations with employers. As early as 1869, about a year after he became General Secretary of the Amalgamated Malleable Ironworkers, John Kane became the workers' secretary to the Board of Arbitration and Conciliation for the Manufactured Iron Trade of the North of England, on the initiative of David Dale, a director of the Consett Iron Company and Honorary Secretary of the Iron Manufacturers' Association. For some years Dale had been trying to get his fellow manufacturers to agree to the establishment of some form of conciliation in the industry, and at last he had succeeded.[2] This Board for the North of England became, if not the model, at least the forerunner, of other Boards established in the 1870's and 1880's, and an account of its activities was very much in the forefront of the deliberations of the Royal Commission on Labour in 1892,[3] although this is perhaps not surprising once it is realized that amongst the Commissioners were David Dale and Edward Trow who had succeeded to both Kane's secretaryships at his death in 1876, as well as A. J. Mundella who had been instrumental in establishing joint conciliatory machinery in the Nottingham Hosiery industry in the early 1860's.[4] The Webbs, for their part, regarded David Dale as a 'shrewd leader of the employers' who sold John Kane and 'a whole subsequent generation of iron workers' an advantage 'at the cost of adopting the position of their opponents'[5]—an interpretation which is in no

[1] Lincoln Evans in Pugh, *Men of Steel*, op. cit., p. xiii.

[2] A. J. Odber, 'The Origins of Industrial Peace, The Manufactured Iron Trade of the North of England', *Oxford Economic Papers*, New Series, Vol. 3, 1951, pp. 207–9.

[3] The Royal Commission on Labour, *Fifth and Final Report*, H.M.S.O., 1894, paras. 83 (p. 32), 108 (p. 42), 113 (p. 43) and 138 (p. 51).

[4] Odber, op. cit. See also J. R. Hicks, 'The Early History of Industrial Conciliation in England', *Economica*, Vol. 10, 1930, pp. 25–39, and for Edward Trow, the evidence of William Whitwell to the Royal Commission on Labour, *Minutes of Evidence*, Group A, H.M.S.O., Vol. 2, 1892, Qq. 14,978 and 14,984, pp. 318 and 321.

[5] S. and B. Webb, *History*, op. cit., p. 324.

way altered by the later judgment that it was 'a condition of union survival at that time'.[1]

The point at issue is the fact that joint industrial councils, composed of workers' and employers' representatives, were associated in the iron and steel industry with the explicit intention of automatically adjusting wages to rise and fall with steel prices. 'The advantages claimed for this system', reported the Royal Commission on Labour, 'are (1) that it obviates disputes about wages, at any rate, during fixed periods; (2) that it promotes a feeling of co-partnership and common interest between employers and employed; (3) that it enables employers to calculate what will be the cost of production, in wages, for some time ahead, and, therefore, to enter into long contracts with some feeling of security; (4) that it causes alterations in the rates of wages to take place gradually and by a series of small steps, instead of suddenly and at a bound'.[2] Of course, bargaining as such is not ruled out altogether by such a device. The scales had to be agreed upon in the first place and were varied from time to time by further bargaining. Thus, although it had no fixed time for meetings, the Cleveland Joint Committee of Ironmasters and Blast Furnacemen, which was established by a Wages Sliding Scale Agreement in 1879, met altogether forty-one times in the ten years between 1882 and 1891, and many questions were discussed at each meeting.[3] As the Chairman of the Midland Iron and Steel Wages Board said to the Royal Commission, 'the existence of a sliding scale does not in any way get rid of the necessity for a board of conciliation—I think a board is absolutely necessary'.[4] The leaders of the steelmen's unions, indeed, were opposed to the establishment of sliding scales, except where they were negotiated through the medium of a board of conciliation.[5]

It must be understood that the operation of joint conciliation

[1] Clegg, Fox and Thompson, op. cit., p. 23.
[2] *Fifth and Final Report*, op. cit., para. 109, p. 42.
[3] Evidence of John Dennington, *Minutes of Evidence*, op. cit., Q. 14,477, p. 290.
[4] Evidence of Benjamin Hingley, *Minutes of Evidence*, op. cit., Q. 15,601, p. 353. See also the evidence of John Hodge who was opposed to the sliding-scale, but very much in favour of boards of conciliation, ibid., Qq. 16,385–6, p. 390, Q. 16,404, p. 391, and Q. 16,452, p. 393.
[5] Sharp, op. cit., p. 59.

boards in the industry did not lead immediately to all disputes being solved by discussion without further disagreement. During the first five years of its existence, for example, the Board for the North of England called in an arbitrator to settle wage rates on six occasions, as against four when adjustments were agreed in joint discussion, and in subsequent years the proportion of arbitrated agreements seems to have increased.[1] Similarly, it was reported to the Royal Commission on Labour that on the Cleveland Joint Committee 'of the thirty-one questions in 1880, eight were withdrawn, five were settled at the meetings, three were left for the firms themselves to deal with, and fifteen were referred to arbitration'.[2] The willingness of both employers and unions to go to arbitration rather than to risk a strike seems to be the really important factor here, especially since the pressure on the joint boards apparently came from the unions.[3] Hence the explanation for the decline in the number of strikes and the success of the conciliation machinery must be sought for elsewhere than in the operation of the sliding scale as such.

This conclusion needs further justification, especially in view of the reference to industrial peace in the industry made earlier. Without being apparently willing to commit himself to any definite explanation of the peaceful nature of the industry, Sharp nevertheless gave equal weight to the sliding scale as to 'the high proportions of skilled men in the industry who earn comparatively big wages and fear, more than anything else, the invasion of the unskilled which might result from industrial dislocation'—a factor with which the sliding scale was 'by no means unconnected'. Indeed, Sharp's mention of the fact that 'the selling price sliding-scale survived only in this industry and in certain minor quarrying work up to 1940' seems further to suggest that he thought it to be the main reason why the iron and steel industry's record of industrial peace made it one of the model industries in Great Britain.[4]

Unfortunately, strict statistical measures of increase in wages

[1] Carr and Taplin, op. cit., p. 72.
[2] Evidence of John Dennington, *Minutes of Evidence*, op. cit., Q. 14,479, p. 290.
[3] Ibid., Qq. 14,480–1, p. 290.
[4] Sharp, op. cit., p. 58.

and prices in the industry do not exist to check this argument, largely because of the lack of satisfactory information on the one hand, and the variations from job to job, from firm to firm, and from region to region, on the other. However, a comparison of the level of wages at 30th June, 1925 with those of 4th August, 1914, does not altogether support Smart, for labourers received increases of from 56 per cent to 75 per cent, whereas steel smelters on the basic process received 26 per cent and those on the acid process 33 per cent[1]—a declining differential which was also operative amongst steel smelters in that the higher paid amongst them received smaller increases than the lower.[2] The general argument from the standpoint of an aristocracy of labour maintaining its differential is, as a matter of fact, altogether unsatisfactory in this context; for, while between 1895 and 1927 wages in the iron and steel industry rose by 103 per cent[3], for the country as a whole the total wages bill rose by over 200 per cent.[4]

Moreover, in terms of the general economic state of the country during the inter-war years, especially those of what has been called 'the black decade', 1921–1931,[5] it is not at all easy to understand how it was that the will to maintain industrial peace did not disappear. Not only was the trend of real wages on the whole unfavourable to workers in the industry,[6] but unemployment remained consistently at about double the national level.[7] At the same time, for the whole of these ten years many firms in the industry paid no dividends at all on ordinary share capital.[8] In the light of the Marxist analysis the basis for serious

---

[1] Committee on Industry and Trade, *Survey of Industrial Relations*, H.M.S.O., 1926, Table, p. 79.

[2] Ibid., footnotes (F) and (G) to the Table.

[3] Thomas H. Burnham and G. O. Hoskins, *Iron and Steel in Britain*, Allen and Unwin, 1943, Table 74, p. 196.

[4] E. H. P. Brown and P. Hart, 'The Share of Wages in National Income', *The Economic Journal*, Vol. 62, 1952, Table 1, pp. 276–7.

[5] Burn, op. cit., Ch. 15.

[6] Ibid., Table 35, p. 407.

[7] Trades Union Congress, *66th Annual Report*, Weymouth, 1934. Report of the Economic Committee on Socialization of the Iron and Steel Industry, Table, p. 195. The Chairman of this Committee was Arthur Pugh, General Secretary of the I.S.T.C.

[8] Carr and Taplin, op. cit., p. 365. Burnham and Hoskins, op. cit., Table 85, pp. 254–5.

industrial conflict was surely there and, of course, these were in fact 'troubled years',[1] but the sliding scale was adhered to in spite of falling prices, and the machinery of conciliation was preserved. The question is, therefore, that of whether there were other economic factors peculiar to the iron and steel industry which made for the successful avoidance of disputes. Or is the explanation to be sought for elsewhere?

In his analysis of the industry, Pool argued that 'a number of factors combined to create a situation in which steadily increasing real earnings could be secured without the trade unions having to fight the employers continuously'.[2] These were an 'enormous' rise in the technical efficiency of the industry, the payment of wages on a tonnage basis as well as on a sliding scale fixed on prices,[3] and 'the relative unimportance of wages as an item in total costs'.[4] These arguments appear to be equivalent to the assertion that it was in the interests of the employer to meet the demands of the unions, at least up to a point, since it was more profitable to keep on producing even at a higher wages cost than to engage in a possibly expensive strike or lockout. A militant policy on the part of the unions, from this point of view, would be worth while since it would succeed without strike action. However, it is open to question whether this analysis is correct as it stands, on the ground that surely the employers would have a sticking point somewhere. Ten years without paying a dividend on ordinary share capital seems on the one hand too easy a victory for the unions, while double the national rate of unemployment seems on the other hand too easy a victory for the employers.

It should, of course, be noted that at the *economic* level Pool's explanation does not obviously contradict the Marxist analysis as developed in these pages. Rising productivity according to Marx is related to technological unemployment and hence to an increase in the capital/labour ratio, making wages less important a cost of production. It should also be accompanied by changes in the organization of the industry in the general

[1] Carr and Taplin, op. cit., Ch. 40.
[2] Arthur G. Pool, *Wage Policy in Relation to Industrial Fluctuations*, MacMillan, 1938, p. 174.
[3] Ibid., pp. 174–6.
[4] Ibid., p. 177.

direction of socialization and by growing class consciousness and political consciousness on the part of the workers, as expressed in the activities of their unions. From this point of view the development of, and reliance upon, joint conciliation machinery, can only be understood as part of the reorganization of the industry collectively, while growing dissatisfaction with capitalism should be accompanied by the consideration that such machinery required further modification if it were to serve a revolutionary purpose. At the same time, granted that Marx himself was correct in his assertion that 'the development of the industrial proletariat is, in general, conditioned by the development of the industrial *bourgeoisie*',[1] the most important fact to account for would apparently be that of the failure of employers to pay dividends *while still continuing in business* for as long as ten years. Had important changes occurred in the organization of industry by this time?

The answer to this question would seem to lie in the direction of the *corporate* revolution, identified by Berle and Means during the period in which the iron and steel industry in Britain was experiencing its most acute depression. Their argument was simply that the development of property ownership since the industrial revolution had resulted in a division of labour at the top of industrial organizations. Whereas earlier the capitalist entrepreneur had performed three different functions within the enterprise, at this stage in the development of capitalism three separate persons were required, each performing a separate function. These were 'that of having interests in an enterprise, that of having power over it, and that of acting with respect to it',[2] or stockholding, directing, and managing. Management was the first to be clearly differentiated, 'hired' managers appearing fairly early on the scene. The invention of joint-stock company law was the next step, leading eventually to shareholders who had no control over the enterprise and whose interest in it was solely that of receiving the maximum return for their investment, 'compatible with a reasonable degree of risk'.[3] The result of this specialization of function

---

[1] Karl Marx, *The Class Struggles in France* in Marx and Engels, *Selected Works*, op. cit., Vol. 1, p. 136.
[2] Adolf A. Berle and G. C. Means, *The Modern Corporation & Private Property*, MacMillan, 1932, p. 119.
[3] Ibid., p. 121.

amongst managers, directors and shareholders was that the control of the enterprise fell into the hands of the directors, a body of shareholders who might in fact be the legal owners of a very small fraction of the voting stock.

Marx himself, of course, had recognized that such a divergence of roles was occurring even in his time, when he referred to joint stock enterprise as 'the abolition of capital as private property within the framework of capitalist production itself'.[1] In this sense it might be argued that all Berle and Means did was to provide documentary evidence to prove that Marx was right; but it can also be argued that in addition they paved the way to the more precise understanding that industrial enterprise in the twentieth century could be conducted by directors whose *main* interest in the business was no longer confined to profit on the capital they, or their fathers, had invested. The analytical distinction between ownership and control, that is to say, is now more clearly seen exemplified empirically as a type of industrial government—whether or not Marx was also correct to describe it as 'a mere phase of transition to a new form of production'.[2] In this new system the directors merely make use of their share ownership to obtain, and to retain, the legal right to ensure themselves an income in the form of directors' emoluments. This does not mean that profit-making has necessarily become unimportant to them, but it does mean that capitalism as a system of gain 'without production' as the Webbs saw it,[3] has given way in some sense to a type of 'production without gain', that is, production without an inevitable declaration of dividends. Joint stock enterprise, once the directors become a self-perpetuating oligarchy, can continue in business through a depression lasting for ten years or so, without paying anything to its shareholders, because in such an oligarchy the ordinary shareholders, for reasons described in detail by Berle and Means, have lost all control over the directors, except for very exceptional circumstances.[4] Provided

[1] Marx, *Capital*, op. cit., Vol. 3, p. 427.

[2] Ibid., p. 429.

[3] Sydney and Beatrice Webb, *The Decay of Capitalist Civilisation*, Allen and Unwin, 1923, p. 104.

[4] Robert A. Gordon, *Business Leadership in the Large Corporation*, University of California Press, 1961, Ch. 8.

that the directors can continue to make sufficient profit at the end of the year to cover the fees which they have already drawn to meet their personal expenses, they will have no incentive other than to continue in business, even although the value of the ordinary shares of the company on the stock market fall to disastrously low figures, seen from their position as shareholders.

From this point of view it would appear that the large iron and steel companies who failed to pay dividends on share capital between 1921 and 1931, were nevertheless able to continue in business because the only protest the ordinary shareholders could make was to sell their stock, the value of which fell very low. The industry, indeed, 'became discredited as a field of investment for capital'.[1] Unfortunately, it is not known whether there were protests by shareholders at company meetings. Nor is it known how far the divergence of ownership from control had proceeded at that time. What evidence there is, however, points to a general trend in the direction predicted by this assumption. In 1865, for example, only 11 per cent of the 70 directors studied by Erickson were salaried administrators, that is directors whose careers were 'primarily as employees of limited companies and partnerships and they reached the top by virtue of executive experience rather than investment'.[2] In 1875–95 the comparative figure for 160 directors was 24 per cent, in 1905–25 for 184 directors 30 per cent, in 1935–7 for 120 directors 41 per cent, and in 1953 for 73 directors, 48 per cent,[3] so that it is most unlikely that the pattern described as a corporate revolution by Berle and Means had not also occurred in this industry.

Looked at from the angle of attempting to account for the perpetuation of the machinery of conciliation, the assumptions underlying the presentation of this evidence—and it cannot be too forcibly emphasized that these are assumptions and not concrete data in their own right—are simply that the control of iron and steel enterprises has fallen into the hands of directors with a background of salaried careers in the industry who have become accustomed to regarding their fees and emoluments,

---

[1] Burnham and Hoskins, op. cit., p. 261.
[2] Charlotte Erickson, *British Industrialists: Steel and Hosiery, 1850–1950*, Cambridge University Press, 1959, p. 50.
[3] Ibid., Table 19, p. 51.

as directors, as a stable form of income. Hence it has become more important to them to keep their enterprises in production than to become involved in strikes or lockouts which might interfere with the smooth run of orders. This does not mean that they necessarily give in to every demand that is made on them, as witness the rather more than usually protracted strike of craftsmen in 1956,[1] but it does mean that they have a vested interest in early settlements of disputes. It is also likely that they have what has been termed a 'managerial' ideology with respect to business as compared with the 'classical' ideology of ownership-dominated enterprise of the older type. That is to say, in terms of the public image of the enterprise such directors stress 'the role of preffessional managers in the large business firm, who consciously direct economic forces for the common good,' whereas the 'classical' type still stress 'the model of decentralized, private, competitive capitalism, in which the forces of supply and demand, operating through the price mechanism, regulate the economy in detail and in aggregate'[2] As applied to employer-employee relations the 'managerial' version of the business creed characterizes employment as typically involving 'both parties in participation in *an authoritarian and hierarchical organization*', whereas the classical version stresses the employment situation as '*a voluntary contract* between equal individuals' in a market situation where 'labour service is the commodity exchanged, while the wage or salary is the price'.[3]

In this sense it is not unreasonable to assume that these are organization-minded men—men who think of the solution of problems in terms of organizations and in the creation of 'machinery' whereby the interested parties get together to 'hammer out' a compromise which may be treated as a precedent —as compared with the 'classical' conception of individuals coming to decisions of a relatively idiosyncratic and arbitrary

---

[1] Ministry of Labour: *Report of a Court of Inquiry into the Causes and Circumstances of a Dispute between the Iron and Steel Trades Employers' Association and the National Joint Trade Unions' Craftsmen's Iron and Steel Committee*, H.M.S.O., August 1956, paras. 39–46, 76–8.

[2] Francis X. Sutton, *et al.*, *The American Business Creed*, Harvard University Press, 1956, pp. 33–4. The details of this 'creed' were established from an examination of printed matter of all kinds coming from firms and businessmen. See the Appendix, p. 406.

[3] Ibid., pp. 108–9.

nature.[1] The history of the iron and steel industry from the 1930's is a history of accelerated organization building of this kind. Quite apart from mergers and amalgamations between firms,[2] the British Iron and Steel Federation emerged as an important centralizing and standardization agency without, it is true, power to impose a veto on company plans, but with apparently considerable moral influence.[3] By the end of the Second World War this had extended to industrial relations' matters, the 1945 Constitution of the Central Council providing that 'no decisions on any major issues of policy should be taken by member associations or agreements entered into which were in conflict with the advice of the Central Council'.[4] Although it would be clearly an error to assume that this constitution has worked without some objections, it may nevertheless be taken as an indication of the extent to which measures for the organizational solution of problems had been accepted as fitting by the directors of steel firms.

Thus, the machinery of collective bargaining within the industry, the joint negotiating arrangements for blast furnaces, heavy steel production and maintenance work,[5] can be taken as but merely another example of organizational devices set up to deal with the complexities of large-scale operations in modern conditions. This is what is implied in this context by the sociologists' emphasis on the institutionalization of industrial relations, or even the institutionalization of class conflict,[6] and

---

[1] It should perhaps be noted that the Consett Iron Company, which produced both David Dale as an employer and John Kane as an employee, not only pioneered 'good' industrial relations in the company, but is also remarkable as an early example of large-scale stockholding, having 660 shareholders in the mid-1860's with the 12 largest shareholders owning 11,000 of the 40,000 shares (Burn, op. cit., p. 254), and 'professionalisation' amongst managers. (H. W. Richardson and J. M. Bass, 'The Profitability of Consett Iron Company before 1914' in *Business History*, Vol. 7, 1965, pp. 85–9.)

[2] B. S. Keeling and A. E. G. Wright, *The Development of the Modern British Steel Industry*, Longmans, 1964, pp. 3–4.

[3] Ibid., p. 15.

[4] Ibid., p. 151.

[5] Ministry of Labour, *Industrial Relations Handbook*, H.M.S.O., revised edition 1961, pp. 41–6.

[6] Ralf Dahrendorf, *Class and Class Conflict in Industrial Society*, Routledge and Kegan Paul, 1959, pp. 64–7.

it raises in a different form one of the problems touched upon at the end of the last chapter, namely the extent to which large and complex trade unions are staffed by organization-minded leaders who are more like the people with whom they bargain than the people whom they represent. It also raises the further question of whether union militancy on their part has given way to complacency and compromise—a weakening of whatever revolutionary class consciousness they had previously shown.

It is important to avoid a circular argument here. Because trade union leaders are instrumental in maintaining the joint-negotiation machinery for collective bargaining, it should not be assumed that they necessarily have a vested interest in maintaining it in its present form. The alternative position was well put by Arthur Pugh, in moving the adoption of the Report of the Economic Committee of the T.U.C. which put forward a scheme for the nationalization of the Iron and Steel Industry to the Trades' Union Congress in Weymouth in 1934. This scheme included Workers' Councils, Regional Joint Boards, and a National Board for the Industry. 'In a socialised industry', Pugh said, 'adequate machinery of negotiation and conciliation for composing differences must be provided';[1] and he went on to develop this view against Charles Dukes of the General and Municipal Workers' Union, who objected to the references in the Report to the possibility of conflict between workers' representatives and Government representatives, asserting: 'I do not visualize that sort of conflict in a socialised industry'.[2] In the present context, Pugh's position is taken as demonstrating a militant outlook *vis-à-vis* employers. While wishing to maintain the machinery of collective bargaining, he was concerned with the future of the industry under private auspices, doubting whether capitalist organizations with a 'primary concern for financial interests, and certainly without due regard to the claims of labour whether by hand or brain' could put the industry on its feet.[3] It should be understood that Pugh wanted strong workers' representation on bargaining machinery, presumably because he thought the need for it

[1] T.U.C., *66th Annual Report*, op. cit., p. 362.
[2] Ibid., p. 372.
[3] Ibid., pp. 360–1.

would still be there *vis-à-vis* representatives of the state once the industry was nationalized. This may not be equivalent to class consciousness as the Marxist understands it, but it is certainly equivalent to union militancy in that framework of ideas, as it has been outlined above, and the demand for the *socialisation* of the industry indicates that it was a form of militancy with revolutionary implications.

Pugh's attitude, indeed, is significant especially when looked at from the point of view of the Leninist doctrine that revolutionary views are not self-developed within the working class and amongst trade union leaders but induced in them by intellectuals from outside. One historian of the British iron and steel industry who could hardly be accused of Marxist sympathies, has nevertheless dealt with the nationalization issue in precisely these terms. Heading this section of his book—'Philosophers Decide'—he gives every appearance of believing that the reason why the Labour Party decided to nationalise the steel industry after the Second World War was because its leaders had come under the spell of Professors Harold Laski and G. D. H. Cole and the New Fabian Research Bureau; and because the Trade Union leaders were reluctant supporters of the Party's policy.[1] Yet, as he himself admits, publications advocating steel nationalization, beginning with Ingot's *The Socialisation of Iron and Steel* in 1936, appeared *after* the Iron and Steel Trades' Confederation, of which Arthur Pugh was General Secretary, had come out in favour of public ownership. It is true that the New Fabian Research Bureau was established in 1931 but there is no indication that it in any way influenced the I.S.T.C. and as late as 1935 Pugh was a signatory of *The Next Five Years* which was mainly a Liberal declaration.[2] The movement of the I.S.T.C. towards nationalization would seem to have been independent of a trend in thinking on the part of Labour intellectuals in the same direction. In this respect it might well be claimed that the Labour Party followed the T.U.C. and the T.U.C. followed the I.S.T.C.

The sequence of events ran as follows. In the autumn of 1930

[1] Duncan Burn, *The Steel Industry 1939–1959*, Cambridge University Press, 1961.
[2] E. Eldon Barry, *Nationalisation in British Politics*, Cape, 1965, p. 146, n. 35.

the I.S.T.C. presented a scheme for the reorganization of the iron and steel industry to the Labour Government of the day.[1] Dissatisfied with the response the union began to publicise its ideas, holding a number of meetings in the spring of 1931 and publishing its scheme as a pamphlet in the summer.[2] At that time neither the terms 'nationalization' nor 'socialisation' were used. The aim was a 'public utility corporation' through state intervention but this was envisaged as a form of public control, rather than public ownership;[3] although it was not long before the Confederation was complaining that such control was 'being prevented by the obstruction arising from the conflicting interests of private enterprise'.[4] By 1933 its official journal was calling for 'ownership and control' by the nation, for the nation, as 'the only means whereby this great industry can be made to serve the national interests, and labour, combining the resources of hand and brain in the industry, be given an undisputed position in all that involves its future progress and development'.[5]

At this time the T.U.C. was clearly influenced by the I.S.T.C. and not the driving force behind its deliberations. In 1931 it had accepted the scheme for public control by a narrow majority. The point of disagreement however was not the issue of control versus ownership, but the protective tariffs favoured by the I.S.T.C. and opposed by the miners and the engineers.[6] Two years later its Economic Committee, under Pugh's Chairmanship, turned to consider the iron and steel industry, and submitted its Report on Socialisation, referred to above, which was accepted at the Weymouth Congress in 1934. The Labour Party's new policy statement, *For Socialism and Peace*, adopted by the Annual Conference of the Party in the same year, incorporated in summary form the proposals of the Economic Committee of the T.U.C.

The link between the two bodies was, of course, very close. The Labour Party had two representatives on the Economic

---

[1] Pugh, *Men of Steel*, op. cit., pp. 456–7, 465.
[2] I.S.T.C., *What is Wrong with the British Iron and Steel Industry?*, 1931.
[3] Pugh, op. cit., p. 457. Barry, op. cit., p. 468.
[4] Quoted in Pugh, op. cit., p. 468.
[5] Quoted in Pugh, op. cit., p. 491.
[6] Barry, op. cit., p. 349, n. 112.

Committee, Hugh Dalton and T. E. Williams, with Herbert Morrison as a substitute. Can these be regarded as intellectuals inducing militancy with respect to public ownership in a much larger body of trade union leaders? About the views of T. E. Williams, the Royal Arsenal Co-operative Society's nominee on the National Executive of the Labour Party, little is known. Dalton, however, is clearly a self-confessed enthusiast for the nationalization of the iron and steel industry. On April 17th, 1944, the Policy Committee of the Labour Party Executive accepted with 'a few small amendments' his paper on 'Full Employment and Financial Policy'. This contained a reference to the nationalization of the industry. 'I had a fight', Dalton wrote later, 'to get this reference to iron and steel. Some of my colleagues jibbed at it. But my experience and observations as a Minister had fortified my opinion, formed some years before, that iron and steel must stand in the first flight of industries to be nationalized by the next Labour Government'.[1]

Elsewhere, however, he is at pains to record that the 'practical plan for socialising the Iron and Steel Industry' which was incorporated in *For Socialism and Peace* in 1934, had been drawn up by the Iron and Steel Trades' Confederation, 'James Walker, the Confederation's nominee on the National Executive, having a large part in it. It had been discussed and agreed with our Policy Committee, and then submitted to, and approved by, the T.U.C. at Weymouth in September, 1934'.[2] James Walker, it is true, is said to have been 'a steady ally' of Dalton,[3] but it seems most unlikely that if the latter had been the driving force behind the proposals to nationalize the industry he would not have said so. In 1944, moreover, the T.U.C. issued a pamphlet on Post-War Reconstruction which advocated the nationalization of iron and steel, independently of Dalton.[4] All the evidence therefore, seems to point to this form of anti-capitalist militancy on the part of the Iron and Steel Trades' Confedera-

---

[1] Hugh Dalton, *The Fateful Years, Memoirs 1931–1945*, Muller, 1957, pp. 422–3. See also pp. 432–3, where Morrison proposes to drop the reference to iron and steel.

[2] Ibid., p. 53, n. 1.

[3] Ibid., p. 103.

[4] See Herbert E. Weiner, *British Labour and Public Ownership*, Stevans, 1960, pp. 66–7.

tion having been internally induced and not wished upon it from outside.

The question of whether this was genuine class consciousness rather than what Lenin called trade-union consciousness is, indeed, altogether another matter. All that has been argued here is that in the 1930's the leaders of the Iron and Steel Trade's Confederation advocated control of and eventually public ownership of the industry because they did not believe that the existing owners could, *as a matter of fact*, continue to run the industry efficiently. In such a circumstance it might also be argued that what they were chiefly concerned with was the unemployment which faced so many of their union's members at that time and hence that, with the wartime and post-war booms, their demand for nationalization would disappear. This is precisely what Barry following Rogow has argued,[1] although clearly their case has to face a major difficulty in that the official policy of the union,[2] as well as that of the National Union of Blastfurnacemen,[3] has been unequivocally in favour of nationalization. It might well have been true, of course, that the senior officials of the unions in 1951, Evans and Callighan, were lukewarm because of 'their experience of the successful operation of Government supervision over the Industry by the Iron and Steel Board, on which they sat;'[4] but if this were the case it is equally clear that this was temporary only since by 1964 the Executive Council of the I.S.T.C., at any rate, was fully supporting nationalization on the ground that unemployment was once again on the increase because those who controlled the industry showed 'no sign of a cohesive effort to achieve a planned growth'.[5] Whether or not the leaders of the union were responding to pressure from below, the fact remains that publicly they had been in favour of nationalization consistently for over

[1] Barry, op. cit., p. 377. See also Arnold A. Rogow, *The Labour Government and British Industry*, Blackwell, 1955, pp. 333–4.

[2] Pugh, op. cit., pp. 578, 589.

[3] Owen, *Ironmen*, op. cit., p. 37.

[4] Keeling and Wright, op. cit., p. 168. As against this it has been said that they had no wish to press the nationalization issue *faster* than the Government was willing to act. See George W. Ross, *The Nationalisation of Steel*, MacGibbon and Kee, 1965, pp. 75–6.

[5] I.S.T.C., 'Executive Council Statement', *Men and Metal, The Journal of the Iron and Steel Trades Confederation*, Vol. 41, No. 10, October 1964, p. 181.

thirty years. In this sense it seems undoubtedly true that the kind of militancy expected by Marx, or at least certain aspects of it, has emerged within the industry, in spite of the fact that the trade union organization did not achieve the unity which his system of ideas also implies. Militancy, even to the point of demanding the end of capitalist ownership, that is to say, is not incompatible with the perpetuation of separate unions for different occupational groups within an industry. The question that remains is the extent to which the special circumstances of the membership of the unions could come to be seen by them as less significant than their common situation of exploitation by their employers.

8

CLASS CONSCIOUSNESS AND POLITICS

So far, events in the history of the British steel industry may be said to fit reasonably well into the Marxist set of predictions that revolutionary class consciousness will develop within a section of the working class as it organizes itself effectively for trade union activity, even if, as has been shown, this does not necessarily mean that that organization will take the form of a single union covering all the workers in the industry. What this discussion has not yet demonstrated, however, is whether the steel unions' support of nationalization, directed against the economic interests of the capitalist owners and employers of the industry, was indicative of sectional thinking only, or whether it was seen by the unions as one aspect merely of the wider class struggle, the rejection of capitalism altogether. Was their demand for nationalization, that is to say, at bottom no more than economic unionism, albeit with revolutionary implications, or had it more fundamental significance? How far was it part and parcel of a transition to struggle at the political level, inspired by a general consciousness of solidarity with other sections of the working class? Briefly, it is the task of this chapter to attempt to answer these questions.

There can hardly be any doubt that the leaders of the steel unions were in the vanguard when it came to the establishment of working-class organizations transcending narrow union interests. John Kane, for example, was one of the trade unionists who supported George Potter in the calling together of the Conference of Trades in 1867, a meeting described as 'the largest and most representative gathering of trade union leaders ever held'.[1] He was present as one of the thirty-four delegates who formed the first Trade Union Congress in the following year,[2] and again in 1869,[3] when he became a member of the Parliamentary Committee,[4] the Executive Committee of the new organization. John Hodge, similarly, became active in the T.U.C. not long after he reached national office in his union. Appointed general secretary of the Smelters' Union in 1886, his name appeared for the first time in the list of members of the Parliamentary Committee in 1892,[5] the year he was President of the Congress at Glasgow.[6]

Nor was this action on their part primarily conceived as a form of industrial organization which might be a substitute for, or compensation for, the lack of trade union unity in a single industry. From the beginning, the Trades' Union Congress was 'an embodiment of trade union solidarity in the political rather than the industrial sphere; its main purpose, that is, was originally to organize trade unions in political agitation for their own defence rather than for joint action in trade affairs'.[7] At that time, 1868, a Royal Commission was sitting to inquire into trade union complicity in the explosion of a can of gunpowder in a workman's house in Sheffield, and indeed into the practice of 'rattening' and the activities of trade unions generally'.[8] The first Trades Union Congress discussed this Royal Commission and, largely as a result of Kane's influence, passed a resolution which was critical of it and in favour of legislation to protect trade union funds.[9] In his speech, Kane drew attention to the composition of the Royal Commission which he described as a body of 'lawyers, landed proprietors and manufacturers', not 'worthy of the confidence of trade union-

---

[1] Benjamin C. Roberts, *The Trades Union Congress, 1868–1921*, Allen and Unwin, 1958, p. 37.

[2] Ibid., p. 46. See also Albert E. Musson, *The Congress of 1868*, T.U.C., 1955, p. 36.

[3] Roberts, op. cit., p. 57.

[4] Ibid., p. 381. Musson, op. cit., p. 43.

[5] Roberts, op. cit., p. 381.

[6] Ibid., p. 375.

[7] Musson, op. cit., p. 10.

[8] Webb's *History of Trade Unionism*, op. cit., pp. 242–4.

[9] Musson, op. cit., p. 36.

ists'.[1] He was already convinced of the need for working-class representation in Parliament, having been active in the establishment of the Northern Reform Union in 1857;[2] and in 1874, with the agreement of his union,[3] he was a candidate, albeit unsuccessful, for Middlesbrough with a radical programme and sponsored by the Labour Representation League.[4] There can hardly be any doubt that in his case support for the T.U.C. was scarcely to be distinguished from support of independent working-class political activity generally.

John Hodge's activities demonstrate a similar attitude of mind. At the Bradford Trades Union Congress in 1888, he moved an amendment intended to get T.U.C. support for the principle that Labour representatives in Parliament should act independently of the two main political parties.[5] He himself became a Labour Representation Committee candidate in 1900, a ballot of the Steel Smelters' Union having decided upon independent action the preceding year.[6] It is hardly surprising, therefore, to learn that his union became affiliated to the Labour Representation Committee in 1901, along with forty other unions, including the National Federation of Blastfurnacemen.[7] During the First World War, as a result of Lloyd George's re-organization in 1917, Hodge became the first trade union Minister of Labour—indeed, the first Minister of Labour, since this was a new Ministry. His acceptance of the post was 'endorsed by the executive',[8] and at later District Council meetings of the union resolutions were passed expressing appreciation of the appointment.

All this, of course, could still be interpreted rather narrowly as indicating an acceptance by the steel workers of the traditional *status quo*, rather than as an expression of their desire to

[1] Quoted in Roberts, op. cit., p. 47.

[2] George D. H. Cole, *A Short History of the British Working Class Movement, 1789–1947*, Allen and Unwin, 1948, p. 189.

[3] Pugh, op. cit., p. 48.

[4] Roberts, op. cit., p. 80. The L.R.L. sponsored 13 trade unionists for the General Election of 1874, of whom 2 were elected.

[5] Ibid., p. 119.

[6] Hodge, op. cit., pp. 137–8.

[7] Henry Pelling, *The Origins of the Labour Party, 1880–1900*, 2nd edition, Oxford University Press, 1965, p. 230.

[8] Pugh, op. cit., p. 203.

put an end to capitalism. Other evidence, however, suggests that political activity on the part of the steel leaders was not carried on independently of forms of class consciousness with revolutionary implications. In 1888, for example, after some nine years of passing resolutions on other ways of dealing with the land question, the T.U.C. declared itself in favour of the nationalization of land and instructed its parliamentary committee to ensure that the issue was raised in Parliament.[1] Only five unions voted against this proposal, none of them steel unions, and support for land nationalization, it is said, came consistently from W. Snow of the Cleveland Blastfurnacemen and E. Trow of the Darlington ironworkers, among others.[2] Four years later the T.U.C. passed unanimously a resolution for the nationalization of coal mining.[3] Over forty years before the iron and steel unions saw the necessity for state ownership in their own industry, that is to say, they were supporting it for land and for the mines. This is important, clearly, because it does not fit into the classical Marxist scheme of the development of class consciousness, as that has been described here. Instead of the leaders of the steel unions being driven more and more towards collaboration with other sections of the working class as they came to accept the conclusion that there was no solution to unemployment for their members while capitalism lasted, their support for other people's anti-capitalist proposals predated any evident awareness of their own economic and political dilemma.

Nor, apparently, were these views induced in them by middle-class intellectuals outside the trade union movement. John Kane, for example, even before he became General Secretary of the Society of Malleable Ironworkers and before he became instrumental in the establishment of conciliation machinery with the steel employers, was responsible for the affiliation of his union to the International Working Men's Association, but there is no evidence that he had read and understood the doctrines that Marx hoped to propagate through the International. What seems reasonable, to two students of the International at any rate, is that Kane's attention to the Association was drawn by William Sylvis, the leader of the Ironmoulders'

---

[1] Barry, op. cit., p. 65.
[2] Ibid., p. 75, n. 96.
[3] Ibid., p. 120.

Union in the United States. Sylvis was secretary of the National Labour Union of America which was associated with the General Council of the International, and he was in close contact with Kane because of the large numbers of iron-moulders who were emigrating to America at this time.[1] It was a sense of working-class organizational solidarity which led Kane to support the international, not a political ideology of a more intellectual type.

This sense of solidarity may be illustrated in another way. In 1926 when the General Strike was called, Arthur Pugh, who was General Secretary of the Iron and Steel Trades Confederation, was also chairman of the T.U.C. As such he soon became wholly involved in the business of negotiating with the government, and with the miners. Described by one author as 'an honest right winger'[2] he is said to have displayed evident relief when the strike was eventually called off,[3] but although he was undoubtedly lukewarm about the whole affair and never came out openly in favour of, or against, the strike, it seems nevertheless clear that he was quite willing to act out to the full his part in the strike as chairman of the committee which had been set up to control it; and the I.S.T.C. was prepared to back him in this respect even against the advice of the president, John Hodge.[4] Of course, it could be argued in simple terms that the steelmen had no option. Once the miners were out in strength, steelworks could not continue in production for lack of coal. On the other hand, the union could have heeded Hodge's warning that support for the General Strike might damage the conciliation machinery that had been built up with the employers, and they could have asked Pugh to retire from his extra-union commitments. The fact that the steel leaders decided to support the T.U.C. argues for a sense of organizational solidarity that transcends sectional interests. Similarly Pugh's readiness to exhaust his strength in the attempt to bring about a solution to the strike which would be satisfactory to his colleagues on the T.U.C. demonstrates a sense of solidarity

[1] Henry Collins and C. Abramsky, *Karl Marx and the British Labour Movement, Years of the First International*, MacMillan, 1965, pp. 75-6.

[2] Julian Symons, *The General Strike*, Cresset Press, 1957, p. 138.

[3] Ibid., pp. 235-6.

[4] Hodge, op. cit., pp. 326-30.

with them in a struggle which they were hardly prepared to meet.[1]

It should be emphasized that this solidarity may properly be interpreted as indicative of revolutionary class consciousness in the sense that it exemplifies a willingness to stand shoulder to shoulder with the members of other working-class organizations in opposition to employers who are regarded as constituting a class apart. As was argued in the first part of this book,[2] such a concept of revolution should not be confused with violent political activity intended to overthrow an existing regime by force. From this latter point of view it is clear that the leaders of the T.U.C. in 1926 were not revolutionaries. Whatever later judgements of history might decide about their lost opportunities and their attitudes, it does not seem unreasonable to claim that they were certain in their own minds that, even were the trend of events to push them in this direction, they would not be able to run the country as an alternative government. Indeed, the strike does not appear to have been thought of in these terms at all. The Labour Party had no faith in it and left the T.U.C. largely to carry on alone, its leaders being content to make pacific speeches in the House of Commons.[3] The whole history of trade union participation in British politics, both before 1926 and afterwards, is a history of acceptance of the constitutional machinery with the express purpose of using it legally to improve the situation of the working class. Insofar as deliberately, or willy-nilly, this has actually resulted in the piecemeal erosion of the capitalist system of exploitation, such participation is, of course, revolutionary in the present context.

This should not be read to imply that there were not trade union leaders in 1926 who might be termed revolutionaries in the other sense, but they were throughout in a small minority, and certainly the iron and steel unions did not number them in their midst. For example, within the trade union movement at this time the Minority Movement was actively concerned with increasing the interest of trade unions in Communist Party politics, or in its own terms, with converting 'the

---

[1] Alan Bullock, *The Life and Times of Ernest Bevin*, Vol. I, Heinemann, 1960, pp. 328–31.

[2] See above, pp. 21–3.

[3] Symons, op. cit., Part 3, Ch. 6.

revolutionary minorities existing in the various industries, into revolutionary majorities'.[1] Only amongst the miners was it at all successful at the leadership level, when A. J. Cook was elected general secretary in 1924.[2] The steel unions were hardly influenced at all, and when in 1928 one of the members of the executive committee of the Iron and Steel Trades' Confederation was billed as a Minority Movement speaker at a South Wales meeting, the central office of the union promptly circularized all branches to the effect that the individual concerned had no authority so to commit the Confederation. At the next election for the executive he failed to get returned.[3] The steel leaders' approach to politics, that is to say, was uniform with their approach to industry—the creation and support of institutions for collective, political action through Parliament, analogous to the joint industrial councils for collective bargaining with employers.

Thus, although the I.S.T.C. has no permanent claim to a seat on the National Executive Committee of the Labour Party, it has always put up a candidate, usually with success.[4] It has always sponsored Labour Party candidates for Parliament[5] and from 1929, at least, it has always had one M.P. if not more.[6] In the 1924 Labour Government one of its sponsored members held a minor Ministerial post—Treasurer of the Household.[7] No Ministerial posts were offered to its sponsored M.P.'s in 1929[8] or in 1945,[9] although one of them became Parliamentary Secretary to the Minister of Supply,[10] and the General Secretary at the time, Lincoln Evans, became a part-time

---

[1] Quoted in Henry Pelling, *The British Communist Party, A Historical Profile*, Black, 1958, p. 26.

[2] Leslie J. MacFarlane, *The British Communist Party*, MacGibbon and Kee, 1966, p. 131. Cook had resigned from the Party in 1921, ibid., p. 130.

[3] Pugh, op. cit., p. 436.

[4] Martin Harrison, *Trade Unions and the Labour Party Since 1945*, Allen and Unwin, 1960, Table 28, p. 309.

[5] Ibid., Table 26, p. 265.

[6] Ibid., Table 27, p. 267.

[7] Victor L. Allen, *Trade Unions and the Government*, Longmans, 1960, Appendix III, p. 238.

[8] Ibid., Appendix IV, p. 259.

[9] Ibid., Appendix V, pp. 291–2.

[10] Pugh, op. cit., p. 586.

member of the newly created Iron and Steel Board.[1] In this respect it is likely that the steel unions accepted the general line of development within the T.U.C.—namely increased service on Government Committees[2] so that by the middle of the century it was represented on bodies which are a part of the establishment of government. Its politically revolutionary activities, as this concept is used here, have been through the medium of a constitution which permits of social change through legislation and administrative decision making. This is why it has been possible for observers to write of the I.S.T.C.'s 'invariable support of the platform' at Labour Party Conferences.[3] It is, in the terminology of such discussions a 'right-wing' organization which is proud to state that it will 'not falter in its support of official policy. There will be no dividing of the ways to delight our political opponents'.[4]

This discussion has been concerned largely with the I.S.T.C. because this is the union about which secondary source material is most abundant, and it is not known how far other unions of steelworkers followed similar practices, although in connection with the Labour Party it has been said that the National Union of Blastfurnacemen has taken a political line which has been 'almost identical' with that of the I.S.T.C.[5] The discussion has also been confined to trade union leadership. It is pertinent, therefore, to ask how far the rank-and-file members shared the policies of their leaders, how far they were in the vanguard urging their representatives forward on the issues raised; or how far they were merely content to endorse, or passively accept, official policy in much the same way as their leaders gave support to the Labour Party.

The answers to such questions are not easy to find. If the official histories of unions equate 'the union' with its leadership, as on the whole they do, how is it possible to discover what in the past the rank-and-file have believed? One approach might be through the device of an examination of unofficial strikes, where these are recorded as indicating dissatisfaction with union policy, as for example occurred in Ebbw Vale during

[1] Ibid., pp. 573-4.
[2] Allen, *Trade Unions and the Government*, op. cit., Ch. 2.
[3] Harrison, op. cit., p. 212.
[4] *Man and Metal*, 1958, quoted in Harrison, ibid., p. 212.
[5] Harrison, op. cit., p. 188.

the First World War;[1] but here again, as the official policy of the iron and steel unions throughout their recent history has been in the direction of the establishment and maintenance of collective bargaining machinery and away from strikes, and hence as the union leaders have been very hostile to unofficial strikes as threatening such machinery, it is likely that the recording of such strikes will not be altogether accurate. Nevertheless, it does seem that on the whole unofficial strikes were rare. Even if steelworkers were not always satisfied with what their leaders said and did, they do not seem to have shown their feelings in such action. Nor has their dissatisfaction emerged in any marked manner in other ways. During the First World War, for instance, the shop steward who before 1914 was regarded as a minor agent merely of the District Committee, became in some industries a spokesman of the rank-and-file worker and a negotiator with managements. This new development began earliest on the Clyde where a strike against the Goverment's policy for the mass introduction of dilution of labour in munitions in the winter of 1915–16, was also a protest against the union leaders' support of the government. 'The Clyde Organization', it is recorded, 'was soon imitated elsewhere. Shop stewards multiplied all over the country; Shop Committees, Works Committees, and Conveners sprang up, and in one town after another Workers' Committees or Shop Stewards' Committees on the Clyde model were created. Throughout, whatever the status of the individual stewards might be, this wider movement remained absolutely unofficial, if not definitely anti-official, and had no relation to the constitutional machinery of the Trade Union movement'.[2]

Thus what has been called a Shop Steward's and Workers' Committee Movement was established which was not only often in conflict with the official trade union movement, but was also revolutionary 'in the sense that most of its leading members held that the abolition of capitalism was one of its principal objectives'.[3] Yet, this Movement was largely confined

[1] Pugh, op. cit., p. 276.
[2] George D. H. Cole, *Organised Labour, an Introduction to Trade Unionism*, Allen and Unwin, 1924, p. 61.
[3] Branko Pribićević, *The Shop Stewards' Movement and Workers Control*, Blackwell, 1959, p. 85.

to the engineering industry, with some extension to mining and the railways in 1918. It affected the steel industry to the degree that strikes of miners, bricklayers, and engineering and electrical maintenance workers brought steelworks to a standstill in 1919 and 1920, but members of the I.S.T.C. do not seem to have been involved.[1] Similarly, the Minority Movement seems to have had little support in the industry, although there were individual cases of attempts to influence branches of the I.S.T.C. in South Wales.[2] It is, indeed, likely that the rank-and-file members of the union were, and are, more conservative in outlook than their leaders. In 1947 when the repeal of the Trades and Disputes and Trades Unions Act of 1927 became operative, only 41 per cent of the I.S.T.C. members were already paying the political levy, a proportion which was increased to 89 per cent by the change in the law.[3] This latter figure compares with 76 per cent for the members of unions as a whole, whereas in 1945 the figure for those who 'contracted in' for the whole country was 48 per cent.[4] The conclusion surely presents itself that the change from below average to above average support for the Labour Party was not a result of conviction on the part of the steelworkers, but an artefact of the manner in which contracting-in and contracting-out were practised in those years. On this issue steelworkers were more apathetic than otherwise.

Or again, a survey of workers' attitudes in a single steelworks, carried out in 1954, showed that although most of the workers interviewed had experienced both nationalization and denationalization of the works, 'neither event seems to have aroused very much external expression of feeling'. Asked whether they would rather work for a private firm than for a nationalized industry, 43 per cent of production workers said they would, while 27 per cent said they would not. 'Moreover, where the preference was expressed, it was very seldom put in terms of political principle. Spontaneous comment usually referred to the greater security and superior amenities given to workers by nationalization'.[5] There is little of the revolutionary,

[1] Pugh, op. cit., pp. 296–300.
[2] Ibid., p. 300.
[3] Harrison, op. cit.
[4] Ibid.
[5] Scott, *et al.*, *Technical Change*, op. cit., pp. 182–3.

even in the very general sense, in such an approach to the issue. Indeed, at this same works it was reported that most union members attended branch meetings only when there were items on the agenda which affected the wages and conditions of their own group in the workplace, and they so resented 'interference' from other groups to make it the custom to vote only on what concerned themselves and to refrain from voting on claims made by other groups.[1] The rank-and-file attitude to trade unionism, it would seem, was primarily economic in Lenin's sense. Interest in the wider activities of the union was limited, except for a few who showed a working-class, and often Labour Party, orientation.[2]

The conclusion, therefore, is that the mass of union members, although perhaps loyal to their union and consciour of solidarity with it, lack class consciousness in the wider sense. A much smaller body of union militants, those who become lay officials and from whom the union leaders are recruited, have such class consciousness and display it in support of the official union policy of working with and through the Labour Party. In this respect, therefore, the leadership is in the vanguard and the rank-and-file are relatively passive, or perhaps even indifferent in so far as revolutionary class consciousness is concerned. They do not act to prevent their leaders from advocating policies of nationalization for their own and other industries, but they show little initiative about such policies themselves. Far from the drive for the ending of capitalism coming from the conditions of the workers themselves, the facts suggest that in the steel industry at any rate, the drive comes from leaders who in many respects have long since ceased to belong to the working class. These are what C. W. Mills called the 'New Men of Power', men who do not appear to derive their revolutionary class consciousness from middle-class intellectuals in the Labour Party, but derive it and, historically speaking, have always derived it independently. Since this is not what might have been expected from the analysis of Marxism presented in the first part of this book, it would appear relevant to look for some alternative explanation.

[1] Charles J. Parsons, *Workplace and Union*, unpublished M.A. thesis, University of Liverpool, May 1960, p. 249.
[2] Ibid., p. 252.

Class Consciousness and Politics

A possible approach is to be found in a discussion by Michels of the reasons why such a significant proportion of the leaders of different socialist parties in Western Europe came from a middle-class background. Many of these were intellectuals, especially Jewish intellectuals. Thus it is likely that one explanation is to be found in the hypothesis that the determining factor is whether or not such members of the middle classes are refused social recognition.[1] This hypothesis does not cover all cases, but in the present context it suggests that the 'New Men of Power' may turn to political ideologies of an anti-capitalist sort because although they are recognized for wielders of power in the context of collective bargaining, they are not socially recognized by the people with whom they are bargaining. There is a certain degree of inconsistency or discrepancy between their status in one area of their lives and that in the other.[2] Whether they want it or not, they have certainly not been assimilated socially into the status level of society which their power entitles them to in the economic sphere. It is, that is to say, the very success of the trade union *organizations* as instruments for the pursuance of militant trade union policies that pushes the men who rise to the top of such organizations in the direction of anti-capitalism, quite independently of the teachings of middle-class intellectuals on the one hand and of the experiences of their members on the other. This is why revolutionary class consciousness on their part pre-dates developments in capitalism which on the unamended Marxist theory should precede the emergence of such consciousness. It also explains the nature of their revolutionary outlook, for their emphasis seems always to be on the *unfitness* of the capitalists to wield their power and their *inability* to deal with the problems of large-scale production because of the divisive nature of the competitive system. Hence the solidarity of trade union leaders is primarily with other trade union leaders and with those of their members who will become the trade union leaders of the future. Organization-consciousness is fundamental to this outlook. The creation and

[1] Michels, op. cit., Part 4, Ch. 2, *passim*. See also R. Bendix, 'Social Stratification and Political Power', *American Political Science Review*, Vol. 46, 1952, pp. 357–75.
[2] Gerhard E. Lenski, *Power and Privilege*, McGraw-Hill, 1966, pp. 86–8, 288–9, 408–10.

maintenance of powerful organizations, and of federations and other associations of organizations, is for them the best solution to the problems facing them.

This, it should be understood, is no more than the sketching of a set of hypotheses somewhat at variance from those of the Marxist framework used in this study of industrial relations. It nevertheless does not altogether contradict them; for the historical argument still remains untouched, namely that the trend in the development of capitalism is towards the creation of such organizations. The main difference is that their ideology is seen to spring from the working of such organizations and not from the economic and social experiences of the working class in industry. However, it still remains open to question how far such experiences may be responsible for the development of the trade union organization in the first place. Thus, from this point of view the notion of status inconsistency is an elaboration of, not an alternative to, the Marxist system.[1]

---

[1] It is perhaps worth noting in this connection that well-paid manual workers who have *descended* the social scale, both in their own work experiences and by reference to their parents and siblings, and hence may also be thought of as experiencing status inconsistency, tend to take a markedly instrumental view of employment, thinking of it primarily in terms of pay and not attending trade union meetings, etc. John H. Goldthorpe, *et al.*, *The Affluent Worker: Industrial Attitudes and Behaviour*, Cambridge University Press, 1968, pp. 158–66.

9

THE VANGUARD OF THE PROLETARIAT

The Marxist approach to industrial relations, as it has been outlined here, consists of a set of hypotheses intended to explain the behaviour of capitalists and proletarians within their organizations in the industrial context. However, there is another view of the matter taken by Marxists themselves, which sees it not only as an explanatory theory, but also as a guide to action. This emphasizes the tasks to be undertaken by convinced Marxists who wish to work for the downfall of capitalism and towards the advent of the classless society. These two approaches are not necessarily contradictory; for it is not conceived that revolutionary class consciousness by itself can change the course of history. What Marxists hold is that such action 'can shorten and lessen the birth-pangs'[1] of the birth of the new society. In this the Communist Party acts as the vanguard of the Proletariat[2], or, rather, as Marx himself put it, Communists are 'practically, the most advanced and resolute section of the working-class parties of every country'. Everywhere they 'support every revolutionary movement against the existing social and political order of things'.[3]

Historically, this has been interpreted in two ways. On the one hand individual Marxists have worked within any working-class or revolutionary organization that came to hand, attempting to guide it towards class-conscious anti-capitalism of a

[1] Marx, *Capital*, op. cit., Vol. I (Preface), p. 10.
[2] Kuusinen, op. cit., p. 410.
[3] *The Communist Manifesto*, Marx and Engels, *Selected Works*, op. cit., Vol. I, pp. 46 and 65.

Marxist variety. On the other they have formed separate
Communist Parties and organizations which sometimes have
made use of, and sometimes have fought other working-class
parties or organizations. Thus in 1928 there was a change in
policy in the Communist-controlled Minority Movement in
this country. The members who previously had been encouraged
'not to organize independent revolutionary unions or to split the
revolutionary elements away from the existing organizations
affiliated to the T.U.C.'[1] were now encouraged to build up
'independent leadership of the working class' as an alternative
to the existing trade union bureaucracy, an aim that was interpreted in the form of establishing break-away unions. Two
such unions were organized in 1928, the United Mineworkers
of Scotland, and the United Clothing Workers in the East End
of London.[2] Both bodies had a precarious existence, and they
were wound up in 1935 and 1936.

Another break-away union, largely syndicalist in origin,
which was formed about this time by London busmen, was
accused by Mr. Ernest Bevin as being the responsibility of
'unauthorized and irresponsible persons not connected with the
industry at all, but with the Minority Movement and the
Communist Party'.[3] However, although some Communists
were involved and although a leading Communist of the time
claimed that the Party was influential amongst this section
of the busmen, it seems reasonably clear that both these individuals were overestimating what the Party had achieved.
All the evidence available seems to show that this was a popular
movement among busmen, and however much its policy with
regard to the Spanish Civil War, to the Soviet Union, and to
Communist affiliation to the Labour Party was inspired if not
dictated, by Communists, its industrial policy was the result, in
the main, of influences working within the territory of the
Board and the T. and G.W.U.[4]

The Communist Party, indeed, had apparently abandoned
the idea of separate unions by this time and had reverted to its

[1] Pelling, *The British Communist Party*, op. cit., p. 26.
[2] Ibid., p. 56. See also MacFarlane, op. cit., pp. 255–60, 265–74.
[3] *The Times*, 29th July 1935, quoted in H. A. Clegg, op. cit., p. 106.
[4] Ibid., p. 108. For a different interpretation see V. L. Allen, *Trade Union Leadership*, op. cit., pp. 63–73.

previous policy of working within the existing trade union machinery. Here it had some limited success, but only so long as the opinion of the leadership did not harden to keep in line with the Labour Party's firm rejection of the Communist Party's request to affiliate. In 1928 the Trade Union Congress instructed its General Council to enquire into 'disruptive elements' in the movement, and the *Report on Disruption in the Unions*, presented to Congress the following year, was largely concerned with the activities of members of the Communist Party, the Minority Movement, and associated organizations.[1] A few years later the General Council took the inevitable step. It circulated what became eventually known as the 'Black Circular' of October 1934—two circulars, in fact, addressed to Unions and to Trades Councils on the position of delegates to the latter being 'connected in any way with either Communist or Fascist organizations or any of their ancillary bodies'.[2] The General Council asked for the views of affiliated unions on this matter and reported that 41 unions were in agreement with proscribing the Communist Party while 10 were not in agreement.[3] A motion at the Margate Congress, moved by J. C. Little of the A.E.U. condemning this policy was lost by 1,944,000 votes to 539,000, and an attempt to move the reference back of this part of the General Council's report was lost by 1,869,000 to 1,427,000 votes.[4] From this time on, official union policy was overtly designed to prevent the extension of Communist influence in the unions.

Such effective proscription was continued for some nine years, until indeed the entry of Russia into the Second World War, and that country's subsequent war victories changed the ordinary rank-and-file union member's conception of what Communism meant. The Party's recorded membership, for example, leaped up from 22,738 in December, 1941 to 56,000 in December, 1942,[5] and by 1943 the T.U.C. General Council felt more or less obliged to withdraw the Black Circular possibly because 'the enthusiastic efforts of the Communists in the

---

[1] MacFarlane, op. cit., p. 249.
[2] General Council's Report, *Report of Proceedings of the 67th Annual Trades Union Congress*, Margate, 1935, p. 260.
[3] Ibid., p. 261.
[4] Ibid., p. 280.
[5] Pelling, *The British Communist Party*, op. cit., Appendix A, p. 192.

factories from 1941 onwards won them the respect of their fellow-workers'.[1] From this time on the Party's influence grew. Using techniques, designed before the war, but operated more successfully after 1941, Communists took advantage of the relative apathy of the trade union membership to fill the posts of Secretary, Chairman and Treasurer of Trade Union branches with Party members,[2] and although the enthusiasm for the Communists gradually died away afterwards, the momentum they had acquired gave them control in some unions and partial control in others for some years after 1945, in spite of the return of the T.U.C. General Council to the policy of banning Communists from union office in October, 1948.[3]

In all this, however, it seems clear that support for Communists was a reflection of their militancy in industrial rather than in political affairs. The *Abridged Report* of the 1960 Policy Conference of the E.T.U. for instance, claimed that support of the union's Communist leadership was 'given to the men and not to the political beliefs they held and whilst they continue to give us the service that they have given to us in the past, we would continue to give them our fullest support'.[4] Throughout the post-war years the Communist Party's electoral support was minimal, and its national membership gradually fell from 45,435, in 1945 to 24,670 in 1958.[5] Its success in local union branches and in getting members elected occasionally to high office in some unions cannot be accounted for in terms of any swing towards the political policies avowed by the Party, and the explanation must be sought elsewhere.

Both Bob Darke's description of the tactics on which he himself was employed and more general knowledge of the constitution of trade unions suggest that, economic and political issues apart, one reason for the contrast between the political failure and the union success of the Party lies in the fact that manipulation of any trade union electoral system in this country

[1] Ibid., p. 135.

[2] Bob Darke, *The Communist Technique in Britain*, Collins, 1953, p. 52.

[3] Allen Hutt, *British Trade Unionism: a Short History*, 4th edition, Lawrence and Wishart, 1952, p. 177.

[4] Quoted in R. Bean, 'Militancy, Policy Formation and Membership Opposition in the Electrical Trades Union, 1954–61', *Political Quarterly*, Vol. 36, 1965, p. 184.

[5] Pelling, *British Communist Party*, op. cit., pp. 192–3.

is open to any resolute minority. While it is true that 'most unions are alive to the danger and endeavour to keep a careful check on their ballots', it is also true, 'that it is extremely difficult to control the conduct of elections in every detail, and some mistakes and perhaps frauds are bound to escape detection'.[1] Particularly where the level of voting is low and where the votes are cast for a large number of candidates it is possible for a small group with a determined policy to be far more successful in pushing forward its favourite candidates than any other less well organized group. However, the relative ease of such victories should not be misinterpreted. 'In practice it requires an iron will and the relentlessness of a tiger',[2] and energetic Labour Party supporters, and also Conservative and Roman Catholic trade unionists, have successfully mobilized support for their candidates',[3] at the expense, it might be added, of the Communists. Looked at from this point of view, elections in trade unions may sometimes, if not always, be seen as a battle-ground between rival factions, with the great majority of members either standing aloof or being used to provide support for the group with the best electoral organization of the moment, and in such a circumstance it is not surprising that the Communist Party might be more influential than its official membership might be deemed to warrant.

None of this detracts from the conclusion that 'the record of the British Communist Party since its foundation has been one of herculean efforts but of tantalizing disappointments'.[4] Nor does it fit easily into the Marxist analysis of developments under capitalism. To the extent that the Communist Party might be thought to be the most revolutionary class-conscious, political organization of intellectuals and members of the working class, its influence amongst trade unionists should have grown as business units have grown in size, since the leadership of the class movement of the proletariat was said by Marx to be assumed by the workers of big industry.[5] Of course, it may

[1] Benjamin Roberts, *Trade Union Government and Administration in Great Britain*, Bell, 1956, p. 247.
[2] Darke, op. cit., p. 72.
[3] Roberts, *Trade Union Government*, op. cit., p. 256.
[4] Pelling, *British Communist Party*, op. cit., p. 182.
[5] Marx and Engels, *The German Ideology*, op. cit., p. 58.

equally be argued that the Party has usually been seen as struggling to defend the U.S.S.R. and hence to be defining the fight against capitalism in these terms rather than in terms of the future of the British economy, which was perhaps why it was so much more popular from 1941–1945. Yet there is no evidence of an alternative influence in trade unions which was informed by a revolutionary class consciousness of an explicitly Marxist persuasion. Short of rejecting the Marxist explanation altogether, therefore, the nature of 'revolutionary' class consciousness in British trade unionism must be described in other terms.

This, of course, is what was attempted in the previous three chapters. The iron and steel industry was selected for study as likely to be in the vanguard of technological development and change; and the history of trade unionism in that industry was scrutinized for evidence which might be interpreted as indicating that iron and steel unionists gradually came round to the view that there was no solution to the problems of the working class other than the supersession of the capitalist system of production. Two kinds of evidence were found which supported this interpretation. In the first place, the steel leaders apparently without opposition from, if not with the active support of, the rank-and-file of the membership, were instrumental in the establishment of the Trades Union Congress and early supporters of the Labour Party, and they have continued to sustain these bodies throughout their history. The measures of their enthusiasm for them, as outlined in Chapter Eight, may be taken as the measures of their class consciousness, to the extent that the rationale for their continued existence has been seen by the unionists in class terms. Secondly, the iron and steel leaders have been advocates of nationalization, not only for their own, but for other industries, because they have believed that employers *as a class* were no longer capable, if they ever had been, of organizing these industries efficiently in the fact of competition from abroad, and by reference to technological advances which could be beneficial not merely to themselves, but to their employees and to the community as a whole. This is class consciousness of a radical, if not revolutionary nature;[1] and

---

[1] In a survey of the steel industry from 1951 to 1963 the Executive of the I.S.T.C. concluded: 'the question is whether a *nationalised* steel industry could have done worse if it tried', *Executive Council Statement*, op. cit., p. 182.

it occurred very early on in the creation of working-class organizations to propagate it. In this sense it seems fair to claim that the Iron and Steel Trades Confederation, and probably the other steel unions, have been in that vanguard of the proletariat; but it also fair to ask how far in the vanguard have they been. Are there any other unions who have as a matter of fact been to the fore of the iron and steel unions in this respect? and if so why?

The sequence of events, it will be recalled, have been dealt with in terms of union solidarity, union militancy, class consciousness and revolutionary ideology, and both union solidarity and union militancy have been shown to be rather more complicated than at first sight they appear. There are, for example, no industrial unions in Great Britain, although 'the National Union of Boot and Shoe Operatives comes very close to the mark, and the National Union of Mineworkers could be slipped by without too much dishonesty'. The I.S.T.C., indeed, is a union which is confined to a single industry rather than one which covers it entirely, and as such it is one among many others, including the National Union of Railwaymen, the National Union of Dyers, Bleachers and Textile Workers, and so on.[1] Similarly, union militancy has not been defined simply by reference to strike intensity, which would have put mining and quarrying as well as textiles well to the fore of the metal and engineering industries;[2] yet the alternative which was employed in Chapter Seven, namely the establishment of joint negotiating machinery with employers, places the iron and steel industry alongside the cotton industry, mining and the railways.[3] In all this it is clear that the mining industry emerges as also part of the vanguard of industrial militancy, and it is, therefore, relevant to enquire whether the unions in this industry led, or followed in the rear of the Iron and Steel Trades Confederation.

In so far as trade union solidarity between unions is concerned, it is clear that although no miners were present at the

---

[1] Hugh A. Clegg, A. J. Killick and R. Adams, *Trade Union Officers*, Blackwell, 1961, p. 15.

[2] C. Kerr and A. Siegel, 'The Interindustry Propensity to Strike: an International Comparison' in Arthur Kornhauser, *et al.*, eds., *Industrial Conflict*, McGraw-Hill, 1954, p. 211.

[3] Sharp, op. cit., Part One, *passim*.

Trades Union Congress of 1868[1] they were represented there-after and played as prominent a part in the activities of the T.U.C. as the steel workers' leaders. Indeed, Alexander MacDonald of the National Association of Miners was elected a member of the first permanent committee of the T.U.C.—the Parliamentary Committee—when it was established in 1871[2] and he was chairman of the committee in 1872 and 1873.[3] Another prominent miners' leader, John Normansell, attended the second Trades Union Congress in 1869, where he read a paper on the best means to secure the direct representation of labour in 'the Commons House of Parliament',[4] a topic which proved to be very much in the fore of attention on the miners' part at that time and for many years afterwards; for, although they did not join the Labour Representation League when it was formed in that year, the miners fought the 1874 election independently and had the pleasure of seeing Alexander MacDonald and Thomas Burt elected, out of the four candidates they put up.[5] A policy of independent representation of miners' candidates was followed for over thirty years, and when the Labour Representation Committee was formed in 1900 the miners' leaders considered it to be 'but a flash in the pan like so many other projects aforetime'.[6] Possibly because the miners' grievances against the landlords predisposed them to alliance with the Liberals,[7] there had been a tendency over the years for the miners to stand as Liberal-Labour candidates. For example, six of the eleven Lib-Lab. M.P.'s in 1885 were miners.[8] In 1905, however, the miners put forward sixteen candidates, five as 'Miners and I.L.P.' Eleven were elected, and five other miners as Lib-Lab.[9] Affiliation with the Labour Representation Committee was by this time a regular feature of Annual Conferences of the Miners' Federation of Great Britain,

[1] Musson, op. cit., pp. 35–6.
[2] Ibid., p. 47.
[3] Roberts, *The Trades Union Congress*, op. cit., p. 377.
[4] Robert P. Arnot, *The Miners*, Vol. 1, 'A History of the Miners' Federation of Great Britain, 1889–1910', Allen and Unwin, 1949, p. 51.
[5] Ibid., pp. 289–90.
[6] Ibid., p. 352.
[7] Pelling, *Origins of the Labour Party*, op. cit., p. 291.
[8] Arnot, op. cit., p. 291.
[9] Ibid., pp. 363–4.

and in 1909 independent representation on their part came to an end, although with the special understanding that the miners would not come on to the Labour Party's Parliamentary Fund until the following general election.[1]

The comparison between sixteen miners' M.P.'s and fifty other Labour M.P.'s in 1905 emphasizes the extent to which the miners took representation in Parliament seriously. At every general election this century the miners have put forward by far the largest group of sponsored candidates,[2] and they have had the largest group of M.P's, amounting to as many as forty-two in 1929.[3] They have had a representative on the National Executive Committee of the Labour Party for every year between 1935 and 1959,[4] and in all these respects may be said to have been more active in a political sense than any other trade union, not excluding the steel unions. A very large proportion of miners' representatives, relatively speaking, have been Cabinet Ministers in Labour Cabinets—10 in 1924, 6 in 1929, 13 in 1945 and 9 in 1951.[5]

At the same time it is reasonably clear that this political action was class-conscious in the sense that this term has been used in these pages, and the development of such class consciousness more closely fits the sequence of the Marxist set of hypotheses than does the history of the steel unions. For example, as early as 1892 the T.U.C. passed a resolution for the nationalization of the mining industry, moved and seconded by two miners from Scotland,[6] and although this preceded a similar resolution at the fifth Annual Conference of the Miners' Federation of Great Britain by two years'[7] it demonstrates the extend to which the miners were seeking to carry other trade unions with them. However true it was that not Marx, but Henry George lay behind these measures, as behind the demand for the nationalization of the land four years previously, the

[1] Ibid., p. 367.

[2] Harrison, op. cit., Table 26, p. 265.

[3] Ibid., Table 27, p. 267.

[4] Ibid., Table 28, p. 309.

[5] Allen, *Trade Unions and the Government*, op. cit., pp. 238, 259, 292 and 293.

[6] Arnot, op. cit., p. 184.

[7] Robert P. Arnot, *The Miners*, Vol. II, 'Years of Struggle, 1910–1930', Allen and Unwin, 1953, pp. 127–8.

emphasis on 'the good of all' in such resolutions is indicative of a move away from sectional interests merely.

This should perhaps not be pressed too far; for there is a sense in which it is possible to interpret the behaviour of the miners in relation to their fellow unionists in the T.U.C. and the Labour Party, as largely motivated by the needs of the mining community. Thus the General Strike of 1926 was first and foremost a miners' strike, and when it was called off after nine days, the M.F.G.B. fought on alone for over six months.[1] The 1935 election, similarly, was fought by the miners as a miners' election—a vote for the Labour Party was a vote for nationalization, 'not only for an immediate amelioration of your conditions, but for a definite policy of dealing adequately and effectively with all our mining problems',[2] and it is significant that from being probably the most politically active and militant section of the Labour Party up to 1939, the record of the National Union of Mineworkers in the post-war years has been 'one of almost consistent orthodoxy'.[3] 'Every attempt to commit the N.U.M. conference to left-wing policies during the Bevanite period and since has been unsuccessful'.[4] Once the mines were actually nationalized, that is to say, the miners' leaders ceased to be revolutionary about ending capitalism in other industries, or rather, they continued to support the demand for such measures, but without the fire and enthusiasm that they had employed in their own cause.

At the same time within their own industry they have become more involved in problems of an administrative rather than a protest nature. Such preoccupation with 'sitting on joint committees with management and working to solve problems which traditionally were managerial' has been said to 'disturb the confidence of rank-and-file union members in the integrity of their own officials', and has been suggested as a possible explanation for the 1,200 or so strikes per year since nationalization, 'not one of which has had union recognition';[5] but this

---

[1] Arnot, Vol. II, op. cit., Ch. 14.
[2] Robert P. Arnot, *The Miners*, Vol. III, 'In Crisis and War, 1930 onwards', Allen and Unwin, 1961, p. 163.
[3] Harrison, op. cit., p. 138.
[4] Ibid., p. 140.
[5] Scott, *et al.*, *Coal and Conflict*, op. cit., p. 22.

should not be interpreted as indicating that the rank-and-file of the miners have been more revolutionary in their class consciousness than their leaders. Conflict within the industry is directed towards wage levels and wage differentials, demonstrating largely what Lenin referred to as trade union rather than class consciousness. Marked anti-capitalist tendencies and political agitation, including considerable support for the Communist Party in some mining areas, were features of the inter-war years;[1] and they have decreased considerably with the virtual disappearance of unemployment and with the improved wages position of this section of the working class.

Of course, the analysis is rather complicated by the introduction of government measures to control unemployment and by nationalization programmes aimed to further these and to increase productivity, neither of which were foreseen by Marx in quite this sense. This means that the higher level of technological development in the industry and the onset of centralization have not been achieved by the capitalist owners themselves. Hence their power to induce revolutionary class consciousness may be said to have been countermanded by the very fact that directly and indirectly the miners' agitations of the pre-war period were successful. Once private ownership of the means of production had been superseded by state ownership the need for revolutionary action within the industry disappeared. However, this interpretation in no way affects the issue that in the inter-war years when, as compared with the steel industry, the level of technical production was low and the degree of centralization smaller, the extent of revolutionary class consciousness amongst miners was greater. Clearly, the examination of the Marxist approach in the first four chapters of this book would not have suggested the miners as the vanguard of the proletariat in Britain, or elsewhere for that matter, and it would seem to be necessary to consider why this should be.

One suggestion which has been made, at least by reference to what has been called the 'strong corporate spirit' of the miners, is that 'this is due partly to the conditions of their work which involves mutual dependence, but even more to the fact

[1] Arnot, op. cit., Vol. III, pp. 179–82, T.U.C., *67th Annual Congress Report*, op. cit., pp. 262–3.

that coal mining leads to the growth of the colliery village, a homogeneous community which produces a powerful sense of solidarity'.[1] Such communities are usually geographically 'isolated', and they 'develop their own codes, myths, heroes and social standards. There are few neutrals in them to mediate the conflicts and dilute the mass. All people have grievances, but what is important is that all the members of each of these groups have the same grievances; industrial hazards or severe depression unemployment or bad living conditions (which seem additionally evil because they are supplied by the employer) or low wages or intermittent work. And here is a case where the totality of common grievances, after they have been verbally shared, may be greater than the sum of the individual parts. The employees form a largely homogeneous and undifferentiated mass—they all do about the same work and have about the same experiences. Here you do not have the occupational stratification of the metal or building crafts. . . .'[2]

Put into Marxist language this argument suggests that militancy is a product of *social* alienation and of polarization. Where the working class, or some section of it, is homogeneous in its occupations and relatively isolated, revolutionary class consciousness is at its highest. Where it is occupationally heterogeneous and dispersed amongst other occupations in a community, its group consciousness, and hence its class consciousness will be low. Marx believed that the historical trend was in the direction of class consciousness, and he also believed that technological advance would lead inevitably to occupational homogeneity. Events, however, have not supported this latter conviction. Hence in so far as he was right in believing that class consciousness and occupational homogeneity were linked, it is to be expected that the historical trend has been away from rather than towards class consciousness. A more highly developed industry, like steel, has always had greater occupational diversification than has coal. Hence the degree of class consciousness amongst rank-and-file steel workers has been less than amongst miners. At the same time, as the British coal industry has become more technically advanced, revolutionary class consciousness has declined, although the relation-

[1] Sharp, op. cit., p. 8.
[2] Kerr and Siegel, op. cit., pp. 191–2.

ship has been masked by the organizational changes which have accompanied nationalization, itself largely prompted by technological considerations.[1]

On the other hand, the previous discussion of events within the steel industry has emphasized that the trend within the industry has been regularly in the direction of increased militancy, set within the context of organizational efficiency and collective bargaining action. The history of the coal mining industry does not fit easily into this pattern. The original demand for nationalization, for example, was made long before mining employers and union leaders had developed the kind of machinery for joint consulation which had *preceded* a similar demand by the steel unions for their own industry. Indeed, initially coal mining lagged behind the iron and steel trades in the development of conciliation. 'As late as 1870, there seems to have been no standing machinery of any sort in operation in coal mining for the adjusting of differences, whether arising at one colliery or of a more universal nature. The only settlement of disputes other than by resort to industrial conflict before that date was of a fortuitous and precarious nature.'[2] From about this time, possibly influenced by the iron and steel industry's conciliation machinery,[3] local joint committees became more common, but although they were later supplemented by district and even county conciliation boards, negotiations at the local level still remained the dominant feature of collective bargaining in the industry. The Miners' Federation wanted a single national conciliation board to replace district boards and instructed its national committee to take steps to this end in 1910,[4] but the owners rejected a request for a national meeting on the ground that 'no useful purpose would be served';[5] and it was wartime experience rather than effective action by the miners' leaders which eventually led to negotiations being conducted at the national level. The owners, however, remained hostile to this procedure and after the defeat of the

[1] Robert A. Brady, *Crisis in Britain*, University of California Press, 1950, Ch. 3, *passim*.
[2] Sharp, op. cit., p. 11.
[3] Ibid., p. 13.
[4] Ibid., p. 25.
[5] Arnot, *The Miners*, Vol. II, op. cit., p. 85.

miners in the 1921 lockout and more especially after the failure of the 1926 General Strike 'the number of separate District agreements was increased and the Miners' Federation of Great Britain as such was excluded, to all intents and purposes, from wage negotiations'. The result was that the Federation became seriously weakened internally and subject to dissension.[1]

Right up to the outbreak of the Second World War the Federation continued to advocate centralized conciliation machinery so that wages might be determined from a national formula; and on behalf of the employers the Mining Association continued to resist this in terms of the 'great variations in cost of production between different fields and the considerable variation in profits'.[2] Once again the onset of war led to the creation of national machinery. In January, 1936 a Joint Standing Consultative Committee for the industry had been set up, consisting of representatives from the Mineworkers' Federation and the Mining Association. Although it was empowered to consider 'all questions of common interest and of general application to the industry, not excluding general principles applicable to the determination of wages by district agreements' it had no power to deal with the wages in any district or with any other issue which a district defined as purely local;[3] and when the war broke out its main function turned out to be that of making cost-of-living adjustments to a scale of wages which was fixed at a level already determined in each district. There was no machinery for ensuring that district questions could be transferred to the Joint Standing Committee whenever necessary. After a number of disputes had revealed the serious weakness of this situation, a government Board of Investigation, chaired by Lord Greene, recommended a National Conciliation Scheme which would have such powers. This recommendation was accepted by both sides of the industry and became effective from May, 1943.[4]

It is possible that this National Conciliation machinery would have continued after the war even if the industry had

[1] Arnot, *The Miners*, Vol. II, op. cit., pp. 368–9.
[2] Sharp, op. cit., p. 47.
[3] William H. B. Court, *Coal*, H.M.S.O. and Longmans, Green, 1051, pp. 231–2.
[4] Ibid., pp. 234–5.

not been nationalized, since the miners' leaders[1] and the Chairman of the Mining Association are known to have favoured its continuation.[2] Nevertheless, it seems reasonably clear that on the owners' side at least there might have been some opposition. Thus Foot wrote, 'Colliery owners, big and small, should for all purposes accept a joint responsibility for the efficient management of the Industry in the interests of the Nation; and can only discharge that responsibility if, as far as main principles and policies are concerned, they take a national and not a local or sectional view, and are prepared to accept and faithfully to carry out all decisions that may be designed to that end'[3]—a passage which suggests that the Mining Association had some doubts about the extent to which the individualism of the owners might frustrate the plan it was proposing as an alternative to nationalization. Certainly the miners' leaders believed that the future of centralized machinery was in doubt. They rejected the Foot plan on the ground that 'any reorganization sponsored by the colliery owners must of necessity be hampered by the interests of individual colliery owners'.[4] They put their faith in the nationalization of the industry which the Labour Government made effective in 1945.

This should not be interpreted as meaning that the drive behind nationalization on the part of the newly formed National Union of Mineworkers was solely, or even chiefly, derived from a demand for centralized collective-bargaining machinery. Nor does it mean that the steel workers supported this demand in order to give the miners what they had already achieved without nationalization. But it does mean that nationalization was seen as necessarily involving measures for the integration of the trade unions into negotiation procedures at every level of an industry, *right up to the top*; and it also means that the unification of conciliation, as well as industrial unionism, was regarded as essential to effective action on the workers' side. Certainly the Act of Nationalization provided integrated

---

[1] Arnot, *The Miners*, Vol. III, op. cit., pp. 369–98.

[2] Robert Foot, *A Plan for Coal*, The Mining Association of Great Britain, 1945, pp. 42–3.

[3] Ibid., pp. 61–2.

[4] Political and Economic Planning, *The British Fuel and Power Industries*, P.E.P., 1947, p. 280.

collective-bargaining machinery for coal;[1] and it seems that an American observer was quite justified in remarking that 'unquestionably, the N.U.M. has worked more closely with the Coal Board than it ever did with private owners'.[2] As a result of nationalization, 'the N.U.M. has shifted, psychologically, from 'protest unionism' to 'administrative unionism', from a distant position where it stood as a challenger of the system of ownership and operation to a more intimate position where it stands as a sponsor and friend of the new order which is in large part its own child. Despite the undeniable vigor with which the traditional bargaining role of a union is still fulfilled, union officials today must spend a large amount of their time and energy serving with management on joint committees . . . and concerning themselves with the problems of the industry, the same problems that keep management awake at night'.[3]

Equally unquestionable seems the conclusion that the degree of centralization in negotiations since nationalization has led rank-and-file miners to lose some of their sense of participation in them,[4] or at least to feel that their leaders are co-operating too much with the Coal Board to the disadvantage of the membership.[5] As one study has put it, the men demand 'firm opposition to the management',[6] the local trade union branch officers are ambivalent and inconsistent; and occasionally strikes have been called to persuade regional officers of the union to take up local grievances with local managements.[7] The rank-and-file interpret union militancy in terms of dealing with day-to-day grievances to their own benefit—a good example of Lenin's trade union consciousness. The union leaders interpret it in terms of the operation of a public utility

[1] William Haynes, *Nationalization in Practice*, Harvard University Press, 1953, op. cit., p. 218. See also the Ministry of Labour, *Industrial Relations Handbook*, pp. 68–73.

[2] Haynes, op. cit., p. 218.

[3] George Baldwin, *Beyond Nationalization*, Harvard University Press, 1955, p. 51.

[4] Haynes, op. cit., p. 219.

[5] Baldwin, op. cit., pp. 52–3.

[6] Norman Dennis, *et al.*, *Coal is Our Life*, Eyre and Spottiswoode, 1956, p. 106.

[7] Ibid., p. 104, for an example in the area.

directed towards strengthening the economy of the country for the benefit of the community as well as of the miners. Hence when there was some possibility that a Conservative Government might decentralize the mining industry 'there was complete unity in the N.U.M. National Executive, including left, right and centre. The Executive passed a resolution which resisted any attempt of the Tory Party to destroy nationalization, and declared that if the Tory government attempted to interfere with the national structure of the industry by decentralization on a district basis, which would mean returning to the pre-war disruption of our coal economy, it would be resisted with every legitimate means at our disposal'.[1]

All this suggests that the intentions of the miners' leaders, possibly even as far back as the 1890's, have been characteristically different from those of the union members, although the intensity of their involvement in Labour Party politics may well have been derived from the solid backing which they received from the mining communities. In their case the readiness of the workers to become engaged in fierce disputes with their employers provided the basis from which they derived the militancy of their own demand for measures to put an end to capitalism. Of course, it is not difficult to understand why straight trade union consciousness should have been so militant in this industry, especially in the nineteenth century. Wages have always been a major element in production costs and mechanization, as measured by the proportion of coal cut by machine rather than by pick and shovel, accounted for no more than 8 per cent of the ouput as late as 1913.[2] In such a circumstance rank-and-file miners might very well be conscious of their employers' profits depending upon the hard, physical labour of the workers. Nor was there much incentive at this time for the owners to increase their mechanization. As compared with the steel industry, the fortunes of which were severely threatened by foreign competition between 1875 and the outbreak of the

---

[1] Abe Moffat, *My Life with the Miners*, Lawrence and Wishart, 1965, p. 94. This quotation is all the more interesting because Moffat never disguised his membership of the Communist Party and his dissatisfaction with the form nationalization had taken.

[2] Andrew M. Neuman, *Economic Organization of the British Coal Industry*, Routledge, 1934, Table 8, p. 43.

First World War,[1] the coal industry may be said to have flourished, so that by 1914 the miners had moved into the ranks of the aristocracy of labour.[2] Thus, although at first sight it seems reasonable to explain the inter-war militancy of the miners, both inside Parliament and outside, in terms of the serious deterioration in their economic circumstances, which occurred between 1918 and 1939,[3] their pre-1914 militancy cannot be explained in the same terms. What seems to be a more viable hypothesis is that it was the very failure of the miners' leaders to prevail upon the coal owners to operate what they believed to be satisfactory collective-bargaining machinery, which strengthened their resolve to take political action for the same ends, and the nationalization of the industry was therefore a means by which this might be achieved.

Two conclusions follow from this argument. In the first place, the perpetuation, and indeed the consolidation of centralized collective bargaining when an industry is nationalized, which the steel leaders' emphasized as necessary in the 1930s,[4] suggest that the historical trend in industrial relations in Britain has been not simply towards class consciousness which will abolish capitalism, but towards what might be called 'organizational consciousness' to create permanent machinery for dealing with grievances in the industrial context. In this sense the replacement of the capitalist owners of the coal industry by representatives of the state was seen also as the opportunity for creating both a more efficient technical organization of production and a more workable means whereby the union leaders could put their members' case before their employers. In the case of the steel industry, for some time it was believed that the same results might be achieved without public ownership, if the Iron and Steel Board could hasten on the technical development necessary in the highly competitive post-war world, since the nature of steel management had been considerably changed

[1] P. L. Payne, 'Iron and Steel Manufactures' in Derek H. Aldcroft, ed., *The Development of British Industry and Foreign Competition, 1875–1914*, Allen and Unwin, 1968, pp. 71–99.

[2] A. J. Taylor, 'The Coal Industry' in Aldcroft, op. cit., p. 43.

[3] Court, op. cit., pp. 117, 229–32 and 266. By 1938 the wages of an adult mine-worker stood 81st in a list of 96–100 manual workers.

[4] See above, p. 100–1.

by a 'corporate revolution' and centralized collective bargaining was already the norm. The subsequent support for the nationalization of the industry in 1964 arose from the conviction that private ownership was failing *on the technical side*.

The second conclusion is that this organizational consciousness was a characteristic of the activists in the mining and indeed the steel unions rather than of the rank-and-file. This does not mean that the latter members were *more* anti-capitalist than their leaders. As has been emphasized in this chapter and earlier,[1] the concern of most union members seems throughout to have been limited to demands for better wages and working conditions, and their dissatisfaction with their leaders, to the extent even of forming two short-lived breakaway unions in mining in 1947 and 1948[2], was derived from their belief that in such matters they were not militant enough, rather than that they should be trying to create a classless society. The leaders for their part were so concerned with the administrative tasks of operating an economically efficient form of public enterprise that they continued to believe they could find the answer to their members' problems by improving the machinery of negotiation and bargaining. Thus class consciousness may be said to contain two features which are not necessarily complementary. Negatively it consists of the recognition of the employer as a *class* enemy whose welfare varies inversely with that of his employees. For the most part, trade union leaders and rank-and-file members have agreed in this, at least while industry has been owned privately. Positively it entails the beliefs that members of the exploited class will be able to solve their industrial difficulties by creating organizations to fight employers and to replace them altogether eventually. Rank-and-file members of unions have tended to accept the first of these positive beliefs, their leaders to emphasize the second.

Even so brief an examination of the vanguard notion as this, therefore, suggests that the Marxist analysis is too broadly formulated as it stands. There is some need to consider in rather more detail the extent to which the leaders of the trade unions might be said to be in the vanguard of their members,

[1] See above, pp. 84–5 and 115–6.
[2] Surrendra K. Saxena, *Nationalisation and Industrial Conflict*, Nigjhoff, 1955, pp. 37–8.

so that the emphasis might not be placed quite so much as it has, on the miners being more class-conscious than the steel-workers, but rather on the union activists being more positive in their conception of the post-capitalist society than the rank-and-file. In sociological terms, what is required is the supplementation of Marx's class conflict notions by hypotheses about the role of the 'revolutionary' élite in social change. The alienation thesis, that is to say, might still be of some significance in explaining why it is that certain groups of workers show militant solidarity earlier than might have been expected from a knowledge of the technical and organization levels of their industry, but what is important in the study of transition to the next epoch is not this class consciousness as such, but how it is translated into political and social change; and the argument of this chapter has been that in this respect the miners have not been noticeably more successful than the steel-workers. They have placed more of their representatives in Parliament, it is true, but there is no evidence that these men have emerged as an effective political force more prominent than any other group of Labour M.P.'s. In this respect the circumstances of their members have not been matched by positive constructive measures which might be said to put them in the vanguard in the new society; but what this means must be postponed until after the élite issue has been given some attention, and it is to the notion of the trade union leader as a member of the 'revolutionary' élite that this study now turns.

10

THE 'REVOLUTIONARY' *ÉLITE*

The notion of an élite has often been contrasted with that of a class, especially in the analysis of the control of political systems by a 'governing élite' as compared with a 'ruling class'. The distinction in this case is between an organized minority *superior* to an unorganized and largely passive majority, and a dominant and organized minority *in conflict* with a subject majority which is also organized, at least in part.[1] Looked at from this point of view it is obvious that there are certain difficulties involved in incorporating the elite concept into the Marxist framework of ideas, largely because it has been regarded as a substitute for the class concept rather than a supplementation of it. However, if the term 'élite' is employed merely to refer to 'groups which emerge to positions of leadership and influence *at every social level*—that is to say, as leaders of classes or of other important elements in the social structure',[2] it seems reasonable to assert that a governing élite may exist as part of a ruling class, and that a revolutionary élite may emerge as the leadership of a subject class, without any violence necessarily being committed upon the Marxist conception of society and history.

The vanguard of the proletariat would clearly be an élite in this sense, although it should always be recognized that its superiority over the non-élite from which it has emerged is derived solely from its revolutionary class consciousness and the understanding of the historical process which this entails. It is

[1] Thomas B. Bottomore, *Elites and Society*, Watts, 1964, p. 31.
[2] George D. H. Cole, *Studies in Class Structure*, Routledge and Kegan Paul, 1955, pp. 105–6. Italics in the original.

not derived from any of the other attributes, such as the possession of special moral fibre and intellectual power *per se*, which have been regarded as essential to the concept, by those sociologists who have been instrumental in developing a set of ideas for understanding the place of élites in society.[1] Nevertheless, the notion of 'excellence' which is virtually never dissociated from the élite concept implies a difference of quality between leadership and led which is in major respects foreign to Marx's own thinking, however much he may have believed scientific socialism to be superior to any other form of social thought.[2] This suggests that considerable care should accompany the employment of the concept in the present context, and much more attention must accordingly be paid to the emergence and role of revolutionary leaders in the transition from capitalism than has been accorded to them so far.

It was, of course, Lenin rather than Marx or Engels who was most open to the charge of élitist tendencies in his thinking, especially when contrasting the 'spontaneity' of the workers with the 'consciousness' of the Social Democrats. Lenin believed, as has been already noted,[3] that left to themselves workers would develop nothing more than what he called trade union consciousness. Such 'spontaneity' as demonstrates itself in strikes, and even riots, is at best only an embryonic realization that the economic system might possibly not be permanent. The strikes which had occurred in Russia in the 1860's and 1870's, for example, Lenin thought to be a good case in point; for, they showed that the workers had begun '—I shall not say to understand, but to sense the necessity for collective resistance But this was, nevertheless, more in the nature of outbursts of desperation and vengeance than of *struggle*'.[4] By implication a group, such as the Social Democratic Party, which had the necessary understanding, was a revolutionary élite; and Lenin saw its task to be one of education and propaganda, to teach and

[1] The outstanding names here are Gaetano Mosca, Vilfredo Pareto, Karl Mannheim and Theodor Geiger. See Piet Thoenes, the *Elite in the Welfare State*, Faber and Faber, 1966, Part I, *passim*.

[2] See Bendix on the intellectual mastery of historical laws by the vanguard of the proletariat, 'Marx believed that the few were merely ahead of the many, but not above them', *Work and Authority*, op. cit., p. 344.

[3] See above, p. 49.

[4] Lenin, *What is to be done?*, op. cit., pp. 374–5. Italics in the original.

to show the proletariat what its historic mission was, as described in Marxist writings about the materialist conception of
history. In fact the creation of an effective organization for this
purpose was Lenin's major contribution to the making of
revolutions,[1] and in this sense the Bolshevik Party was the first
example in history of the concrete manifestation of a bridge
between the gap in Marxist theory and practice.[2]

What is not so clear in all this is how *on Marxist grounds* such
a party fits into the intellectual formulation of the materialist
conception of history. Lenin's own insistence on the independent role of intellectuals largely begs the question; for, to assert
that 'in Russia, the theoretical doctrine of Social Democracy arose
quite independently of the spontaneous growth of the working-
class movement; it arose as a natural and inevitable outcome
of the development of ideas among the revolutionary socialist
intelligentsia'[3] in no way answers the question how such ideas
could ever be effective in the drive towards revolution. In a
very definite sense Lenin left confused the relationship
between the *origin* of an idea and its *adoption* by the people most
able, and in Marx's eyes *destined*, to make use of it. In his subsequent analysis of the conditions for the success of the Bolsheviks
he managed to find a way round this issue, but only at the cost
of introducing an elitist notion in the form of the superior moral
qualities of the revolutionary leadership. The 'iron discipline
needed for the victory of the proletariat', he wrote, is maintained not only 'by the class consciousness of the proletarian
vanguard and by its devotion to the revolution, by its per-
severance, self-sacrifice and heroism'. It depends also on 'its
ability to link itself with, to keep in close touch with, and to a
certain extent, if you like, to merge with the broadest masses of
the toilers'.[4] However, even this formulation is unsatisfactory
since it still leaves unexplained how it is that intellectuals with
a middle-class background, like Marx, Engels, and Lenin
himself, could find it easier so to 'merge' with the masses than

[1] Vladimir I. Lenin, *'Left-Wing' Communism, an Infantile Disorder*, in V. I.
Lenin, *Collected Works*, Vol. 31, Progress Publishers, 1966, pp. 23–6.
[2] Georg Lukacs, *Histoire et Conscience de Classe* (History and Class Consciousness), Editions de Minuit, 1960, p. 338.
[3] Lenin, *What is to be Done?*, op. cit., pp. 375–6.
[4] Lenin, *'Left Wing' Communism*, op. cit., pp. 24–5.

it was for the 'natural' leaders of the working class, the elected trade union representatives and officials.

One possible approach to this problem would seem to lie in the analysis of the nature of trade union organization insofar as it sets limits to what those who are most active can perceive as relevant to the needs of the working class. Lenin, it is true, did not tackle this issue in this form, but he was aware that the routine of everyday activity was likely to condition the outlook of those most subjected to it. Discussing the difficulty of the Soviet regime during the period of famine in 1918, he said that the minority of class-conscious workers' leaders had a special difficulty in impressing on the rest the need for strict discipline and adherence to the Bolsheviks' plans for the control of the country. 'Among the broad masses of the toilers there are many (you know this particularly well; everyone of you sees this in the factories) who are not enlightened socialists and cannot be such because they have to slave in the factories and they have neither the time nor the opportunity to become socialists'.[1] At the same time he was also very conscious of what he regarded as the reformist character of trade union organization.[2] Hence it may be argued that a trade union leader's necessary concern with economic reform issues and with collective bargaining is likely to produce an attitude of mind which makes these the rationale for existence and hence is very far from revolutionary in Lenin's sense. However, as was argued towards the end of Chapter Eight,[3] there is one aspect of the trade union leader's social position which is likely to serve as a corrective. In spite of the power which he wields through the backing of thousands of workers in his role of collective bargainer, and in spite of his relatively secure and favoured economic position, as compared with many other members of society, he is not accepted personally into the ranks of those who manipulate and control the major social instruments of the industrial system. In ideological terms he is not assimilated[4] by the class with which he

[1] Vladimir I. Lenin, 'Report on the Current Situation to the 4th Conference of Trade Unions and Factory Committees of Moscow, 27 June 1918', *Collected Works*, Vol. 27, Progress Publishers, 1965, p. 468.

[2] Hammond, op. cit., Ch. 10, *passim*.

[3] See above, pp. 117–18.

[4] Goldthorpe and Lockwood, op. cit., pp. 148–52.

might otherwise identify and may even perhaps attempt to identify, this leads him to revolutionary opinions and to revolutionary actions in the sense of this book, because there is no alternative open to him *while he remains a trade union leader* but to work for the kind of society where the leaders of working-class organizations are accorded genuine recognition and esteem simply because they are leaders of such organizations.

It is important to recognize that this fits much more securely into the Marxist framework of ideas than Lenin's revisionist proposals. As Marx saw it, 'consciousness' and especially 'effective consciousness', which is what he saw as the scientific appraisal of the human situation, were products of a human being's social situation. In particular, the organization of the workers into factory hands, and following this, their organization into trade unionists, were successive steps in the development of conditions conducive to the growth of class consciousness. From this point of view the élite of leaders must be more revolutionary than the rank-and-file because such an élite is nothing more than those members of the working class who *because of their position in a trade union,* are emancipated from the stultifying effects of factory employment. They have the time and the opportunity at least to consider what such employment entails and how it affects the human personality. This does not mean that in their activities they are necessarily revolutionary in the ordinary empirical sense; but it does mean that their actions will have revolutionary implications in the theoretical sense of the term insofar as the conduct of successful strikes and successful peaceful collective bargaining forces employers to greater competition and rivalry amongst each other and hence speeds up the polarization process. Moreover, as Marx constantly emphasized, the final stages in the transition from capitalism would comprise a series of political events in which class conflict would become increasingly intensified. Clearly this can only mean that as a matter of fact trade union leaders will become more and more involved in political activity, either through their membership of political parties, or because some part of the functions of a trade union becomes political. Such activity itself implies that the social distance between them and the membership will increase, since the situation of the workers in the factory remains unchanged while the revolutionary consciousness of the leaders increases, the more they become involved in political struggles with their opponents. In this sense it is reasonable, even within the Marxist framework of ideas, to talk of a revolutionary *élite*.

There is also a sense in which it is possible to talk of some kind of *qualitative* difference in the personalities and outlook of the leadership as compared with the rank-and-file. A man does not rise to the top of the trade union hierarchy over night. He usually spends many years in union activity before he becomes fully involved in the type of negotiating and political behaviour referred to above. Thus, the average age (median) of the 18 British general secretaries, studied by Roberts in 1952, was 49 at the time of their election, or appointment to office. The youngest was 37 when he became general secretary, the oldest 56. The average age of 63 full-time national officers was 43 when they reached this grade, with a range of from 28 to 59. 33 of these men had followed more or less the same career pattern. On average they were 24 (range 17–32) when they obtained a local, part-time office in their union, 34 (range 24–44) when they became full-time officers at district level, and 43 (range 32–52) when they moved to headquarters.[1] Before his appointment, that is to say, a general secretary probably spends 15 years wholly employed by his, or more rarely some other union, and 10 years before that employed part-time.

Moreover, if he previously had been a shop steward or other 'lay' officer of his union, he would have spent much of his own time and some of his firm's engaged in union business. In the survey by Clegg, Killick and Adams, it was reported that 'shop stewards of all kinds gave nearly eleven hours a week to their work, over six hours out of their working time, and over four and a half hours of their own time. Convenors spent little more of their own time on union business (just over five hours), but averaged eighteen hours of their working-time'.[2] These figures are rather higher than those published for the Royal Commission on Trade Unions in a subsequent study. Nevertheless, the

---

[1] Roberts, *Trade Union Government*, op. cit., pp. 272–4. Details of the unions covered are listed in a footnote on p. 268. Included are the British Iron and Steel and Kindred Trades Association, and the National Union of Mine Workers.

[2] Clegg, *et al.*, op. cit., p. 154.

sample of shop stewards on this later occasion were occupied
for as long as six hours a week on trade union business, 'four
hours spent in working time or during breaks, and two hours in
the steward's own time. Senior stewards spent a total weekly
average of ten hours on their various duties.'[1] In this respect it
might be argued that trade union business and trade union
involvement offer a man a way of escape from the day-to-day
routine of manual work, whether he eventually chooses full-
time employment with a union as an alternative career pattern,
or not; but only a small minority of a union's members are in
any sense willing, if only to a very limited degree, to take on
what has sometimes been seen as too responsible or too thank-
less a task.[2] For example, only 15 per cent of the members of a
general union showed any interest in the office of shop steward,
and two-thirds of these were also interested in promotion within
the firm to the rank of supervisor, leaving 5 per cent interested
in being or becoming a shop steward as such.[3] The Royal
Commission's study, similarly, demonstrated that shop stewards
often lost pay from their employers as a result of their union
activities, amounting to as much as £2 in an average week in a
small minority of cases.[4] Altogether, then, it would appear that
men and women who are so prepared to carry on negotiations
on behalf of their fellow workers and to spend some, if not a
great deal, of their leisure time voluntarily on these and other
duties, form a very special, if small part of the population.

Of much greater significance than such qualitative differences, however, is the nature of the tasks which such an élite
has to face. In terms of the Marxist analysis revolutionary consciousness of whatever variety is of little use in the transition
from capitalism to a new world order, unless it results in action
which actually leads to changes in the social system. In drawing
a distinction between the revolutionary élite and the rank-and-
file, therefore, the emphasis should be on the extent to which the

---

[1] William McCarthy and S. Parker, *Shop Stewards and Workshop Relations*,
Royal Commission on Trade Unions and Employers' Associations, Research
Papers, 10, H.M.S.O., 1968, p. 17.
[2] Joseph A. Banks, *Industrial Participation*, Liverpool University Press,
1963, p. 65.
[3] Ibid., Table XI, p. 66.
[4] McCarthy and Parker, op. cit., p. 17.

leadership brings about effects which the rank-and-file does not. This implies that in the analysis of class consciousness what people say is of less significance than what they do, and beyond this lies a further implication of the Marxist framework of ideas about history, namely, that what they can do is inevitably related to their social circumstances as these are determined by the technologies available to them and the economic organization of their everyday lives. In the case of the trade union leadership, as this has so far been described in the case of the iron and steel industry, the critical issue is the extent to which over time effective collective-bargaining machinery was created by them *vis-à-vis* the employers and the state, especially in the sense that the operation of such machinery has weakened the power of employers to extort surplus labour from their employees. From this point of view the fact that John Kane supported the International Working Men's Association[1] was paradoxically of much less significance as a form of revolutionary activity than his endeavours along with a leading employer[2] to make the Board of Arbitration and Conciliation for the Manufactured Iron Trade of the North of England an effective machine for settling disputes without recourse to strikes or lockouts. It is true that he persuaded the Society of Malleable Ironworkers to affiliate to the International but the latter had very little influence on the nature of class conflict in Britain. The appeal of such an organization was that it offered to augment domestic political and industrial struggles with the power of international combination. Except for the tailoring trade,[3] and on one occasion for the engineers of Newcastle and Gateshead,[4] there was not much the International could do for the British trade union movement, and it is noteworthy that its membership consisted largely of builders, cabinet makers, bookbinders, etc., workers in trades whose techniques had been affected little or not at all by the industrial revolution.[5] Hence its demise in 1874 after only ten years of existence in no way affected the fortunes of the employees in the British iron and

[1] See above, p. 109.
[2] See above, p. 90.
[3] Collins and Abramsky, op. cit., pp. 68–72, 83–4.
[4] Ibid., pp. 219–20.
[5] Ibid., p. 76.

steel industry. Similarly, the fact that the steel unions supported the demand for the nationalization of the land and coal mining over forty years before they saw the need for it in their own case[1] may be interpreted as implying that they had created for themselves machinery for the effective prosecution of collective bargaining which the unions in these other employments lacked —just as the miners' demand for the end of private enterprise may be interpreted in part as a response to the coal owners' refusal to accept a centralized system of negotiation with the unions.

The significance of this point that consequences are a better indication of revolutionary class consciousness than intentions, no matter how fiercely they are avowed, may be underlined by reference to the consideration of the question, whether the miners' leaders were able to achieve as much on the basis of legislation as the leaders of the iron and steel unions had been able to achieve without it. 'In the nine years of nationalization,' wrote Jenkins in 1956, 'the National Union of Mineworkers has revolutionized the miners' conditions. It has sharply improved their earnings, developed a good pension scheme and negotiated the best compensation-for-redundancy agreement in Great Britain. At national level, too, the union has secured full information and an effective right of veto on those plans of which it disapproves; many miners have been promoted but the essential character of the industry has remained unchanged. Real power is even more concentrated now than in the private owners' day and it is heavily infiltrated with representatives of the great oligopolies which dominate British life'.[2] Three of the eleven members of the National Coal Board at that time were, it is true, trade union leaders or ex-trade union leaders,[3] and this may be said to compare favourably with the lack of such people at the top of the iron and steel industry, all of whom were company directors, whereas only one National Coal Board member and one division chairman of the Coal Board were company directors. However, five of the N.C.B. members were technical or professional managers by origin (45·5 per cent),

[1] See above, p. 109.
[2] Clive Jenkins, *Power at the Top, A Critical Survey of the Nationalised Industries*, MacGibbon and Kee, 1959, p. 128.
[3] Ibid., p. 117. One was an ex-miner.

147

as were six of the nine division chairmen (66·7 per cent), none of whom were trade unionists.[1] Although the organization of the two industries was obviously very different, this degree of professional managerialism in coal-mining compared with the 49 per cent referred to earlier for iron and steel in 1953[2] is very striking. Power at the top, whether linked with capital owner-ship or not, is very much the kind of power which the so-called 'corporate revolution' has introduced into private enterprise, namely control by people whose *access* to positions of command is determined not by property ownership as such but through the possession of managerial expertise and experience. These are the men who sit on joint industrial councils with the full-time leaders of modern trade unions, whether the industry is nationalized or not.

Moreover, in spite of Jenkins' conviction on the point, it is by no means the case that the improved position of the miners, when this is looked at by reference to the state of other manual workers, was a simple consequence of nationalization. Indeed, their relative condition in the matter of earnings between 1946 and 1953 seems to have remained largely unchanged.[3] The great improvement had already taken place, in wartime.[4] Hence it may well be, as the General Secretary of the Miners' Federation had declared prior to nationalization, that 'nearly all the improved conditions of the mine workers ... (arose) ... either directly or indirectly as a result of national negotiations and national machinery',[5] although of course, this centralized collective bargaining was perpetuated and consolidated by the Act of 1946 and subsequent measures. The main significance of nationalization, therefore, from the point of view of the Marxist framework of analysis, is that it has redirected the fruits of surplus labour from the tables of the owners of mining capital into other places, and it is open to question whether this is capitalism under a new guise—new in form but not in

---

[1] Ibid., p. 43.
[2] See above, p. 97.
[3] Baldwin, op. cit., pp. 151–4.
[4] Haynes, op. cit., p. 38.
[5] Ebby Edwards, 'A National Union for All Mine Workers in Great Britain', *The Colliery Guardian*, 17th November 1944, quoted in Haynes, op. cit., p. 188.

content[1]—or a rather different type of exploitation of the subject class.

It should be emphasized that the appointment of trade union leaders to positions of authority in the National Coal Board has been paralleled by the appointment of others to positions of similar influence in the machinery of the modern state. This includes the unpaid membership of the very large number of advisory committees which have now become part of the day-to-day business of government. Whereas in 1931–32 there was only one Government committee on which the T.U.C. was represented, by 1938–39 the number had risen to twelve. By 1948–49, it stood at 60, rising to 81 in 1953–54, but dropping again to 65 in 1957–58.[2] In part, this increase reflects the growing use of such committees over the years, from 200 standing and 400 *ad hoc* committees before the Second World War to 484 standing and 366 *ad hoc* committees in 1958,[3] although this represents growth at a rate of about half that of the increased employment of T.U.C. members on such bodies. The representatives of employers' trade associations sit with them. Indeed, some employers' associations came into existence during the Second World War as a direct result of governmental encouragement.[4] Together with senior civil servants, the union leaders and employers on these advisory committees are said to decide 'a large part of the nation's economic business . . . with only the barest reference to the electors' representatives in parliament';[5] and since wages and conditions of employment are usually outside their terms of reference, direct conflict between the representatives of the trade unions and the trade associations is rare. On many of the issues discussed, it seems that 'there is no reason why employers and unions should hold differing views, but even where employers and unions are in disagreement, they still talk to the Government more than they argue with each other'.[6] Over time, the members of such advi-

[1] James Harvey and K. Hood, *The British State*, Lawrence and Wishart, 1958, pp. 226–7. See also Mandel, *Traité*, op. cit., pp. 150–1.
[2] Allen, *Trade Unions and the Government*, op. cit., pp. 32–4.
[3] Political and Economic Planning, *Advisory Committees in British Government*, P.E.P., 1960, pp. 9–10.
[4] Jack W. Grove, *Government and Industry in Britain*, Longman, 1962, p. 60.
[5] Ibid., p. 159.
[6] P.E.P., *Advisory Committees*, op. cit., p. 72.

sory committees get to know each other personally and become on Christian-name terms.[1] In a very real sense, the trade union leaders have moved into the administrative centre of the modern British state, even if their claim that the government now treats the Trade Union Congress as 'a sort of industrial Parliament'[2] expresses a wish rather than describes a reality.

Indeed, the T.U.C.'s concern at the decline of trade union representation on the Boards of the nationalized industries[3] and their later assertion that 'there is now a growing recognition that at least in industries under public ownership provision should be made at each level in the management structure for trade union representatives of the work people employed in these industries to participate in the formulation of policy and in the day-to-day operation of these industries',[4] indicate that they see *participation* in administration as the trade union role in the future. From time to time, it is true, they may complain about some of the individuals who are appointed to sit with them, as when the I.S.T.C. objected to the post of Group Managing Director for the National Steel Corporation being filled in 1967 by 'an outspoken opponent of nationalization, with what can only be described as rather suspect attitudes towards trade unions'[5]; but there is no evidence of a widespread demand from union leaders that ex-company directors as such and other erstwhile capitalist employers should not play as much part as ex-trade union leaders in the administration of public enterprise.

Clearly, this is a very different interpretation of the course of events under capitalism from what might have been expected of a revolutionary élite in Lenin's analysis. For him, there could be no doubt that such behaviour on the part of trade union leaders was *chauvinistic*.[6] The explanation for the difference lies in his

[1] Ibid., p. 71.

[2] Trades Union Congress, *Trade Unionism*, the evidence of the T.U.C. to the Royal Commission on Trades Unions and Employers' Associations, November 1966, p. 66.

[3] 'Workers' Participation in the Nationalised Industries', Trades Union Congress, *96th Annual Report*, 1964, p. 321.

[4] T.U.C., *Trade Unionism*, op. cit., p. 97.

[5] 'Notes and Comments', *Man and Metal*, Vol. 44, 1967, p. 225.

[6] Vladimir I. Lenin, *Opportunism and the Collapse of the Second International*, 1915, in Lenin, *Collected Works*, Vol. 22, op. cit. Such an attitude is described

conception of revolution and the part played in it by insurrection. A revolutionary élite was one which aimed at *seizing* political power, and a successful revolutionary élite was one which removed the existing wielders of power from office, by violent means if necessary.[1] It is true that, with Marx and Engels, he looked forward to the eventual 'withering away' of the state but he recognized that it would 'obviously be a lengthy process'.[2] After removing the old ruling class, that is to say, the revolutionary élite would find itself obliged to become controllers of the state machine during the period of the dictatorship of the proletariat, which he described as 'the organization of the vanguard as the ruling class for the purpose of suppressing the oppressors'.[3] There is no room here for the notion of a 'revolutionary élite' *sharing power* with the former representatives of the capitalist class.

Lenin's emphasis on the paramount need for revolutionary political activity of a violent sort and his insistence on the necessity for trade unionists to cease to be satisfied with economic struggle merely, arose in part from the weak position of Russian trade unions throughout the whole period of the pre-revolutionary era. Article 318 of the penal law of 1874 had 'imposed varying sentences of prison or exile on those organizing a society which stimulated hatred between employers and workers'.[4] A law on associations, passed in 1906, eased this situation a little but strikes remained illegal and unions were unable, on pain of legal penalty, to make preparations for strike action. This did not mean that trade unions were not organized, nor strikes, even successful ones, conducted. Indeed, the revolutionary

---

as 'class collaboration, repudiation of the dictatorship of the proletariat, repudiation of revolutionary action, unconditional acceptance of bourgeois legality, confidence in the bourgeoisie and lack of confidence in the proletariat. Social-chauvinism is the direct continuation and consummation of British liberal-labour politics', p. 122.

[1] It is possible that Lenin saw violence as always necessary. See his *Thesis and Report on Bourgeois Democracy and the Dictatorship of the Proletariat*, in Lenin, *Collected Works*, Vol. 28, Progress Publishers, 1965, p. 458.

[2] Vladimir I. Lenin, *The State and Revolution*, in Lenin, *Collected Works*, Vol. 25, Progress Publishers, 1964, p. 454.

[3] Ibid., p. 461.

[4] Hugh Seton-Watson, *The Decline of Imperial Russia*, Methuen, 1952, reprinted 1964, p. 127.

activites of 1905 which led to the Act of 1906 largely consisted of spontaneous and organized uprisings of strikers.[1] Nevertheless, regular collective bargaining of the kind which led to the development of conciliation and arbitration machinery in Britain never took roots in Russia. Moreover, trade unionists and professional revolutionaries alike were very conscious indeed of the presence of the state in economic life. Although *agents-provocateurs* and police spies have played their part in the history of trade unionism in Britain as in all other countries, there is no record of anything quite so ingenious as the deliberate organization of unions controlled from the beginning by the police as in Zubátov's Moscow.[2] Nor is there any case of police-organized, revolutionary agitation to provoke willingness on the part of the ordinary citizen for the state to suppress political movements, quite so extreme as that operated by Azef and Lopukhin.[3] For revolutionaries like Lenin, not trust could be placed in the existing political system. No movement could be genuinely revolutionary unless it set out to conquer the state.[4]

Of course, some of his views as set out in 1905[5] were also coloured by the Webb's *Industrial Democracy* which he had translated into Russian and had published under the title of *The Theory and Practice of English Trade Unionism* in 1900–01. His concern that an aristocracy of labour might emerge in Russia which would not have a Marxist outlook might be said to stem from the evolutionary gradualism of the Webbs' approach. At the same time, it may equally be argued that *even in Marxist terms* Lenin misinterpreted what was happening in the world immediately around him. At the turn of the century, the Russian government 'was not only by far the greatest landowner in Russia, it was by far the greatest capitalist and the greatest employer of labour. Its railways, its mines, its factories of many

[1] James Mavor, *An Economic History of Russia*, revised edition, Russell and Russell, reprint, 1965, pp. 477–97.
[2] Ibid., pp. 188–201.
[3] Ibid., pp. 572–82.
[4] Compare his emphasis that in an autocratic political system, revolutionary activities are best pursued by those 'who have been professionally trained in the art of combating the political police', V. I. Lenin, *What is to be Done?*, op. cit., p. 464.
[5] See above, p. 49.

different kinds were in every part of the country'.[1] Lucrative state contacts played an important part in the development of the Russian productive system and Russian capitalism. For example, some two-thirds of the country's metallurgical output was acquired by the state. The relationship between bureaucratic officialdom and entrepreneurial industrialism was very close. 'Officials sat on many bodies supervising industrial activities'.[2] In his *Development of Capitalism in Russia* (1899) Lenin mentioned none of these things. Instead he concentrated on the rapid growth of machine usage and large scale operations.[3] He preferred to see Russia as an advanced, or at least advancing, capitalist society, and although he was aware that there was within the Marxist framework of ideas another set of concepts which he might have used to analyse events in Russia, namely, those connected with the Asiatic mode of production,[4] in his theoretical formulations he chose to use terminology more suitable for the treatment of capitalism on the model of England, which Marx had always seen as the society in which the vanguard of the proletariat was located.[5]

Thus, in remaining true to the Marxist analysis of revolution and insisting that this can only occur when a 'crucial moment' occurs in the 'revolutionary upsurge' of the proletariat, he argued that it was economic change *tout court* which brought this about. For example, he noted in 1917 that 'the people are close on desperation'[6] as the necessary indication that a revolution was at hand, without also apparently reflecting on the fact that, as in 1905, it was the failure of the government to cope with domestic problems, exacerbated by military defeats, that

[1] Mavor, op. cit., p. 152.
[2] Seton-Watson, op. cit., pp. 118–19.
[3] Vladimir I. Lenin, *The Development of Capitalism in Russia*, in Lenin, *Collected Works*, Vol. 3, Foreign Languages Publishing House, 1960, Ch. 3, *passim*.
[4] Wittfogel, op. cit., Ch. 9, *passim*.
[5] In his *What the 'Friends of the People' Are and How They Fight the Social Democrats* in 1894 he had noted that 'capitalism in Russia has been artificially implanted by the government' but also claimed that the state was 'nothing but the organ of the rule' of the *bourgeoisie*. Vladimir I. Lenin, *Collected Works*, Vol. 1, Foreign Languages Publishing House, 1963, pp. 293 and 196.
[6] Vladimir I. Lenin, *Marxism and Insurrection*, in Lenin, *Collected Works*, Vol. 26, Progress Publishers, 1964, p. 24.

had brought the economy close to chaos. Far from a rising class of capitalists taking over the state from feudal dignitaries and urging it to imperialist adventures as a cloak for outlets and greater profits, the entry of Russia into the twentieth century was heralded by the state itself creating a class of capitalists for its own political purposes, a class which both in terms of numbers and of influence remained relatively weak right up to the revolution of 1917. Lenin himself was sufficiently politically astute to realize that the struggle of trade unions for recognition was of little moment compared with the task of dealing with a massive bureaucratic apparatus of government, but his doctrine, elevated to a universal generalization, has had the invalid implication that the efforts of trade union leaders *everywhere* have been of no serious political or social importance, especially when considered alongside the contrivances of trained and professional revolutionaries.

The alternative view which, of course, is favoured here, is to argue that where the state has not been instrumental in developing capitalist industry, and where there have been no major political catastrophes to bring the people even remotely close to desperation, the part played by trade union leaders in the economic and political events, which indicate that capitalism is giving way to a new social order, is not at all negligible. By the time that the government came to interfere in economic life in Britain, that is to say, capitalist enterprise had for the most part already become large-scale corporate enterprise, the trade unions had become powerful organizations, and business leaders and trade union leaders already had a long tradition of organized collective bargaining, conciliation and arbitration behind them. The transition to a new form of society, which is seen here as the crucial feature of a revolutionary era in the Marxist sense, cannot be understood in a logically complete fashion if the nature of these facts is overlooked or misinterpreted. Thus, the vanguard of the proletariat was not the Communist Party but the élite of trade union activists, loosely organized together through the Trades Union Congress, and effective in a political sense through its committees of liaison with government departments and through their associated and sponsored Members of Parliament.

From this point of view, a political party directly representing this vanguard has never emerged in Britain. The Labour Party, which has served in one sense as the political 'wing' of the trade union movement, cannot be said to have been the product of a 'self-generating' process by which the unions spontaneously developed a political organization to translate their 'revolutionary' consciousness into legislation. Always it has contained a powerful non-working-class element, imbued with pre-Marxist utopian sentiments, which has reduced, 'at least at the ideological level,' domination of the Party by the unions, and 'assured middle-class ideological empathy'.[1] As the Labour vote in the constituencies has grown, the domination of the Party by this element, or at least by people not of working-class origin has increased.[2] Hence, within the British political system recruitment to Parliament has continually emphasized not only that 'workers and their children are unlikely to be included,'[3] but also that workers and their trade union representatives are unlikely to be much included. At no election between 1918 and 1935, when on average the Labour Party received 31·1 per cent of the votes,[4] did the proportion of trade union members in the Parliamentary Labour Party fall below 50 per cent, save in 1929, when the Party received 37·1 per cent of the votes[5] and the trade union representation amongst Labour Party M.P.'s fell to 39·7 per cent. At no election after the Second World War, when the Labour Party received on average 46·5 per cent of the votes,[6] did the proportion of trade union members in the Parliamentary Labour Party rise above 40 per cent, and the highest proportion attained by the union-sponsored candidates, in the election of 1954, was 36·7 per cent.[7] The public recognition of

---

[1] G. W. Ditz, 'Utopian Symbols in the History of the British Labour Party', *British Journal of Sociology*, Vol. 17, 1966, p. 147.

[2] R. Rose, 'Class and Party Divisions: Britain as a Text Case', *Sociology*, Vol. 2, 1968, pp. 129–62.

[3] Ibid., p. 155.

[4] Ibid., p. 134.

[5] David Butler and J. Freeman, *British Political Facts, 1900–1960*, Macmillan, 1963, p. 123.

[6] Rose, op. cit., p. 134.

[7] All percentages of union representation calculated from Butler and Freeman, op. cit., p. 100 for 1918 to 1959, and from David E. Butler and A. King, *The British General Election of 1964*, Macmillan, 1965, pp. 235–6, and *The British General Election of 1966*, Macmillan, 1966, p. 209.

the Labour Party as a serious contender for power, capable of forming an alternative government, has been accompanied by a marked decline in importance of union representatives in the ranks of its Parliamentarians, and it has also been accompanied by some indication of a rift in outlook, not so much perhaps on specific issues as on the kinds of issues about which different sections of the Labour Party have shown themselves willing to take the lead.[1]

All this may be interpreted as further evidence for the point that on the whole the 'revolutionary' élite has sought to attain its ends through administrative measures rather than through legislation. Yet this should not be read as necessarily implying a refutation of the Marxist thesis that eventually the class struggle would move from the industrial to the political front. The considerable increase in administrative business conducted by the government in modern Britain, as compared with that of its predecessors a century ago, has resulted in blurring the distinction between purely political decisions, taken by the government in parliament, and purely administrative decisions, made by the civil service in order to implement what parliament has already decided. Many administrative ordinances today have undoubted political consequences. Many decrees which are *defined* as administrative are in fact political.[2] For the trade union leaders to concentrate on the administration and its activities, therefore, is not for them to abandon political action for less effective practice but to direct their attentions to where the relevant directives are issued. Paradoxically, the trade union leaders' preference for pressure group politics rather than for converting the Labour Party into their own instrument or for creating their own political party *ab novo*, is the measure of their sensitiveness to the changed circumstances of the society in which they operate.[3] To the extent that this analysis has sought to remain close to the essentials of the Marxist approach, that is to say, the emphasis has been placed on the realities of the industrial and political worlds in which the

[1] Samuel E. Finer, *et al.*, *Backbench Opinion in the House of Commons, 1955–59*, Pergamon Press, 1961, pp. 65–8.

[2] Thoenes, op. cit., Ch. 7, *passim*.

[3] John Lovell and B. C. Roberts, *A Short History of the T.U.C.*, Macmillan, 1968, p. 187.

trade unions work. The role of the 'revolutionary' élite can be understood only in terms of the situation in which it finds itself, and an essential ingredient of this is the changed nature of the economic, political and social orders of contemporary British society. However, one important feature of these has so far not been explored, namely, the circumstances of those whom the trade union leaders represent. During the period of review what changes, if any, have there been in employment, property ownership, and power? The next step in the sociological critique of the Marxist approach to industrial relations consists of an attempt to answer this question.

CLASS, PROPERTY AND POWER

One of the most striking features of the process of industrialization over the past hundred years or so has been the continued acceleration of the division of labour and specialization. As measured by the proliferation of occupations this has proceeded at a faster rate than the growth of the total population at working ages. Thus, in 1851 the Registrar-General's 'dictionary' identified about 7,000 distinct occupational titles.[1] At this time the population of Great Britain, aged 15–64, totalled 12·5 million persons of both sexes.[2] By 1901 the comparable figures were 15,000 occupational titles and 23·2 million persons.[3] In 1951 more than 40,000 occupations were listed[4]—an increase of more than 570 per cent over 100 years, while the population, aged 15–64 had risen to a mere 32·6 millions,[5] 261 per cent greater than in 1851. Of course, such 'dictionaries' list many different job names rather than distinct occupations, largely because the same occupation may be referred to by different local words in different parts of the country. Nevertheless, the comparison between the growth of numbers of occupations and

[1] Interdepartmental Committee on Social and Economic Research, Guides to official Sources, No. 2, *Census Reports of Great Britain, 1801–1931*, Her Majesty's Stationery Office, 1951, p. 31.

[2] *Papers of the Royal Commission on Population*, Vol. 2. Reports and Selected Papers of the Statistics Committee, H.M.S.O., 1950, Table 1, p. 189.

[3] Interdepartmental Committee, op. cit., p. 34.

[4] David C. Marsh, *The Changing Social Structure of England and Wales*, Routledge and Kegan Paul, 1958, p. 140.

[5] Registrar-General, *Census 1951, England and Wales, General Report*, H.M.S.O., 1958, Table 40, p. 91. *Census 1951, Scotland*, Vol. III, General Volume, H.M.S.O., 1954, Table 22, p. 34.

that of the working population is too extreme to be considered as no more than an artefact of shifting terminological usage. There can hardly be any doubt that the technical and organizational inventions of modern society have resulted in the population becoming increasingly differentiated in occupational terms.

Sociologically speaking, it is to be expected that such differentation may well result in some forms of social conflict, or at least of social distance.[1] What Caplow has called 'occupational ideologies'—the customs and traditions of an occupation, and the standards of conduct 'which are enforced because of the real or supposed effects which their violation would have on the performance of the job'[2]—may be seen to create attitudes of mind, on the whole common to all those who follow a given occupation, and on the whole distinct from those whose callings are different. Some of these distinctions, to be sure, are likely to be less extreme than others. Amongst the 40,000 or so occupational titles employed for the 1951 census, many no doubt would have been found to refer to ideologies so similar as to make distinctions trivial; and for his part Caplow chose to illustrate his point by describing only the ideologies of the professions, the crafts, factory work, shopkeeping and teaching, without considering further whatever subdivisions of ideological commitment might occur within such broad occupational categories. Yet, the range between the narrow but trivial distinction and the broad but extreme is so great as to leave it very much open to question where the important divisions lie between similarities and differences in occupational ideologies. Particularly when the time factor is introduced to cover changes in the patterns of occupational recruitment and function, produced by developments in technology and industrial organization, the possibility that a hundred years of increasing specialization has widened and increased the number of gulfs within society, should not be overlooked.

The point may perhaps be particularly well exemplified by reference to the situation of the worker in clerical employment.

---

[1] Emile Durkheim, *The Division of Labour in Society*, trans. by G. Simpson, Free Press, 1933, Book 3, *passim*.

[2] Theodore Caplow, *The Sociology of Work*, University of Minnesota Press, 1954, p. 124.

Like many manual workers—for example electricians engaged in maintenance—clerks are employed in many different industries, and they are also employed in administrative and service jobs.[1] The nature of the work they are called upon to do is different in each case. Thus in the civil service 'a clear-cut classification of functions, qualifications, remuneration and criteria of advancement permitted a high degree of standardization of conditions throughout government departments. . . . By striking contrast with this administrative centralization and *Gleischaltung*, industrial and commercial clerks have been scattered among a great number of private firms among which administrative particularism has been the rule. In the majority of these firms the degree of office rationalization has been low, and many of the paternalistic relationships of the counting house have persisted. In particular, the lack of a rigid division between 'clerical' and 'managerial' grades has not resulted in the explicit blockage of mobility for the clerical group which has been typical of the civil service'.[2] Within a single industry the characteristics of clerical work may vary considerably according to the number of workers in a single unit of administration;[3] and within a single firm in America it has been found possible to identify four distinct types of clerical employment—high-level technical, semi-supervisory, varied clerical, and repetitious clerical—each type varying in the degree of intrinsic satisfaction the clerk experienced in his job, the amount of variety he said characterized the work, and the extent to which he expected advancement.[4] Similarly, six Paris insurance companies, studied subsequently, demonstrated not incomparable features.[5]

That the more general distinctions within clerical employ-

[1] Details of total numbers employed in different industries, obtained from the 1951 Census, are given in John R. Dale, *The Clerk in Industry*, Liverpool University Press, 1962, p. 7.

[2] David Lockwood, *The Blackcoated Worker: a Study in Class Consciousness*, Allen and Unwin, 1958, pp. 142–3.

[3] Ibid., p. 77.

[4] Nancy C. Morse, *Satisfactions in the White Collar Job*, University of Michigan Press, 1953, Table 14, p. 56, Table 19, p. 62, Table 20, p. 63, and Table 31, p. 74.

[5] Michel Crozier, *Le Monde des employés de Bureau* (The world of office workers), Editions du Seuil, 1965, Ch. 6.

ment has some relevance to this discussion of the Marxist theses may be seen by reference to the variations in trade union allegiance found within the ranks of clerks.[1] In strict Marxist terms, of course, clerks are not distinguishable from each other, or indeed from manual workers, when they are considered from the angle of their relationship *vis-à-vis* employers. They possess few shares in industrial property. They have no control over the means of production. Like manual workers they are obliged to sell their labour power in order to live. Moreover, both in terms of their salaries and the mechanization of their work there is some evidence of 'proletarianization' of clerks since the beginning of the century.[2] Yet, some demonstrate industrial militancy and political consciousness of as marked a kind as manual workers show, whereas others have apparently laid themselves open to the charge of 'false' class consciousness, because of their very haste to dissociate themselves from the proletariat by making alliance with an employer who exploits clerical and manual workers alike and indiscriminately. However, as Lockwood has pointed out, the analysis of the clerk's position by reference to proletarianization and false class consciousness misses a significant feature of his circumstances. His *market* situation is not identical with that of the manual worker. He still enjoys a higher income than all except craftsmen.[3] He has greater job security and less fear of possible unemployment, that is, 'a relative immunity from the hazards of the labour market which were the lot of the working classes'. He has superior chances of rising to supervisory and managerial posts, pension rights, holidays and conditions of work which are more favourable than those of the manual worker.[4]

[1] Lockwood, *The Blackcoated Worker*, op. cit., Ch. 5. G. Routh, 'White Collar Unions in the United Kingdom' in Adolf Sturmthal, ed., *White Collar Trade Unions*, University of Illinois Press, 1966, Ch. 7. George S. Bain, *Trade Union Growth and Recognition, with Special Reference to White Collar Unions in Private Industry*, Royal Commission on Trade Unions and Employers' Associations, Research Papers, No. 6, H.M.S.O., 1967, Ch. 3.

[2] Francis D. Klingender, *The Condition of Clerical Labour in Britain*, Lawrence, 1935, pp. 18–24, 58–67, 98–9.

[3] G. Mackenzie, 'The economic dimensions of embourgeoisement', *The British Journal of Sociology*, Vol. 18, 1967, pp. 36–8. This study uses American not British data.

[4] Lockwood, *Blackcoated Worker*, op. cit., p. 204.

Indeed, the fact that there remains some possibility of promotion into the ranks of management raises the question of whether the clerk's refusal often to follow the lead of his manual fellow-employers in developing class consciousness of an anti-capitalist sort is a genuine case of false class consciousness or evidence of an approach to the social organization of industry very different in kind. For some non-manual employees at least it is clear that 'there is no identification with the wrong class, but a rejection of a class view of society in favour of a status view'.[1] By this is implied an acceptance of the idea that society, or a single organization within it, is stratified not in terms of the possession or non-possession of power to extort surplus labour, but along lines of superiority and inferiority derived from personal qualities. Of course, such qualities must be thought of in relation to the work assignments of individuals in the employing organization. In general, low income, lack of opportunity to rise in the authority and income scales, strict supervision, and employment in large impersonal work groups seem to lead to worker solidarity and militancy *vis-à-vis* employers, identical to the trade union consciousness of manual workers. The converse of these circumstances, especially as indicated by the opportunity for an employee to rise into the ranks of management or to exercise broadly professional responsibilities, is associated with status consciousness. Among engineers, for example, the distinction between these two positions was found to be reflected in the degree to which they saw their occupational associations as organized to pursue trade union or professional interests.

It should be appreciated that the distinction referred to above is analytical only. Not all the members of the Engineers' Guild, studied by Prandy, demonstrated status consciousness. Some of them were clearly anxious that it should pursue trade union objectives.[2] Not all the members of the Association of Scientific Workers demonstrated class consciousness. Some thought it should not attempt to become involved in collective bargaining because it was the qualifications of individual scientists that determined their salaries, not the power of their association.[3]

[1] K. Prandy, *Professional Employees: a Study of Scientists and Engineers*, Faber and Faber, 1965, p. 38.
[2] Ibid., Table 2, p. 114, and discussion.
[3] Ibid., pp. 165-7.

Indeed, it would seem possible for an individual to think in status terms in some situations and in class terms in others.[1] Thus manual workers, members of a trade union and hence to this degree class conscious, sometimes aspire to supervisory status; and this may be conditioned by a more or less realistic perception of the possibilities open to them. In a Merseyside seed-crushing factory, for example, workers in jobs calling for above the average in terms of the mental requirements of the work and of its skill and responsibility contents, were more likely to be interested in promotion to the rank of supervisor than were other workers, and people in these jobs were more likely to be so promoted.[2]

All this serves to emphasize the point that within a single occupation, or cluster of occupations, the lines of distinction between conditions which lead either to status or to trade union consciousness are far from clear and possibly always shifting. The process whereby, over time, occupations have become more and more sub-divided has been accompanied by a bewildering variety of opportunities for advancement as this is measured by income and authority. Hence, although the Marxist prophecy about polarization has in one sense been fulfilled in that positions of power which enable their occupants 'to transcend the ordinary environments of ordinary men and women'[3] have fallen into fewer and fewer hands, in another it has not been realized because so many different levels of authority are now filled amongst the ranks of the propertyless. As Marx seems to have seen it, the splitting of society into *two* great hostile camps would result from a tendency in the industrial system to make each class more or less homogeneous in most respects. Certainly he thought there was every possibility that the proletariat would become pauperized;[4] and he also believed that the nature of factory work would become so simplified that all personnel would be interchangeable for a great many jobs and the degree

---

[1] Throughout Prandy, following Lockwood and Weber, dichotomizes between class and status consciousness. In the present discussion 'trade union consciousness' has been substituted for 'class consciousness' in the treatment of their ideas.

[2] J. Banks, op. cit., Table XXIII, p. 112, and discussion.

[3] Charles W. Mills, *The Power Elite*, Oxford University Press, 1956, pp. 3–4. Such an elite is 'in position to make decisions having major consequences'.

[4] See above, pp. 38–9.

of alienation which would accompany this process would be more or less uniform.[1] Such dehumanization of the working class, indeed, he thought would lead to the revolution to end all classes. Yet in so far as it is possible to measure so elusive a concept, amongst manual workers alone variations in the nature and conditions of work are such that individuals differ markedly in response to their environments and display several degrees of rudimentary status and class consciousness. Recent research by industrial sociologists[2] seems to indicate that the industrial forms which have emerged over the past hundred years or so are rather more complex than the simple polarization model might suggest; and it is open to question whether such complexity has implications for the Marxist analysis of class conflict.

The reference above to clerical and scientific workers raises a case in point. When, in the *Communist Manifesto*, Marx and Engels wrote about the eventual disappearance of the lower stratum of the middle class, what they had in mind were small tradesmen, shopkeepers, handicraftsmen and peasants, people with sufficient capital to be able to make a living without being obliged to sell their labour power to some employer and yet with not enough to permit them to employ wage workers themselves. Certainly this polarization picture provides no room for the replacement of such an 'old' middle class by a new one, consisting of a white-collar proletariat—clerks and other industrial bureaucrats, production and maintenance engineers and managers, research and development scientists and technologists —although later in his life Marx did acknowledge the existence of a growing new middle class intermediate between workers on the one side and capitalists and land-owners on the other.[3] Of course, it is not altogether true that the old middle class of self-employed persons has disappeared,[4] but as compared with

[1] See above, pp. 76–7.

[2] Amongst other work may be mentioned Stanley E. Seashore, *Group Cohesiveness in the Industrial Work Group*, University of Michigan Survey Research Center, 1954; Leonard R. Sayles, *Behaviour of Industrial Work Groups*, Wiley, 1958; and Robert Blauner, *Alienation and Freedom: The Factory Worker and his Industry*, University of Chicago Press, 1964.

[3] Marx, *Capital*, Vol. III, op. cit., p. 52.

[4] David C. Marsh, *The Changing Social Structure of England and Wales, 1871–1961*, Routledge and Kegan Paul, 1965, Table 38, p. 153, and Table 41, p. 163.

the rising new middle class, this section of the population, in terms of income as well as in numbers, has dwindled considerably.

Behind this development have occurred those changes in technology and organization, referred to in past chapters, which have converted the productive unit from a small scale and relatively simple, social system into a complex collectivity,[1] controlled and administered by a hierarchical system of authority. The number of different occupations required for the operation of such productive units is now considerable; and the variations in power and influence, as well as the monetary and other rewards, which economic collectivities offer, lie at the basis of the distinction between an employee's response in terms of trade union or status consciousness. Moreover, the very fact that this response is by reference to opportunities to rise in the administrative hierarchy further serves to emphasize the extent to which contemporary life values the administrative or managerial role. In this sense it is not inappropriate to talk of a 'managerial demiurge' permeating society,[2] and it is also relevant to consider whether, therefore, this reflects the process of a 'managerial revolution', transforming capitalism and resulting from 'a drive for social dominance, for power and privilege, for the position of a ruling class',[3] on the part of industrial administrators.

In Marx's eyes managers were no more than an aristocracy of the proletariat, mere employees of those who in fact controlled the large industrial enterprises. Possessors of relatively little capital, their income came from salaries which were 'or should be, simply the wage of a superior type of skilled labourer, whose price is regulated in the labour market like that of any other labourer.'[4] From Burnham's point of view the corporate revolution, and more especially the intrusion of the state into economic affairs, has changed all this. From individualistic exploitation of the working class, capitalism has developed into corporate exploitation[5], and those who control the organization in

[1] Talcott Parsons and N. J. Smelser, *Economy and Society*, Routledge and Kegan Paul, 1956, pp. 14–16.
[2] Charles W. Mills, *White Collar*, Oxford University Press, 1951, Chs. 4 and 5, *passim*.
[3] James Burnham, *The Managerial Revolution*, Day, 1941, p. 71.
[4] Marx, *Capital*, Vol. III, op. cit., p. 427.
[5] Burnham, op. cit., p. 125.

this new kind of society form a new ruling class. As he put it, 'those who already for the most part in contemporary society are actually managing on its technical side the actual process of production, no matter what the legal and financial form—individual, corporate, governmental—of the process' are the real rulers of society, and these he defined as managers in his sense of that term.[1] Superficially this has some similarity to the Marxist analysis since Marx wrote of capitalists that it was irrelevant that some of the surplus labour they extorted was passed on to others. 'It is the employing capitalist who immediately extracts from the labourer this surplus value, whatever part of it he may ultimately be able to keep for himself. Upon this relation, therefore, between the employing capitalist and the wages labourer, the whole wages system and the whole system of production hinge'.[2] If Burnham's thesis is correct and his managers on the technical side are a new ruling class, this must be because they immediately extract surplus labour from the workers they employ, however much they may pass some of it on to shareholders, to state functionaries, and to the owners of finance houses.

Burnham's argument, of course, was a revisionist one, that the struggle between capitalists and proletariat had resulted not in a classless society but in a new system of exploitation, the system of corporate exploitation. Just as Marx sought for evidence of the society to come, existing side by side with established capitalist forms, and found it in workers' co-operative production,[3] so Burnham sought for it and found it in state enterprises controlled by managers.[4] It was, however, at this point that his analysis departed from the strict line of logic demanded by the Marxist thesis. Managers, he alleged, operated contemporary industrial organizations for their own benefit. Pointing to the preferential salaries they drew as support of his contention, he added: 'it is the *fact* of preferential distribution that counts, not the form it takes or the means by which it is carried out.'[5]

---

[1] Ibid., p. 80.
[2] Marx, *Wages, Price and Profit*, op. cit., p. 391; *Capital*, Vol. III, op. cit., pp. 372–5. Surplus *value* in this passage is equivalent to surplus *labour*.
[3] Marx, *Capital*, Vol. III, op. cit., p. 431.
[4] Burnham, op. cit., p. 72.
[5] Ibid., p. 124.

Yet, what in the Marxist analysis distinguishes slavery, feudalism and capitalism from one another is not the fact that the ruling class uses the system to its own advantage, but the different ways in which it is done. If there has been a managerial revolution in some Marxist sense of the term, it must be because the managers have introduced a new way of extorting surplus labour from the workers. Otherwise their differential advantage in salary might be said to accrue from the fact that they possess a scarce skill. The alternative, indeed, is to argue that in so far as they also extort surplus labour from those they manage it is because they operate the industrial enterprise as a servant of its capitalist owners or as servants of a state which is 'dedicated to the preservation of the structure of capitalism and . . . staffed by those who fully accept the postulates and objectives of this form of society'.[1] The question at issue, therefore, is whether the corporate revolution[2] extorts surplus labour on a capitalist or some other basis.

As Marx himself pointed out, joint stock enterprise dissociated the ordinary capitalist shareholder from control over it. In the process there was produced 'a new financial aristocracy, a new variety of parasites in the shape of promoters, speculators and simply nominal directors, a whole system of swindling and cheating by means of corporation promotion, stock insurance, and stock speculation'.[3] The 'variety of parasites' were clearly intended to be regarded as of no historical significance, but corporate directors other than purely nominal ones, may be said to be altogether different. Perhaps their most striking characteristic in recent times has been dividend restraint and the use of profits for further investment. 'Although the very fast-growing firms have in fact gone to the capital market for as much as half of their investment finance, the average company quoted on the Stock Exchange has drawn more than three-quarters of its finance from reserves and only 5 per cent from bank loans and less than 20 per cent from capital issues. The corporations have become their own investors;

---

[1] Paul M. Sweezy, *The Theory of Capitalist Development*, Dobson, 1946, p. 249. The whole of Ch. XIII of this book is devoted to an excellent account of the Marxist conceptions of the state.

[2] See above, pp. 90–9.

[3] Marx, *Capital*, Vol. III, op. cit., p. 429.

shareholders are increasingly coupon-clippers'.[1] Shares, indeed, have increasingly come to be treated as equivalent to loans. In Britain, for example, between 1936 and 1951 dividends remained remarkably stable. It was the capital ploughed back into the company which fluctuated widely as profits fluctuated.[2]

Marx's 'social undertakings as distinct from private undertakings', which is how he described joint-stock companies,[3] might thus be now described as controlled by directors, who although they may also be influential members of the capitalist class,[4] are not of necessity any more capitalist in their role of director than the mediaeval lord remained feudal in his control over those parts of his estates that he converted to production employing legally-free, wage labour. To the extent that the modern director retains control over the technical side of production, over the administration of a complex organization, employing research and development scientists and engineers, as well as production and maintenance workers, he remains a manager in Burnham's sense and not merely a finance director.[5] To the extent that the system he uses to exploit his employees benefits himself first—in the form of directors' fees, emoluments, salaries, bonuses, pensions, expense accounts and salaries—and the capitalist afterwards in the form of dividend, the latter may be correctly seen as a kind of survival from a previous epoch and no longer the driving force behind the present epoch's ruling class.[6] Just as capitalism transformed 'feudal landed property, class property, small peasant property in mark communes . . . into the economic form corresponding to the requirements of this mode of production',[7] so what Marx

---

[1] Michael B. Brown, *After Imperialism*, Heinemann, 1963, p. 321, and references cited.

[2] Philip S. Florence, *Ownership, Control and Success of Large Companies*, Cambridge University Press, 1960, pp. 148–53.

[3] Marx, *Capital*, Vol. III, op. cit., p. 427.

[4] Florence, *Ownership, Control and Success*, op. cit., Table IVF, p. 102, and Ch. IV generally.

[5] Burnham, op. cit., pp. 83–4.

[6] For details of the relative importance of salaries and other forms of income in the remuneration of a sample of full-time directors, see Anthony J. Merrett, *Executive Remuneration in the United Kingdom*, Longmans, 1968, pp. 36–7 and 87.

[7] Marx, *Capital*, Vol. III, op. cit., p. 603.

saw as social capitalism and what Burnham has thought of as managerialism, is transforming private, industrial capital into the economic form corresponding to the requirements of the collective mode of production. Just as under capitalism the landowning class 'neither works itself, nor directly exploits labour, nor can find morally edifying rationalizations, as in the case of interest-bearing capital',[1] so under collectivism—which is probably the more appropriate term for this new society[2]— the capitalist class is made to discard 'all its former political and social embellishments and associations'.[3]

For his part, Burnham was convinced that the encroachment of the state into economic life had already doomed private enterprise managed by executive boards. The state, he wrote, 'takes over fully, with all attributes of ownership, section after section of the economy both by acquiring already established sections and by opening up other sections not previously existing', and he instanced 'postal services, transportation, water supply, utilities, bridges, ship-building, sanitation, communication, housing' in support of his thesis.[4] Even where the old form continued, subject of course to the corporate revolution, the state was imposing more and more restrictions on the rights of capitalist property owners, an example of 'control without full ownership'.[5] From Burnham's point of view such control was the significant feature; for, 'ownership *means* control; if there is no control there is no ownership',[6] and presumably a restriction upon control means *ipso facto* a restriction on ownership.

The growth of such state interference might be expected to show itself in some increase in the proportion of occupied persons employed by the state. In Great Britain in 1891, for example, only 0·7 per cent of the working population were employees of the central government in civil occupations and 1·2 per cent in local government service. By 1950 these figures

---

[1] Ibid., p. 809.
[2] Marx remarked that the joint-stock capitalist was 'a collective capitalist', *Capital*, Vol. 1, op. cit., p. 334.
[3] Marx, *Capital*, Vol. III, op. cit., p. 604.
[4] Burnham, op. cit., p. 107.
[5] Ibid., p. 108.
[6] Ibid., p. 92. Italics in the original.

had increased steadily to 4·3 per cent and 6·2 per cent respectively. Employment with the nationalized industries is not included in the former of these last two figures. Such employment added 10·8 per cent to the central government proportion, making in all a civil total of 21·3 per cent in central and local government service.[1] It seems, therefore, that the Labour government's four-year-old nationalization programme had as much impact as nearly sixty years of development without such legislation; and although it is true that there have been no significant changes away from central and local government to private employment, events have not altogether given overwhelming support to Burnham's argument. Direct control over little more than one tenth of the economy, as measured by occupation, is all that is exercised by local government and central government departments, and a further one tenth is all that is under the control of boards of directors who are appointed by public authorities and have no ownership of the means of production in those industries.

At the same time it does not appear that there is much evidence in favour of Burnham's thesis of a *radical* interference by the government over the power of directors in the private sector. It is true that as compared with sixty years ago the state possesses a whole battery of legal and administrative regulations which it may use to direct private individuals to perform, or to abstain from performing, certain economic functions in which it has an interest. It also apparently spends more money on it —as much as 3·2 per cent of the gross national product in 1955 as compared with only 1·0 per cent in 1890, although the meaning of this increase must be read with caution as the figure in 1920–22 was higher than that of 1955.[2] Direct intrusion into the control activities of private boards of directors is in any case very rare. In 1960 the British Government had appointed directors to the boards of only 104 firms registered under the Companies Acts, and extremely few of these were 'genuine trading concerns'.[3] The main mode of interference as contrasted

---

[1] Moses Abramovitz and V. F. Eliasberg, *The Growth of Public Employment in Great Britain*, Princeton University Press, 1957, Table 1, p. 25.

[2] Alan J. Peacock and J. Wiseman, *The Growth of Public Expenditure in the United Kingdom*, Princeton University Press, 1961, Table A-17, pp. 190–1.

[3] Grove, op. cit., p. 70.

with exhortation, that is to say, is still largely financial and indirect; and in all cases private enterprise seems to have responded either individually or through the establishment of trade associations in attempts to influence the government in the ministries or in Parliament. Such pressure group activities,[1] which it should be noted are also pursued by trade unions, are intended to soften the impact of regulations which are found obnoxious and to persuade administrators and politicians to introduce measures which will help rather than hinder private organizations in their affairs. Over time, indeed, industrial trade associations have widened the scope of their undertakings 'chiefly in constructive as distinct from defensive functions'.[2] Although they may not be said to determine broad policy and tend to concern themselves 'with matter of detail, with administrative questions, or with amendments and modifications to legislation',[3] this change may be taken as indicative of the extent to which state power is used by them, as by trade unions, to deal with problems raised by the transition to a collectivist form of society.

In this connection one important area in which the more general intrusion of the state into social life has accelerated intrinsic developments in corporate organization, is worthy of attention. The 'giant size of orders placed by public authorities for modern power stations, modern aircraft, modern defence equipment'[4] is beyond the capacity of most small firms and many even of the larger ones to fulfil. Hence government spending on this scale has led to mergers and to a growth in the size of some firms, whether there has been amalgamation or not, both increasing the concentration of trade in the hands of fewer firms.[5] However, quite independently, this type of polarization process has also been influenced by what Marx always conceived

---

[1] See John D. Stewart, *British Pressure Groups*, Oxford University Press, 1958; Allen Potter, *Organised Groups in British National Politics*, Faber and Faber, 1961; and Samuel E. Finer, *Anonymous Empire*, Pall Mall Press, revised edition, 1966, *passim*.

[2] Political and Economic Planning, *Industrial Trade Associations*, Allen and Unwin, 1957, p. 251—note the eighteen different topics listed on pp. 73-4 concerning 'most of the subjects discussed'.

[3] Ibid., p. 255.

[4] M.B. Brown, op. cit., p. 320.

[5] Evely and Little, op. cit., p. 155, and Table 32, p. 137.

as significant, the continuous evolution of more complex and expensive technological requirements.[1] In so far as it is correct to think of all this as part of a corporate revolution leading to to collectivism rather than to the classless society, the intrusion of the state has served merely to confirm rather than drastically to alter what was inherent in social relationships outside its sphere of control. Its impact on such events has been unintended and largely unanticipated, and in this sense it has continued to play a part not unlike that assigned to it in Marxist analysis, since this allows that it may, for example, 'be used to make concessions to the working class provided that the consequences of not doing so are sufficiently dangerous to the stability and functioning of the system as a whole'.[2] In attempting to ameliorate some of the worst consequences of private enterprise, for instance by nationalization, it has accelerated the transition to the next epoch, but it has not been the driving force behind that change.

The nature of the argument should by now be quite clear. Burnham's belief that capitalism would be succeeded by a managerial society, largely as a result of deliberate state policy, has not been supported by the course of events in advanced capitalist societies. On the one hand, it is not the technical managers but the members of the boards of directors who make the major decisions about the conduct of the enterprise, and its future, at the present time. On the other hand, it is not the state which has determined this development but *spontaneous* changes occurring in the private sphere, as a consequence of the extended division of labour and the organization of productive workers in larger and larger viable units. Moreover, the fact that the nature of property ownership in this sphere has paralleled the development of collective production by becoming collective ownership serves to emphasize the point that this is private enterprise or *voluntary* collectivism, rather than that kind of collectivism which socialists, as opposed to sociologists, have always thought of as correlative to state and municipal ownership of industry, and in the long run essential to socialism. Needless to say, the kind of non-violent, collectivist revolution which has been referred to here has not introduced socialism in

[1] Ibid., pp. 181–3, 187–8.
[2] Sweezy, op. cit., p. 249.

this sense. What has occurred instead, it is now claimed, is the advent of a new, class society.

When he was looking for signs of the society to come in the society of his own day, Marx seized upon producer co-operation as the prototype, mainly for the reason that 'in a co-operative factory the antagonistic nature of the labour of supervision disappears because the manager is paid by the labourers instead of representing capital counterposed to them'.[1] At the time such factories seemed to be flourishing. 163 new producer co-operative societies were registered under the Industrial and Provident Societies Acts between 1862 and 1880.[2] By the end of the Second World War, however, such experiments could be seen to have stagnated, especially by contrast to the expansion of joint-stock enterprise. They existed for the most part in the boot and shoe, clothing and printing industries and were surviving as an adjunct merely of the retail consumers' co-operative movement on which they entirely depended.[3] While there can be no doubt that they had demonstrated the possibility of operating without a capitalist hierarchial framework of authority, their failure to expand equally demonstrates that their continued existence in the future is precarious.

This is important for the interpretation of current industrial *economic* events because of the fact that Marx recognized features of similarity in the direction of the co-operative and the joint-stock systems. 'The wages of management', he wrote, 'both for commercial and industrial managers are completely isolated from the profit of enterprise in the co-operative factories of labourers, as well as in capitalist stock companies'.[4] *Both* had resolved the conflict between capital and labour, the former 'positively', the latter 'negatively'.[5] It is, of course, not altogether clear what he meant by this distinction, but the course of history since his day has surely favoured the negative rather than the positive solution. To the extent, therefore, that the wages of manage-

[1] Marx, *Capital*, Vol. III, op. cit., p. 380.
[2] George D. H. Cole. *A Century of Co-operation*, Allen and Unwin, 1944, p. 158.
[3] Ibid., pp. 394–5. For the position in 1957 see Ken Coates and A. Topham, eds., *Industrial Democracy in Britain*, MacGibbon and Kee, 1968, p. xxxii.
[4] Marx, *Capital*, Vol. III, op. cit., p. 380.
[5] Ibid., p. 431.

ment are paid not by the labourers, but by directors, the dominant form of contemporary enterprise is structurally different
from what Marx conceived to be the future form in a classless
society. What has been termed here 'collectivism', that is to say,
is a new type of class society in *Marxist terms*; and the people
who sit on the boards of control of private and public industrial
organizations constitute a new ruling class of employers, dependent not upon capital, but upon some other source of authority
for their power to extort surplus labour from their employees.

What is the source of this authority? A generation ago Berle
and Means pointed out that 44 per cent of the 200 largest companies in the United States of America were subject to what
they called 'managerial control' and this accounted for 58 per
cent of the companies when they were measured by their
wealth rather than by their number.[1] Managerial control, they
said, exists when directors 'can virtually dictate their own
successors'.[2] When the ownership of a joint-stock company
is scattered through a multitude of shareholders widely dispersed about a country, or around the world, proxy voting
becomes the norm, and the existing board of directors control
the proxies. Thus such forms of enterprise become self-perpetuating oligarchies. The directors decide who will join them on
the board when a vacancy occurs, providing them with a share
if necessary, and it is the directors who appoint all the senior
managers to organise the labour force and the means of production on their behalf. Thus the directors retain control over
the enterprise by virtue of the very fact that it is an oligarchy
and they sit at the top of it.[3]

The board of control of a nationalized industry, it is true, is
not self-perpetuating in this sense since its members are appointed usually by a Minister of the Crown. They are appointed, however, not elected, and once in office they have oligarchical powers not strikingly different from those possessed by the
board of directors of a joint-stock company,[4] and both seem to

[1] Berle and Means, op. cit., p. 94.

[2] Ibid., p. 87.

[3] Margaret Miller and D. Campbell, *Financial Democracy*, Hogarth, 1933,
Ch. 2, *passim*. George H. Copeman, *Leaders of British Industry*, Gee, 1955,
p. 47.

[4] William A. Robson, *Nationalized Industry and Public Ownership*, Allen and
Unwin, 1960, Chs. VI, VIII and IX, *passim*.

consist in the main of the same kind of people.[1] Although parallels with other epochs of history may be misleading, it should be noted in this context that the authority of a mediaeval lord was no less feudal if he were given a grant of land by his sovereign rather than had inherited it from his father. Moreover, although the incomes of the self-perpetuating boards are decided largely by themselves, while those of the nationalized industries are decided in advance by ministerial decree ratified by Parliament, there is some evidence that the latter are determined by reference to what directors in private enterprise pay themselves, and not *vice versa*.[2] Thus the power of such people to fix their own rewards, limited only by what the market will bear and by what the Exchequer can raise from the general public through taxation, together with the control they exercise over hierarchies of subordinates, are the indications that in the industrial field at least, they constitute a new ruling class.

The reference above to feudal inheritance raises a point which Burnham saw as important in his discussion of the managerial revolution and which is also significant here. The Asiatic, feudal, and capitalist epochs are marked by systems of production in which authority is handed down from father to son by reference to a legal device which sociologists refer to as *ascriptive*. Appointment to public or private boards of directors at the present time is, however, not made ascriptively. The emphasis in the collectivist society, that is to say, is on merit, although it should be noted that one of the ideological underpinnings of capitalism was an emphasis on inheritance plus achievement rather than on *mere* inheritance. Nevertheless, as Burnham pointed out,[3] one of the striking features of modern management is the effort top managers make to ensure that their own sons—much more rarely their daughters—are given the kinds of education that will open up the way to promotion to high-ranking jobs. Thus collectivist society continues one of the elements of capitalist ideology, namely its emphasis on 'openness'. Anyone might

---

[1] R. Blackburn, 'The New Capitalism' in Perry Anderson and R. Blackburn, eds., *Towards Socialism*, Fontana Library, 1965, pp. 136–7.

[2] Robson, op. cit., pp. 230–3. For some details on salary comparisons in 1966 see Anthony J. Merrett and D. A. G. Monk, *Inflation, Taxation and Executive Remuneration*, Hallam Press, 1967, pp. 44–7.

[3] Burnham, op. cit., p. 109.

become a capitalist if, by hook or by crook, he could acquire some capital. So, anyone may become a board member if he can gain the right kind of qualifications. The element of exclusiveness remains, however, in the fact that 'disproportionately few, whether in large or small firms, seem to have become top managers after starting at the bottom, or after beginning as manual or clerical workers. The largest single element in top management comprises men who have got financial or scientific qualifications before they entered industry.... In the bigger companies the educational ladder rather than inherited wealth has been the important factor'.[1] The hierarchies are not altogether closed. After all, one per cent of the 182 top managers studied by Clements in 1958 had had fathers in unskilled occupations, and a further two per cent came from a semi-skilled background.[2] More recently Clark has reported comparable figures of 2·5 per cent and 11·8 per cent respectively, or 1·7 per cent and 11·8 per cent if directors are considered alone.[3] In both studies quite large numbers reported that they had begun their careers in industry at the bottom.[4] But, clearly, opportunities to rise to the top are weighted in favour of those who, adapting Clements, may be called the 'crown princes'[5] of industry, the sons of those already at the top, who can afford to send their offspring to Britain's expensive public schools.[6]

That the system is in part open goes some way to accounting for the prevalence of status consciousness, referred to earlier in this chapter, in connection with the discussion of the attitudes of

[1] Roger V. Clements, *Managers: a Study of their Careers in Industry*, Allen and Unwin, 1958, p. 150.

[2] Ibid., Table 10, p. 177. Note that not all Clements' top managers were board members, ibid., pp. 21 and 49.

[3] David G. Clark, *The Industrial Manager: His Background and Career Pattern*, Business Publications, 1966, Table 4.10, p. 68.

[4] Clements, op. cit., Table 29, p. 185; Clark, op. cit., Table 5.5, p. 78.

[5] Op. cit., p. 24, 'Crown princes' are 'men whose start, progress and achievement in business can be largely ascribed to close family links with the ownership or top management of the firm'. For comparable American data see Mabel Newcomer, *The Big Business Executive*, Columbia University Press, 1955, Table 17, p. 53, Table 18, p. 55.

[6] Blackburn, op. cit., p. 117, n. 2, and references cited. See also The Public Schools Commission, *First Report*, Vol. 2, Appendix 8, Section 4, H.M.S.O., 1968, p. 236, and R. Heller, 'Britain's Top Directors', *Management Today*, March 1967, pp. 62–5.

scientists and engineers in industry. So long as the possibility exists for an individual that he might mount the authority hierarchy to the point of sharing in control, to this extent he will shun trade union activity, designed as a challenge to the system. In this sense it is not unreasonable to talk of such men as 'belonging' to industrial organizations, even if the view that they 'have left home, spiritually as well as physically, to take the vows of organization life'[1] might seem to be extreme. Those who are definitely conscious that the avenues for advancement in their case are blocked fairly early on in their careers are men likely to display trade union consciousness *vis-à-vis* the 'professional' organizations of which they may happen to be members. Thus, the class system of contemporary society has become closely associated with the power systems of the industrial organizations, and in the process it has become dissociated from the kind of property system that prevailed in the capitalist epoch. Power nowadays provides access to wealth. Only when converted into educational opportunity does wealth provide access to power, except where some vestiges of capitalism continue to exist. That this system is no longer capitalist may also be seen by reference to the Marxist notion of exploitation through the extortion of surplus labour. Necessary labour, it will be recalled, is the labour which men must undertake to rear their families and to continue to exist themselves. Hence, it might be that 'surplus labour represents what belongs to the labourer but what he does not get. Any income but the labourer's, any expenditure not made by labour comes out of surplus-value'.[2] However, Marx realised that even in a socialist society surplus labour was bound to persist,[3] and indeed might be deliberately extorted within industry to provide schools, hospitals and other services for the general welfare of all and not necessarily as a return to the *individual* labourer for his own benefit. Such a society would be still classless provided that there was no section of it able to acquire preferential claims on the social fund, or alternatively able to keep for itself some part of the surplus product before passing on the rest to be distribu-

[1] William H. Whyte, jnr., *The Organization Man*, Simon and Schuster, 1956, p. 3.
[2] Bober, op. cit., p. 199. Read surplus *labour* for surplus *value* here.
[3] K. Marx, *Capital*, Vol. III, op. cit., p. 953.

ted as general welfare. If the collectivist society is a class society,
therefore, it must be because of the way in which the board of
directors handles labour output in their organization of production.

As an American textbook on business management has emphasized, the essentials of modern business success lie in the
management's handling of cost accountancy and budgeting.[1]
For this purpose it distinguishes between five main divisions of
costs: labour, materials, manufacturing expenses, administrative
expenses and selling expenses. It further distinguishes between
variable, semi-variable and fixed expenses. Now, labour which
'represents the payment to those who actually perform work
on the product',[2] is a variable expense as is the cost of materials,
since both fluctuate directly with fluctuations in output. Manufacturing expenses, which include the cost of supervision, and
selling expenses are semi-variable. But administrative expenses
which 'represent the payments made to personnel and for
materials, equipment, and the services which are necessary for
the administration of the organization as a whole',[3] are fixed.
Thus it may be said that directors' fees, etc., are a first charge
on the organization, both in private and public industry, and
the surplus product is what comes from manipulation of variable
and semi-variable costs. In this respect collectivist society is
more like feudalism than capitalism in that work on the lord's
demesne preceded work on the serf's own plots, whereas capital
makes its claim on the surplus product *after* it is produced. Of
course it is not at all unlikely that increases in the directors'
share of the product are determined by reference to past
surpluses, but this does not alter the fact that budgeting for the
following year starts from the basis of a higher fixed administrative cost factor and calculates its variable labour factor
by reference to this factor and what it estimates its sales chances
to be. The axiom of such business practice, that 'the general
wage level in a business organization and the wage policy itself
must be determined by top levels of management'[4] represents

[1] Lyman A. Keith and C. E. Gubellini, *Business Management*, McGraw-
Hill, 1958, Ch. 22, *passim*.
[2] Ibid., p. 352.
[3] Ibid., p. 353.
[4] Ibid., p. 216.

the point at which class conflict in the collectivist society reaches its crisis. The modern emphasis in accountancy on costing, as compared with the nineteenth-century view that 'proprietorship and property rights alone were of importance',[1] draws attention to what is called 'labour efficiency' as the crucial element in the finances of organizational practice. Power to determine how much shall be allocated to fixed and how much to variable expenses is what distinguishes the ruling class from those whose incomes are regarded as a variable only. No matter how individuals come to be appointed to the boards of control of contemporary industrial organization, it is the fact that they are empowered to make such decisions which entitles them to be regarded as a ruling class, in the Marxist sense.

It should be emphasized that, like everything else in this critique of the Marxist approach to industrial relations, the conclusions of this chapter are tentative only. Rather more research into the evidence for and against the notion of a transition to collectivism needs to be undertaken than has been attempted here, before the modifications in the Marxist analysis which are implied can be regarded as satisfactory. Nevertheless, it is submitted that sufficient data have been presented to make it not unreasonable to pursue the matter further. To the extent that the class and power systems of contemporary society may be said to diverge significantly from those of the capitalist epoch proper, the place of trade unions and of collective-bargaining procedures in such a society might be thought also to have changed from their traditional state to a new one. Indeed, only if such changes have occurred may it be legitimate to conclude that a new era has been entered, rather than that a new stage in capitalism has been reached. It is to the consideration of this issue that it is now necessary to turn.

---

[1] Nicholas A. H. Stacey, *English Accountancy: A Study in Social and Economic History, 1800–1954*, Gee, 1954, p. 38.

12

INDUSTRIAL RELATIONS UNDER VOLUNTARY COLLECTIVISM

The main reason for regarding trade union leaders as a 'revolutionary' élite, it was argued above,[1] is because *in their own interests* they find themselves obliged to work for changes in capitalist society, which will result in their being accorded genuine recognition for the fact that they are the representatives of large and powerful organizations. In this respect capitalism may be said to bear the seed of its own destruction, since it is the development of large-scale units of industrial operation which makes it possible for strong trade unions to emerge. Of course, it is also true that the strength of such unions depends, in part at least, on their amassing considerable funds, which they may use to support their members against individual employers if strike action ever becomes necessary. Moreover, the actual sum of money at the disposal of the leadership at any given moment of time is in some sense of less significance than what has been called 'the levy capacity' of the membership, that is, 'the extent to which the unions could obtain from their members the income necessary to replenish the funds should they be run down by a strike or lockout'.[2]

Clearly, so long as a trade union leader can maintain sufficient confidence in his fellows for them to subscribe *extra* money in a case of emergency, and so long as they themselves are not only willing, but able to meet their union's special need in such contingencies, the financial reserve behind a union's militancy may be regarded as far in excess of its book-keeping record of as-

[1] See above, pp. 142–3.
[2] Roberts, *Trade Union Government*, op. cit., p. 393.

sets, considerable though these may nowadays be.[1] To this extent the power of trade union leaders to make themselves felt *vis-à-vis* employers can be only partially estimated from the direct cost to the latter of a strike as compared with the losses to their employees. Indirectly, there is in operation a reserve force which grows to the degree that the pursuance of a national policy of full employment and social welfare over a long period of years provides a buttress of economic security for the trade union member. Thus, in so far as trade unionists have worked in the past for state interference in economic life to provide social security for the working class, so far have they also, consciously or unconsciously, created the condition whereby the viability of their own organizations has been increased.

The advent and development of such state policies may, indeed, be read as indicating that the final phases of transition from capitalist society have arrived; and one author at least has recognized the dominant features of government interference on behalf of social welfare as characteristic neither of liberalist capitalism nor of its traditional rival, socialism, but those of a new form of society. It is true that in this conception of the Welfare State, Thoenes has argued that its 'guarantee of collective social care to its citizens' is *concurrent* 'with the maintenance of a *capitalist* system of production',[2] but there is nothing in his treatment of the subject, other than references to 'an economic system for the production of goods and services, in which the necessary machinery for keeping it going is the private property of employers whose main aim is still business profits',[3] which is necessarily incompatible with what has been written above about the intrusion of the state into economic life and about the collectivist organization of the modern joint stock company. The main point of Thoenes' argument is that 'in the Welfare State the entrepreneur is simply part of a larger system, the national economy. If all goes well he can enjoy great freedom within this system, but as soon as the vulnerable economy threatens to go a little awry, government regulations are looked for in order to safeguard it. The entrepreneur may perhaps give advice about these regulations; he may register

---

[1] Ibid., Ch. 18, *passim*.
[2] Thoenes, op. cit., p. 125. Italics not in the original.
[3] Ibid., p. 127.

protests against them; he may profit by them; but they are made by an authority that is set above him. Very large firms, of course, can manage to adopt a more independent type of management, so much so indeed that lesser or local authorities, in their turn, can find themselves in a position of semi-dependence upon them. But these concerns, with amongst other things their great internal bureaucracies, are much more like states within the state than examples of free undertakings'.[1] Once the government of a country has accepted responsibility for collective social welfare, that is to say, it finds itself obliged to interfere with the operations of the economic system, even to the extent of nationalization if necessary, in order to carry out the task which its people expect of it, but it will not take over the ownership of the means of production in those instances where it believes it has convincing evidence that private enterprise is 'perfectly capable of providing society quite satisfactorily with the goods and services it needs'.[2]

Such a concept of collectivism implies that the extortion of surplus labour from the employees of economic organizations, private or public alike, will to some extent at least be obscured by state policies designed to guarantee a minimum income to citizens, to ensure their welfare against foreseeable contingencies such as sickness and old age, and to provide medical, educational and other social services as a positive attempt to enhance the quality of their lives. As Asa Briggs has put it, these objectives are effected through the deliberate use of the apparatus of government 'in an effort to modify the play of market forces'.[3] In the case of the labour market, of course, trade unions themselves have always sought in various ways to improve the bargaining power of their members in resistance to what Marx saw as 'the constant tendency of capital . . . to force the cost of labour back towards . . . zero'.[4] State action, however, armed with punishments for those employers who break

[1] Ibid., p. 175.
[2] Ibid., p. 128.
[3] A. Briggs, 'The Welfare State in Historical Perspective', *European Journal of Sociology*, Vol. 2, 1961, p. 228.
[4] Marx, *Capital*, op. cit., Vol. 1, p. 600. 'Zero' in this connection is a theoretical concept, a limit always beyond reach, as Marx himself pointed out, but one towards which 'we can always approximate more and more'.

the law in this respect, is altogether a different kind of intrusion into the free operation of the market from collective bargaining supported by no more than the threat of a strike, which punishes employees along with employers.

In England direct government interference of this kind effectively began with the Trade Boards Act of 1909, later described as 'in reality, the silent abandonment of the doctrine, held for three generations with an almost religious intensity, that wages should be settled, as it was said, by free competition, and free competition alone'.[1] The Act was the result of some twenty-five years' agitation over the plight of workers in the 'sweated trades', employed not in large factories by large employers, but by small men in small, often inadequate workshops, or in their own homes. Most of these workers were beyond the reach of the trade unions who found them difficult to contact, let alone organize. While it is true that 'to some extent the principle of state interference in the wages and conditions of private industry had already been sanctioned by the fair wages resolutions'[2] —that is, 'the expression of the will of Parliament about the way in which the executive should safeguard the interests of workers employed by those to whom government contracts are given'[3]—the employer who tendered for such a contract would always make his estimates high enough to cover any extra wages it might entail; and if he were unsuccessful in his tender there was nothing the government could, or would do, to ensure that his workmen were paid as much on private contracts as they would have been on contracts with the state. The powers of the Trade Boards were much more extensive than this, for all that it was not the government's intention that they should be able to achieve anything more than to determine minimum time and piece rates for four trades only, namely tailoring, paper and cardboard box-making, chain-making, and the finishing or mending of machine-made lace. Yet, with all these limitations, after a slow start, the Boards were effective for a small fraction of badly paid workers. Thus, in 1911 the Chain Board fixed time rates for women workers which resulted in a wage of

---

[1] Richard H. Tawney, *Towards Industrial Peace*, 1927, p. 19, quoted in Frederick J. Bayliss, *British Wages Councils*, Blackwell, 1962, p. 1.

[2] Clegg, Fox and Thompson, op. cit., Vol. 1, p. 404.

[3] Ministry of Labour, *Industrial Relations Handbook*, op. cit., p. 149.

11s. 3d. per week as against earnings of from 5s. to 6s. per week received previously.[1]

Moreover, in spite of opposition from time to time which almost resulted in its being discontinued, the Act remained on the statute book, was broadened after 1918, and was consolidated as the Wages Councils Act of 1959, to regulate terms and conditions of employment in those 'trades or industries where machinery for regulating the remuneration either does not exist or is not, and cannot be made adequate for that purpose, and, therefore, a reasonable standard of remuneration will not be maintained'.[2] Minimum wage legislation, that is to say, now operates where the practice of collective bargaining by means of Joint Industrial Councils does not reach, and it represents a major interference with the unrestricted working of the market for labour in the case of about three and a half million British workers,[3] covered by some sixty councils.[4]

It should perhaps be emphasized that the Councils are not departments of state, composed of civil servants and politicians, but largely autonomous bodies consisting of equal numbers of representatives of employers and employees in the trade or industry concerned, together with not more than three independent members, 'not connected with either side of industry'[5] of whom one is always chairman. The universities have provided about one third to one half of such independents and the legal profession about one third.[6] The Minister of Labour appoints the Council members, but otherwise has no power over their conduct or decisions. He cannot reject or amend proposals which are submitted to him, although he may refer them back to the Council for reconsideration. Eventually he must make a Wages Regulation Order to give a Council's proposals legal effect. In practice, moreover, he appoints members to Councils from the names which are submitted to him by employers' associations and trade unions interested in the trades or industries covered by a Council.[7] Since, too, changes in wages and

---

[1] Bayliss, op. cit., p. 11.
[2] Ministry of Labour, *Industrial Relations Handbook*, op. cit., p. 153.
[3] Bayliss, op. cit., p. 72.
[4] Ministry of Labour, *Industrial Relations Handbook*, op. cit., pp. 216–17.
[5] Ibid., p. 157.
[6] Bayliss, op. cit., Appendix 2, p. 160.
[7] Ibid., p. 103.

working conditions are usually put forward in the first instance by the workers' representatives on a Council, it seems likely that trade union leaders see its operation as an alternative to collective bargaining in those cases where Joint Industrial Councils with employers, for one reason or another, are not viable.

In the depression years, to be sure, some anxiety was felt in trade union circles lest the existence of a Trade Board should weaken workers' interest in trade unionism in those trades where minimum wages were fixed by law,[1] and in the period after the Second World War some hostility has been expressed from time to time by trade unionists against minimum wage legislation as such, accepting it only as a necessary evil and believing that it should be reduced rather than expanded over time.[2] The point here is that the proposals made by Wages Councils in the post-war period have usually followed changes which had already been introduced elsewhere as a result of collective bargaining on the Joint Industrial Councils,[3] and in consequence the minimum wages of trades and industries covered by the Councils have lagged behind, rather than set the pace for the wages of poorly paid workers. Indeed, only for women workers, and then only up to about 1948 and not since, have earnings awarded in this way advanced faster than women's earnings generally.[4] Thus, direct government interference has had the effect of no more than establishing a base line from which comparisons may be made, although in this respect it may be said to have made an impact on that 'historical and moral element'—'the degree of civilization of a country'— which Marx saw as partly determining the value of labour power by adding to the 'natural wants' of the labourer a number of 'so-called necessary wants' dependent upon 'the habits and degree of comfort' which he and his family could come to regard as essential.[5]

The preference of trade union leaders for collective bargaining

[1] Dorothy Sells, *British Wages Boards*, Brookings Institution, 1939, pp. 312–15.

[2] R. L. Bowlby, 'Union Policy Toward Minimum Wage Legislation in Post-war Britain', *Industrial and Labor Relations Review*, Vol. 11, 1957–8, p. 75.

[3] Bayliss, op. cit., p. 73.

[4] Bowlby, op. cit., Tables 3, 4, 5 and 6.

[5] Marx, *Capital*, Vol. 1, op. cit., p. 171.

rather than for Acts of Parliament is important in this context because, as a matter of fact, statutory wage legislation is the only example in England of the free play of the labour market being directly influenced by government action as a permanent policy. During the two world wars compulsory arbitration was also used for this purpose, although only as part of a general attempt to control the use of labour in an emergency, and, therefore, temporary situation and to remove the threat of strikes and lockouts by declaring them illegal. During the First World War such compulsion was not very effective,[1] and when it was decided to introduce a Condition of Employment and National Arbitration Order in 1940 every effort was made to obtain the agreement of the British Employers' Association and the T.U.C.[2] Both these bodies, moreover, agreed that compulsory arbitration should be continued into peacetime, but as soon as it became obvious in 1950–51 that the prohibition of strikes and lockouts no longer had general support within the country, the Order was revoked and new measures were introduced which virtually abandoned compulsion.[3]

Post-war governments, indeed, have relied rather on an indirect approach to interference in the labour market. Following the 'stabilization' budget of 1941 and the formal acceptance by the state in 1944 of responsibility for maintaining a 'high and stable' level of employment,[4] successive Chancellors, irrespective of their political allegiance, have incorporated in their Budgets measures which they have thought to be 'appropriate to correct and anticipate the particular and adverse changes which appear to jeopardize' it.[5] Not only have they been on the whole successful in keeping unemployment low by intervening to increase demand whenever it looked like rising, but they have also won over the *confidence* of businessmen that the state could and would interfere in this way whenever necessary.[6] The

---

[1] Henry M. D. Parker, *Manpower: A Study of Wartime Policy and Administration*, H.M.S.O., 1957, pp. 10, 11.

[2] Ibid., pp. 134, 448 et seq. See also Sharp, op. cit., Part II, Ch. 7.

[3] Ministry of Labour, *Industrial Relations Handbook*, op. cit., pp. 145–8.

[4] John C. R. Dow, *The Management of the British Economy, 1945–60*, Oxford University Press, 1965, p. 1.

[5] Gilbert Walker, *Economic Planning by Programme and Practice in Great Britain*, Heinemann, 1957, pp. 154–5.

[6] Dow, op. cit., p. 364.

result of over twenty years of success in this regard has been to make the general public expect much more of the government than it ever did in the past.

The nature of the Welfare State's intrusion into economic life should not be misunderstood. Because trade union leaders have sought to maintain the system of Joint Industrial Councils independent of government interference, and because the government seems largely to have respected their wishes and those of the employers in this matter, it should not be assumed that the trade unions have maintained unchallenged control over the market for labour during the period of full employment since the end of the Second World War. Rather what has happened is that the nature of markets generally has changed. Quite apart from collective bargaining and welfare policies interfering with free competition, the production of goods by large and permanent industrial organizations has led to prices being fixed, no longer by supply and demand as in the days of classical capitalism, but by administrative fiat. Such 'administered' prices are 'set by individual companies and kept constant for periods of time' even in cases, such as steel production, where some costs such as those for scrap fluctuate more or less in the classical manner.[1] Of course this does not mean that prices are inflexible. What it means is that they are adjusted by firms to meet aggregate costs over a predetermined period, because they have come to learn that full employment largely guarantees that the higher prices will be paid by the consumer. In turn, the trade unions press for wage increases to meet the rising cost of living and the firms adjust their prices further to meet their new wages bill.[2]

This inflationary trend since 1945 has been interpreted in the main as a wages-prices spiral, in spite of the fact that other factors, such as import costs, have also played an important part in the process; and the wages factor has been accorded prime of place in the causal sequence. Thus, according to one

---

[1] Gardiner C. Means, *Pricing Power and the Public Interest*, Harper, 1962, p. 11.

[2] Dow, op. cit., Ch. 13, *passim*. See also his 'Analysis of the Generation of Price Inflation: a Study of Cost and Prices Changes in the United Kingdom, 1946–54', reprinted from *Oxford Economic Papers*, Vols. 8 and 9, 1956–7, National Institute of Economic and Social Research Reprint Series, No. 9.

author, there were some six occasions between 1945 and 1965 when the British economy was faced with a major crisis in its balance of payments position. In every instance the same broad approach was taken by the government of the day, whether it was Conservative or Labour in its political affiliations. Through 'excessive' wage demands trade unions have been accused of exerting an upward, inflationary pressure on prices. Through 'restrictive' practices, they have been said to exert a downward pressure on productivity. Through strikes, overtime bans, and working-to-rule, they have been seen to have had a depressing effect on total production.[1] Appeals for 'restraint' in making wage adjustments have been addressed to trade union leaders and employers alike; and although the idea of a national 'incomes' policy has gradually come to replace that of a national 'wages' policy, it is primarily through control of wage demands that governments have thought the way to a solution of the country's financial problems might be found.

Trade union leaders in particular have been subjected to requests to put the national interest in the forefront of their union's policy determination; and it is noteworthy that since the war the T.U.C. General Council has been most reluctant to propose any resolution which would seem critical of the government's wage and economic policies, although member unions have not been quite so circumspect. However, 'even union officials who reject the attitude of relatively uncritical positive commitment where issues of national interest are concerned, have to couch their rejection in terms which show that they are aware of national interest issues. Indeed agreements between representatives of different unions over wages policies often take the form of arguments about alternative ways of furthering the national interest.'[2] Thus one feature of trade union participation in the affairs of state, referred to above,[3] has been the correlative pressure on the leadership as a whole to accept general state welfare measures which might sometimes be interpreted as opposed to, and sometimes even at the expense of, the militant pursuit of the vested interests of the

[1] Victor L. Allen, *Militant Trade Unionism*, Merlin Press, 1966, Chs. III and IV.
[2] Ibid., p. 54.
[3] See pp. 147–50.

members of individual unions. This does not mean that they have not continued to use collective-bargaining machinery for the benefit of their members, but that they have been under regular constraint to do so in such a fashion as not to endanger the government's efforts to preserve the stability of the economic system as a whole. It is, to be sure, this aspect of the ideology of the Welfare State which makes possible a Communist interpretation, stressing the function of such a state as 'preventing further intensification of the existing conflicts in capitalist society'.[1] The point of emphasis here, by contrast, is that the trade unions are willy-nilly impelled to accept the ideology because it is part of the collectivist ethos they have for so long been maintaining.

One aspect of the Communist criticism is, however, worthy of further attention. Full employment has been accompanied by remarkably little evidence that there has been genuine redistribution of income within the country.[2] Although a great deal has been written about the supposedly strongly egalitarian tendencies of post-war legislation and governmental decrees,[3] the statistical foundations for the analysis of incomes received *before tax* are so shaky as to be almost valueless as a form of verification for the argument. Nor do they include estimates for what is apparently a growing practice on the part of industrial organizations to reward certain of their employees, usually executives and senior management personnel, with untaxable benefits in kind, such as assistance with house purchase or the provision of housing at nominal rents, the provision, repair, insurance, maintenance and running of cars, assistance in the purchase of expensive education for their children, the provision of free meals, entertainment, travel and other expenses allowances.[4] In looking at statistics of wage movements, *vis-à-vis* the movements of other kinds of income over time, therefore, it is important always to remember that one of the most striking features of the collectivist economy is not recorded, namely, the

[1] S. Zawadzki, 'The Origin and the Idea of the Concept of a "Welfare State"', *Polish Western Affairs*, Vol. 6, 1965, p. 253.

[2] Ibid., pp. 260–1.

[3] See the references in Richard M. Titmuss, *Income Distribution and Social Change*, Allen and Unwin, 1962, pp. 15–16, 194–5.

[4] Ibid., Ch. 8, *passim*.

power of those with authority in organizations to charge against 'running expenses' services to employees which are not regarded as part of their incomes for taxation purposes, and, of course, it is a concomitant of the conception of such organizations as exploitative bodies that senior personnel are more likely to benefit from the use of such power than those lower down in the hierarchy of authority.

Nevertheless—in so far as it is reasonable to make comparisons between occupational groups in terms of the average incomes received by men—managers and other administrative personnel received incomes which advanced most rapidly between 1913/14 and 1960, with foremen close behind, while skilled manual workers lagged slightly behind the semi-skilled, who lagged behind the unskilled.[1] If this may be interpreted as representing some kind of redistribution of income, it would apparently suggest a trend toward equality amongst the working class, but in the opposite direction across power lines. However, rather more striking than the changes between occupations is the rigidity of the income structure over time.[2] Far from the transition from capitalism to a new epoch being marked *inter alia* by income polarization, what seems to have occurred is a general rise in the level of living for all incomes[3] while the pattern of differential rewards between occupations has remained very much as it was in the later days of free enterprise capitalism. It is hardly necessary to add that poverty has not disappeared. Even under welfare state policies it has been estimated that some 280,000 families had incomes, 'excluding any assistance allowances they received', which were less than their requirements, as measured by reference to the national assistance scales current at the time of the enquiry in 1966.[4] In 70,000 of these cases the father of the family was in full-time employment. Some of these were fathers of large families, but 25,000 had incomes from such employment which

[1] Guy Routh, *Occupation and Pay in Great Britain, 1906–60*, Cambridge University Press, 1965, Table 47, p. 104. The percentage increases over the period are estimated to have been as follows: Managers 925, Foremen 898, Skilled manual 804, Semi-skilled 842, Unskilled 849.

[2] Ibid., Ch. 4, *passim.*

[3] Ibid., pp. 55–6.

[4] Ministry of Social Security, *Circumstances of Families*, H.M.S.O., 1967, p. 8.

were insufficient for a family of four (two children), and a further 20,000 had income insufficient for a family of five (three children).[1] Although pauperization as Marx foresaw it has not occurred, poverty alongside affluence remains as a feature of the new society.

In terms of collective bargaining the stability of the income structure may be interpreted against the background of what Knowles has called the 'institutionalization of wage settlements',[2] namely the increasing standardization of wage-settlement practices and the interdependence of wage and salary bargains.' Wages are by now highly 'structured', that is to say, in each industry there is what is known as a wage 'structure' of prescribed regular payments for work in special circumstances, and of prescribed principles for extra payments in special circumstances; and the nature of the structure itself influences the kind of wage changes that can be made at any time'.[3] The point to notice here is that trade union leaders engaged in collective bargaining find themselves inevitably forced to regard as unalterable the division of labour and the organizational structure of industry which has been built up over the past hundred years. The kind of occupational diversity described in the previous chapter, which modern technical and organizational knowledge has produced, carries with it a differential rewards system which collective bargaining can influence but little. Indeed, in presenting the case for a wage award to a Joint Industrial Council a trade union leader is obliged to take the wages structure largely for granted and to put forward a special plea for those of his members whose circumstances have deteriorated in some way because of exceptional events not fully appreciated by those who control the structure. It is in this sense that a collective bargain may be said to demand 'a degree of social justification which a private bargain can ignore'.[4]

Thus, one of the most popular arguments in favour of wage

[1] Ibid., Table III3, p. 11.
[2] K. G. J. C. Knowles, 'Wages and Productivity' in George D. Worswick and P. H. Ady, *The British Economy in the Nineteen-fifties*, Oxford University Press, 1962, p. 520.
[3] Ibid., p. 516.
[4] Barbara Wootton, *The Social Foundations of Wages Policy*, Allen and Unwin, 1955, pp. 73-4.

increases which have been advanced during the inflationary period since the beginning of the Second World War has been that of compensation for those employees whose wages have failed to keep pace with the rising cost of living. As Wootton has pointed out, the factual element in this argument—whether or not wages and salaries have as a matter of fact fallen behind —is of less significance than the assumption that they *ought* not to do so. 'This principle is invariably taken for granted—never argued on its points'.[1] Yet, it is unavoidably conservative in essence, for it implies that in keeping in step with the cost of living everyone ought to keep in step with everybody else. Even more obviously conservative in this respect, however, has been another principle which Wootton has identified as almost equally popular as the cost of living argument. This is the assertion that wage claims may be validly propounded by reference to increases received by workers in other industries and occupations. 'The principle involved is simple: it is assumed that any occupation in which wages can be demonstrated not to have kept pace with the general advance as shown by this index' (sc. the Ministry of Labour's index of wage movements) 'has a *prima facie* case for an increase in pay'.[2] Here again the attempt to maintain differentials in a situation in which price and wage changes are inflationary should be noted; for, at bottom these arguments rest on the ethical assumption that no one ought to be worse off than he was, relative to other people, before these movements were perceived to take place. In this sense the modern institutionalization of wage settlements may be interpreted as being, at least in part, a form of defensive action by trade unions to ensure that their members' comparative position in society should not be impaired by full employment.

Of course, none of this should be read as contradicting the indication that some levelling of incomes *amongst wage workers per se* occurred between 1913/14 and 1960, as the figures quoted from Routh attest.[3] Some narrowing of the differentials between skilled, semi-skilled, and unskilled manual employees clearly

---

[1] Ibid., pp. 125–6.
[2] Ibid., p. 131.
[3] See above, p. 190, footnote 1.

took place, especially during the periods of the two world wars,[1] although between the wars and after 1950 the trends seem to have been in the direction of widening them.[2] In part the explanation for these differences may be sought in the tendency of the unskilled to be the most unemployed, even under conditions of full employment,[3] so that in the inter-war period in particular the skilled workers advanced relatively to other manual workers. Since 1950 the persistence of full-employment policies has made it more difficult for them to repeat the earlier postwar reversals on the operation of labour market mechanics alone, but it is possible that they have achieved some widening of differentials simply by virtue of the strength of the protest that their status has weakened *vis-à-vis* other manual workers.[4] In this sense, therefore, it appears correct to talk of the 'concept of a proper hierarchy of rates' as being 'deeply ingrained in current thought on wage questions'.[5]

At the same time this need not be seen as contradictory to the fact that over fifty years some narrowing of differentials has occurred, because the ever increasing coverage of manual employment by national agreements on a flat-rate or percentage basis for *all* workers may well have had this effect, especially in periods of fairly rapid growth of trade unionism itself.[6] The institutionalization of collective bargaining, that is to say, brings within the framework of the bargaining process a whole list of those lower-paid workers who are slower to become organized than the aristocracy of labour, but in the long run this diminution of differentials cannot go very far since the process also seems to entail the institutionalization of wage regulation in the form of an accepted wages structure that resists much encroachment from below.

---

[1] Routh, *Occupation and Pay*, op. cit., pp. 109 and 123. K. G. J. Knowles and D. J. Robinson, 'Differences between the Wages of Skilled and Unskilled Workers, 1880–1950' in the *Bulletin of the Oxford University Institute of Statistics*, Vol. 13, 1951, pp. 109–27.

[2] Routh, *Occupation and Pay*, op. cit., pp. 128–32. For a comparison with Directors' and Executive Incomes, see Merrett and Monk, op. cit., Table IV, p. 47.

[3] Routh, *Occupation and Pay*, op. cit., Ch. 3, *passim*.

[4] H. A. Turner, 'Trade Unions, Differentials and Levelling of Wages', *The Manchester School of Economic and Social Studies*, Vol. 20, 1952, pp. 227–8.

[5] Wootton, op. cit., p. 135.

[6] Turner, 'Trade Unions, Differentials . . .', op. cit., pp. 232 et seq.

Satisfactory empirical verification of hypotheses about the impact of trade unionism on wages is, unfortunately, hard to find and the issue is still very much open to disagreement.[1] Nevertheless a brief examination of what has been happening to clerical employment suggests that the relationship between the success of unions in organizing an occupation and the narrowing of differentials is worthy of further investigation. Between 1911 and 1961 the total number of occupied clerks in Great Britain increased by 260 per cent, as compared with 29 per cent for the total occupied population and 2 per cent for all manual workers.[2] In some sense, it might be claimed, this is a measure of the rate of growth of collectivism, both in the administration of an increasing number of large organizations and in the general expansion of bureaucracy in industrial and governmental affairs. The women amongst clerks appear to have prospered relatively successfully over this period but male clerks' average earnings increased by only 589 per cent between 1913/14 and 1960 as compared with the 704 per cent received by skilled manual workers and the 749 per cent received by the unskilled.[3] In manufacturing, moreover, only about 10·5 per cent of all clerks were unionised on 1st January, 1964[4]—a percentage less than that for trade unions as a whole in 1892[5].

Thus the differential between clerical and manual occupations has declined, for all that clerks, male and female alike, still earn more on average than semi-skilled and unskilled manual workers; and this redistribution of income has occurred during a period in which trade union density generally has increased from 17·9 per cent to 42·6 per cent.[6] It is difficult to avoid the impression that the lack of trade union consciousness amongst clerks, whether caused by their employers' unwillingness to recognise white collar unions[7] or not, is a major feature in this process; and this raises the questions of whether, as collec-

---

[1] For an excellent introduction to the problems and the literature see Richard Perlman, ed., *Wage Determination, Market or Power Forces?*, Heath, 1965.
[2] Bain, op. cit., Table 1, p. 5.
[3] Routh, *Occupation and Pay*, op. cit., Table 47, p. 104.
[4] Bain, op. cit., Table 16, p. 27.
[5] Ibid., Table 9, p. 14.
[6] Ibid. The figures are for 1911 and 1964.
[7] Ibid., Ch. 5, *passim*.

tivism proceeds and clerks become organized occupationally into larger and larger units with relatively smaller chances for advancement, they will eventually become as militant in their trade unionism as manual workers, and whether in consequence the gap between the two categories of worker will begin to widen again.

The implications of this possibility should not be misunderstood. Increased militancy on the part of clerical and other white-collar employees does *not* entail that they will necessarily develop class consciousness in the sense of solidarity with manual workers and their unions. As Blackburn and Prandy have pointed out, 'many white collar unions prefer to avoid the unpopular connotations of the word "union" by being known as "guilds" or "associations". Few of them register as trade unions 'even though there are certain legal advantages'. Few affiliate to the Trades Union Congress and to the Labour Party.[1] More generally throughout the world, 'white-collar workers and their unions are as a rule attracted by conservative or even right-wing parties far more than are manual workers'[2] Nor, on a strictly Marxist basis, should this be simply interpreted as false class consciousness. To the extent that 'the commercial worker produces no surplus labour directly' the function in industry performed by clerks is 'to reduce the cost of realizing surplus value'; that is, they help the employer to appropriate the surplus labour which has already been obtained from the manual labourers.[3] Since, therefore, from the Marxist point of view the wages of the clerk are paid out of the unpaid wages of the proletariat, they perform 'unproductive' labour, that is 'all labour resulting in the output of goods and services the demand for which is attributable to the specific conditions and relationships of the capitalist system, and which would be absent in a rationally ordered society'.[4] Class consciousness likely to lead to the introduction of such a 'rationally ordered' and presumably

---

[1] R. M. Blackburn and K. Prandy, 'White-Collar Unionization: A Conceptual Framework', *The British Journal of Sociology*, Vol. 16, 1965, pp. 112–14.

[2] A. Sturmthal, 'White-Collar Unions—A Comparative Essay' in Sturmthal, ed., op. cit., p. 385.

[3] Marx, *Capital*, Vol. III, op. cit., pp. 294–5.

[4] Paul A. Baran, *The Political Economy of Growth*, Calder, 1957, p. 32. This passage is italicized in the original.

classless society, implies the abolition of clerical work as employment *per se*, since presumably in such a society whatever non-manual work would be required for the co-ordination of activities would be performed by the manual workers themselves as part of their own jobs; and clearly there is no indication in the trade union organization of clerks that they look forward to the eventual conversion of the occupation into manual work. Of course, the alternative analysis presented here, that the collectivist is a new form of class society, in no way contradicts this position. The large-scale, bureaucratic organization required in such a society implies an increase in the clerical manual ratio necessary for the exploitative process, and white-collar employees will continue to have interests not in common with, but inimicable to, those of the wage workers, although they may well have interests in common amongst themselves against their employers.

The nature of industrial relations in contemporary British society, as seen from this point of view, should now be reasonably clear. Collective bargaining between employers and employees in highly organized occupations is conducted almost wholly by reference to the right of trade unions to be involved in certain decisions in the factory and by reference to what have become established procedures for dealing with disputes.[1] There is in no sense even an implied challenge to the existence of the authority hierarchy as such. Although there is some evidence that over fifty years strikes about wages, bonus payments etc., and hours of work have declined proportionately as compared with strikes over demarcation issues, dismissals of shop stewards and other workers, the removal of established privileges etc.,[2] such challenge to management prerogative, as these latter causes of strikes imply, has been made in terms of the justice of the case, for example the 'wrongful' dismissal of a steward, and not in terms of the existence of management rights as such. Nor is there any clear indication that unions challenge the methods by which Boards of Management decide their own salaries and

[1] Arthur I. Marsh, *Disputes Procedure in British Industry*, Research Paper 2 (1), Royal Commission On Trade Unions, H.M.S.O., 1966, *passim*.

[2] Knowles, *Strikes*, op. cit., pp. 234-6. W. McCarthy, 'The Reasons Given for Striking', *Bulletin of the Oxford University Institute of Statistics*, Vol. 21, 1959, pp. 24-5.

those of their employees. In so far as trade union leaders are still conducting a class struggle it is in terms of profits and returns going to capitalist investors. They are, as it were, still completing the process of transition from capitalist society.

Perhaps one of the clearest examples of their acceptance of collectivism and the collectivist ideology is to be found in the Trades Union Congress' *Interim Report and Post-War Reconstruction* issued in 1944 which finally put to an end any official support of Guild Socialist or other industrial democratic notions by asserting that the members of the 'governing board of a public industry . . . should be selected by their competence efficiently to administer the industry.'[1] Granted that the 'abolition of management is a prerequisite of industrial democracy',[2] as the nineteenth and early twentieth century advocates of workers' control understood it,[3] the T.U.C., and it may be assumed, the great bulk of trade union leaders could not, and to this day cannot, conceive of a modern industrial system without managers who are *not elected* from below but *selected* from above by those who presumably are best fitted to distinguish between the competent and the incompetent. The 'wider case for industrial democracy' which the Trades Union Congress put to the Royal Commission on Trade Unions and Employers' Associations accepted the 'different levels of management' without question and entered a plea for representations of the workers to participate 'on whatever is the normal body which regularly meets . . . to take decisions'.[4] Although from time to time enthusiasts for workers' self-management see signs in the trade union movement of a revival of interest in 'the aggressive encroachment of Trade Unions on management powers'[5] no persistent trend is manifest towards the kind of co-operative

---

[1] Quoted in Hugh A. Clegg, *A New Approach to Industrial Democracy*, Blackwell, 1963, p. 34.

[2] Ibid., p. 119.

[3] Ibid., Ch. 1, *passim*.

[4] T.U.C., *Trade Unionism*, op. cit., pp. 104–7.

[5] K. Coates, 'Democracy and Workers' Control' in Anderson and Blackburn, eds., op. cit., p. 293. For references to support the view that 'after resting dormant for two generations, the movement for workers' control in Britain has once again begun to stir, reshape itself, and gather force and insight', see p. 293, note 1, and p. 294, notes 1 and 2. See also Coates and Topham, eds., op. cit., Section IV, *passim*.

enterprise which Marx had apparently in mind when he talked of the *positive* resolution of the conflict between capital and labour, namely managers being paid by the workers.[1] Indeed the ambivalent attitude of trade union leaders toward shop-stewards, who might perhaps be seen as an embryonic form of organized worker protest against their subject class position in modern industry, may be seen as a case in point. 'Unions are apprehensive that the shop steward might be used as an instrument for deluding the rank and file into supporting unofficial forms of organization which may seem logical to them, but which may also threaten the established trade union structure'.[2] The defence of the working class against the insecurities of a competitive market economy and the individualism of capitalism drove the English trade unionists to create large scale organizations of their own and to work for Welfare State policies which could bring the market economy under some kind of control. In the process they have created a state of mind on the part of the leadership which can see no alternative to the organization of industry but large-scale collectivities, prevented from too much tyranny over the individual by being balanced against other large-scale collectivities in some kind of economic and political pluralism. In this respect it should be clear that the Marxist analysis of industrial relations as presented in the First Part of this book, even with the modifications which have been introduced from time to time in the chapters of this Second Part, leaves very much unexplained. Private enterprise capitalism, so far from being converted into state, municipal and co-operative enterprise[3] has been replaced by private enterprise collectivism, involving Welfare State politics on a pluralistic basis. However, the implications of this for the development of satisfactory sociological amendments to the Marxist framework of ideas take the study into new areas of enquiry, as the next part will show.

[1] See above, pp. 173-4.
[2] Arthur Marsh, *Managers and Shop Stewards*, Institute of Personnel Management, 1963, p. 20.
[6] See especially p. 55 above.

Part Three

IMPLICATIONS

13

RECAPITULATION AND APPRAISAL

During the past twenty years sociologists have come to recognise clearly a major research problem which the founders of their discipline, a hundred years or so ago, were hardly aware existed. How is it possible to reconcile the stringent demands of scientific social research with the imperative need to understand the manifold and apparently continuous processes of change in ideas and practice which constitute human experience? While it is true that major nineteenth-century sociologists, like Herbert Spencer, were not unconscious of the difficulty of ensuring objectivity and precision in what they were doing,[1] they were so concerned to derive their sociological conclusions from historical 'sequences that extend over centuries or are traceable throughout civilization',[2] that they produced the kind of sociology described by Donald MacRae's unnamed, but allegedly not, apocryphal, historian as 'history with the hard work left out'.[3] The emphasis at the time of Marx, that is to say, was on quick results; and, provided that an author could produce a more or less logically coherent and to all intents credible interpretation of social events, it did not seem to matter very much if the 'evidence' he used to support it was rather of an illustrative than of a verificatory nature.

Mid-twentieth-century empirical sociology, by contrast, intent on the task of finding data which could be validly accepted as genuinely relevant to the research in hand, steadily

[1] Herbert Spencer, *The Study of Sociology*, 1873, Chs. IV–XII, *passim*.
[2] Ibid., Kegan Paul, International Scientific Edition, 1881, p. 106.
[3] D. MacRae, 'Some Sociological Prospects', *Transactions of the Third Congress of Sociology*, Vol. VIII, 1957, p. 302.

whittled down the questions to be studied to what appeared to be manageable proportions. In the process it left itself open to the charge of naïvety in its concern for what its opponents saw as trivialities. At this point in time it could be said that whereas the nineteenth-century sociologists were convinced that what they said was significant even if they were unable to demonstrate that it was true, those of the twentieth century were no longer certain that what they said was significant although they knew quite clearly how to set about determining whether or not it was true.[1] Inevitably, proposals were made from time to time to win advantage from the best of both positions by focusing attention on what have been called *'theories of the middle range*; theories intermediate to the minor working hypotheses evolved in abundance during the day-to-day routines of research, and the all-inclusive speculations comprising a master conceptual scheme'.[2] In this way, it is hoped, significant problems may be tackled objectively and precisely with techniques which are scientifically speaking beyond reproach.

From the point of view of tackling major issues the present study may be read as a response to this plea. If the materialist conception of history and the rest of the Marxist conceptual framework, designed to explain social change from epoch to epoch, may be thought of as one such 'master scheme', deduction from it to organized employer-employee relations in the British steel industry, may be claimed as an attempt to formulate a 'theory' of the middle range. At the same time, the examination of disputes and negotiations between leaders of the steel trade unions and members of the Boards of Directors of steel firms may be seen as an empirical approach towards the verification of such middle range hypotheses as this 'theory' implies. Yet, the frequency with which very few data had had perforce to suffice for evidence, may be read as a salutary warning of the hazardous nature of the exercise. Bridging the gap between

---

[1] Robert K. Merton, *Social Theory and Social Structure*, Revised and Enlarged Edition, Free Press, 1957, Introduction to Part Three, *passim*. Strictly speaking, Merton's contrast is between European writers on the sociology of knowledge and American students of mass communications, but his analysis is applicable to the difference between nineteenth- and twentieth-century sociologists generally.

[2] Ibid., pp. 5–6.

macroscopic speculation and middle-range hypothesis about social change is a yet more of a desideratum than a realizable consummation of sociological research. In this respect the constant repetition throughout these pages of the caveat that any conclusion is no more than tentative is not merely a justifiable precaution but an imperative stipulation in the present state of the subject.

Of course, as a matter of elementary logic it is the case that, no matter how slight the evidence, if it is in fact incontrovertible and if it contradicts a middle-range hypothesis, not only must that hypothesis be false, but also the master scheme from which it has been derived may no longer stand without revision. Verification of one hypothesis through the falsification of its contradictory may, therefore, seem to be a relatively simple affair. The problem for sociology, however, is that the establishment of incontrovertible evidence is a task of inordinate complexity. This is perhaps why the encouragement of concern for the meticulous attention to detail has come to take so central a part in the training of research sociologists at the present time. Yet, if this emphasis is not to degenerate into an obsession so extreme that even middle-range hypotheses are abandoned in favour of very minor working ones, some alternative to certainty must be accepted for most research purposes. The difficulty here is that willingness to tolerate imprecision always leaves open the possibility that the questions raised by doubts about the evidence might have been answered in a rather different fashion from that actually followed.

For example, in the present context the steel industry was selected for study initially because on the basis of the information available it was thought to be in the vanguard of developments in technology and in the scale of its operations. The hypothesis was accordingly proposed that, if the Marxist master scheme were in fact valid, the workers in that industry would be found to be in the vanguard of the evolution of a revolutionary class-conscious proletariat.[1] On the customary interpretation of industrial events in Britain, however, it was shown that this does not appear to have been true, at least before the 1860's. Chapter Six, therefore, proceeded on the assumption that the

[1] See above, pp. 69–70.

disturbances of the earlier period did *not* represent the kind of revolutionary class consciousness which results in a permanent impact on industrial, political and social relationships in the Marxist sense. Such facts as general trade unions, chartism and millenarian movements were treated as irrelevant to the testing of this particular hypothesis, and attention was directed instead towards later trade union organization amongst the 'aristocrats' of labour, sectional in their economic interest, and powerful enough to command respect from their employers.[1]

One alternative which might have been chosen instead would have been to have rejected altogether the original Marxist premise about the primacy of technology and the scale of operations, as contradicted by the evidence. In such a contingency the driving force behind social change could not be claimed to be the continuous discovery of more efficient modes of production which increase the intensity of conflict between capitalists and wage workers, but something else. However, as it stands, this alternative is not satisfactory because it immediately creates the obligation to give content to the empty phrase, 'something else', in the form of a further explanatory hypothesis which will be not only consonant with these facts but which is not contradicted by other incontrovertible evidence and which is also not incompatible with other hypotheses constituting a middle-range 'theory' of the evolution of industrial relations under capitalism. Moreover, with this alternative the fact of technical advance itself and that of the growth in the scale of operations, which have not been disputed, must either be shown to be false, or be accounted for as an independent process or one which is in some sense counterbalanced in its effect by some other *specified* process. Altogether, then, the rejection of an hypothesis of this order carries with it implications which are not lightly to be ignored, and unless the evidence is genuinely beyond doubt, outright rejection does not seem to be the most satisfactory way of proceeding. This is the main reason why in the present instance the alternative interpretation of the facts themselves was preferred.

Nevertheless, reinterpretation carries its own penalties; for, it cannot be made without at the same time requiring certain

---

[1] See above, pp. 70 et seq.

other adjustments in the set of hypotheses that constitute the framework of a middle-range 'theory'. Again in the present context, the recognition of trade unionism amongst British steel-workers as a form of revolutionary activity was only possible on the basis of converting the theoretical concept, 'revolution',[1] into an empirical term devoid of all traces of violence. Collective bargaining with employers, it will be recalled, was seen as an example of union militancy in spite of the fact that it was pursued almost without recourse to strikes.[2] The use of the constitutional machinery of government for welfare purposes and in order to bring about the reorganization of the industry through nationalization was similarly interpreted as the political counterpart to collective bargaining in the industrial sphere.[3] At the same time, the search for evidence of class consciousness amongst steel workers was directed away from verbal manifestations of attitude *per se* and towards overt expression of class unity in concrete behaviour, such as support for the General Strike.[4] Hence, the sequence of organizational forms —trade unions, joint industrial councils, the Trades Union Congress, the Labour Party, government committees—were seen as successive steps in the development, on the one hand, of 'revolutionary' class consciousness on the part of the union leaders and, on the other, of permanent encroachments upon the erstwhile untrammelled right of capitalist employers, leading to the eventual displacement of capitalism by another type of social system.

From this point of view, the trade union organizations which developed in the steel industry in the second half of the nineteenth century, and flourished thereafter, were no more than the *first* positive steps in the process whereby revolutionary class-consciousness became an effective force in the history of the transition from capitalism. From this point of view, therefore, what has been called the period of 'revolutionary trades unionism' from 1824 to 1834,[5] or perhaps from 1829 to 1842,[6]

[1] See above, pp. 21–3.
[2] See above, pp. 89–91.
[3] See above, pp. 108–9.
[4] See above, pp. 110–11.
[5] George D. H. Cole, *A Short History of the British Working-Class Movement*, op. cit.
[6] Sidney and B. Webb, *History of Trade Unionism*, op. cit., Ch. 3.

must be seen as merely a 'false-start' in this process,[1] an attempt
to give organizational form to 'a consciousness of the identity
of interests between working men of the most diverse occupations
and levels of attainment' which, while it was certainly greater
than the 'fragmentary form' in which it had appeared two
generations before,[2] was still insufficiently experienced to distinguish between what was possible and what was not, granted
the conditions of the day. As G.D.H. Cole put it, 'before the
workers could hope to make a great inclusive union of all
sections they had to accustom themselves to combination, and
to learn the management of great forces.'[3] These they mastered
in the course of the next century.

At this juncture it may be objected that this revision of the
Marxist hypotheses has become so drastic that Marx himself
would hardly have been likely to recognize it, had it been
presented to him as his own in his day. After all, when he wrote
in 1855 that he did not think he was 'exaggerating in saying
that the *English Revolution began yesterday in Hyde Park*',[4] he was
referring to mass demonstrations by a large crowd of undifferentiated persons who displayed overt hostility to 'the pro-
cession of elegant ladies and gentlemen . . . in their high coaches-
and-pair with liveried lackeys in front and behind' all the way
from Apsley House up Rotten Row along the Serpentine as
far as Kensington Gardens.[5] To Marx the knowledge that they
were not very far from violence was perhaps an indication that
the class struggle was moving into its last phases, leading
necessarily to the dictatorship of the proletariat and the transition 'to the *abolition of all classes* and to a classless society'.[6]
He certainly did not have in mind a quiet decision by the
leaders of the steel and other trade unions to establish a local
Trades Council for political purposes, although these also date

---

[1] See above, p. 23.

[2] Thompson, op. cit., p. 807.

[3] Cole, *A Short History*, op. cit., pp. 90–1.

[4] Karl Marx, 'Anti-Church Movement Demonstration in Hyde Park',
Neue Oder Seitung, 28th June 1855, English Version in Marx and Engels, *On
Britain*, op. cit., p. 416. Italics in the original.

[5] Ibid., p. 418.

[6] Karl Marx, 'Letter to J. Weydemeyer', 5th March 1852, in Marx and
Engels, *Selected Correspondence*, op. cit., p. 86.

from about this time.[1] Nor does he seem to have expected that the union leaders and the members of the Boards of Directors of the newly-established Joint Stock Companies would before long be getting together to work out effective conciliation machinery which would institutionalize collective bargaining, and eventually institutionalize the wages structure and in this sense assist in making legitimate the authority of a new type of master for the industrial proletariat.[2]

The present amendment of the original Marxist hypotheses, that is to say, is of such a character that it must rank as an example of revisionism so extreme as to imply, as some might have it, not only an abandonment of Marxism as a scientific 'theory'[3] but also 'a revolt against Marxism rather than a "revision".[4] These implications, however, must be vigorously resisted here, not because they are necessarily false in all circumstances, but because they constitute a *non-sequitur* in the present context. The intention behind a revision of hypotheses, as a sociologist sees it, is not a rejection of a 'theory' but its modification to make it a more perfect tool for explanation. Of course this must mean discarding the original formulation. Yet, the search for indisputable knowledge implies that such relinquishment must be seen as a gain, not a loss. To those for whom the actual words of the master are so precious that any amendment is a heresy, a perversion, a reaction against revealed truth, the sociologist must affirm that his primary devotion to his discipline requires that he must follow wherever his scientific finding may lead. If any revision of 'theory' also involves some change in its manner of application—the advocacy perhaps of a different kind of social policy—he would also count this as a gain, to the extent that goals are more likely to be reached if means are based on principles derived from knowledge rather than speculation.

Orthodox Marxists, of course, have always castigated revisionism as a betrayal of the workers' movement, an abandonment of the ideal of the classless society almost within reach.

[1] S. and B. Webb, *History of Trade Unionism*, op. cit., pp. 224–5.
[2] See above, pp. 166–9, 175.
[3] Meyer, *Marxism*, op. cit., p. 130.
[4] Ronald L. Meek, *Studies in the Labour Theory of Value*, Lawrence and Wishart, 1956, p. 211.

Sociologists *per se* must remain unmoved by such rebukes. For all that in their capacity as citizens and as visionaries individuals amongst them may believe that a society cannot be regarded as just, if it permits of the exploitation of man by man, these same sociologists in their capacity as social scientists can allow such beliefs to have no influence whatsoever on their determination to distinguish the valid from the invalid. *Pari passu*, as visionaries they will not be diverted one iota from their convictions of what is morally right and socially just, simply through the discovery that one particular explanatory hypothesis, or one particular set of hypotheses, does not square with the facts. While it is undoubtedly true that it is not always possible for an individual person to keep his pursuit of scientific understanding distinct from his quest for a more perfect social order, and in this sense may be said to confuse matters of fact with matters of value, there is no logically sound reason why such confusion should be elevated into a principle of conduct. Indeed, the rejection of the precept that a scientific position *ought* to entail a moral outlook, and its correlative assertion that of necessity every scientific position *must* involve a moral outlook, leaves the sociologist less untrammelled in his amendment of ideas and the social reformer less hindered in his affirmation of ideals to be realized.

None of this, it must be emphasized, alters the point that what has been presented here as a sequence of events in the evolution of revolutionary class consciousness, directs attention to forms of behaviour which are very different in content from those which are commonly thought of in these terms. That revolutionary élite which Clark Kerr and his colleagues have identified as one of five industrializing élites in modern times, approaches its task through the conquest of state power and the violent removal of the pre-existing ruling class from its position of dominance, drastically changing the 'total culture' in the process.[1] Such a revolutionary élite is composed of 'intellectuals and associated activists' bound together in an exclusive political party faithful to the ideology that history will make it inevitable for them to 'create the future'.[2] It is certainly not composed of people like the British trade union leaders, tentatively feeling

[1] Clerk Kerr, *et al.*, *Industrialism and Industrial Man*, Heinemann, 1962, Ch. 4, p. 96.   [2] Ibid., p. 59.

their way towards a society where social welfare will be guaranteed through their negotiations with businessmen, civil servants and professional politicians. Or again, the world revolutionary élites which Harold Lasswell and his colleagues have seen as the 'violent men', unleashing 'a social revolution in the course of executing its political revolution',[1] are composed of the 'frustrated and vengeful middle groups that had experienced some improved social mobility, gained some economic rewards, and wanted political power'.[2] To the extent that theirs is a case of status inconsistency[3] it is a consequence of their personal life stories rather than a by-product of the ambiguous position in society of the organizations of which they are the elected representatives, as is the case with British trade union leaders.

The existence today of a very different kind of revolutionary class consciousness alongside that which characterizes the institutionalization of collective bargaining, therefore compels attention. Although what has been outlined here may seem to propose a reasonable modification of the Marxist theoretical approach to industrial relations, satisfactory for the purpose of explaining the course of events in Britain, it is very much open to question whether the same set of hypotheses will also serve to account for developments elsewhere in the world. Marx himself, it is true, wrote that 'the country that is more developed industrially only shows to the less developed the image of its own future'.[4] In the conditions of his time he may be excused for devoting his researches to the study of Britain as the exemplar and for concluding that 'before all others' the British working men were 'competent and called for to act as leaders in the great movement that must finally result in the absolute emancipation of labour'.[5] Yet even Marx in his later years began to think that the struggle for freedom might not necessarily take place in Britain itself. 'After occupying myself with the Irish question for many years', he wrote in 1870, 'I have come to the

---

[1] Harold Lasswell, *et al.*, *World Revolutionary Elites*, M.I.T. Press, 1965, p. 457.

[2] Ibid., p. 459.

[3] See above, p. 117.

[4] Karl Marx, *Capital*, Vol. I, op. cit., pp. 8–9.

[5] Karl Marx, 'Letter to the Labour Parliament', 9th March 1854, reprinted in Marx and Engels, *On Britain*, p. 402.

conclusion that the decisive blow against the English ruling classes (and it will be decisive for the workers' movement all over the world) *cannot* be delivered in England but only in Ireland'.[1]

The detailed explication of this argument need not be considered here since it includes a prophecy which has not in fact materialised. What is important, by contrast, is the simple notion that class conflict may be intensified elsewhere than in the country where technical developments are actually most advanced. Marx's preliminary sketch of a 'theory' of colonialism, that is to say, opened up the way to a more complex set of ideas elaborated by Lenin into a 'theory' of imperialism, based on monopoly capitalism,[2] and further developed by later writers into a thesis about the final stages of capitalism taking the form of nationalistic imperialism, dominated by state monopoly, capitalist adventurers.[3] For present purposes this entails showing how the fruits of imperialist investment and overseas trade benefit the working classes at home in Britain, so that, for example, negotiations by trade union leaders in the British steel industry have been as successful as they have because employers have been able to extort surplus labour from workers abroad. Starting from Marx's position, that 'the capitalist class would never resist the trade unions if it could always and under all circumstances . . . avail itself of every rise in wages in order to raise prices of commodities much higher yet and thus pocket greater profits',[4] it is necessary to demonstrate that this is in fact what steel firms did during the relevant period in English history, and that, in consequence, class conflict was intensified in those countries which bought their goods and paid dividends on their capital investments.

That these countries might not be those where anti-capitalist, political revolutions have as a matter of fact occurred is, of course, always possible, so that it may also be necessary to

---

[1] Karl Marx, 'Letter to S. Meyer and A. Vogt', 9th April 1870, reprinted in Marx and Engels, *Selected Correspondence*, op. cit., p. 285. Italics in original.

[2] See above, pp. 44–5. For an excellent account of Marx's ideas on Imperialism see Thomas Kemp, *Theories of Imperialism*, Dobson, 1967, Ch. 2, *passim*.

[3] Kuusinen, op. cit., Ch. 10, *passim*.

[4] Karl Marx, *Capital*, Vol. I, op. cit., p. 340.

provide, independently, an explanation in these terms of what happened in Russia in 1918 and in China, Yugoslavia, Poland, Czechoslovakia, Cuba, etc., subsequently. Ultimately, what is required is a clear demonstration of linkage between these two sets of events—imperialist expansion and Communist revolutions—with the implication that, in spite of complications produced by extraneous factors, it may, or may not, be the case that peaceful trade union negotiations in countries designated as imperialist have been the consequence of the same general developments in capitalism which have led to violent political upheavals in countries where the capitalist social system has been replaced by another, structurally very different. Thus, in strict logic, two possibilities follow from the results of the analysis presented in the previous Part of this book and the alternative conception of revolutionary class consciousness raised now. Either the sequence of events, as yet undescribed, which has led to a social revolution carried through by violence and political coercion is the 'normal' pattern of history in the transition from capitalism, whence British trade union practice is an exceptional form, consequent upon the imperialist opportunities which have presented themselves to a capitalist nation, able early on to take advantage of technical and organizational progress;—or, the peaceful sequence described above is the 'normal' one, and those anti-capitalist violent revolutions which have occurred in the twentieth century have been produced by a chance concurrence of a number of extraordinary factors, including imperialism, in a relatively small number of places.

Doubtless, it would be claiming too much to assert that a decision between these alternatives is available at the present time. Nor will much more be attempted here than to suggest ways in which the problems involved may be tackled, always in the expectation that others may find it profitable to undertake the necessary labour. Indeed, as has been repeatedly emphasized already, the level of treatment which is enjoined by the issues discussed in the Second Part of this book, demanded evidence of a quality rarely to be found, so that all the conclusions drawn are necessarily tentative. This further proposal to test the Marxist framework of ideas now calls for detailed knowledge of at least the same level of sophistication, but for many countries rather than for one. Such encyclopaedic learning is probably beyond the capacity of any one scholar and certainly implies resources not in the possession of the author. Nevertheless, the nature of the Marxist approach to social change in capitalist society and hence to industrial relations during the period of transition, requires that some attention be paid to these questions in an exploratory fashion, if the full implications of the 'theory' in its revised form are to be appreciated. The third and final Part of the work, therefore, begins with an attack on these problems.

Moreover, even apart from the crucial issue of Communist revolutions, what has been achieved so far entails some comparative analysis of other societies than Britain to clarify the significance of proposals to revise. In pointing out, for example, that trade union development in the steel industry did not automatically result in a single industrial union, some reference was made to the fact that in America, by contrast, the United Steelworkers union organizes all steel workers, whether they are employed in process, maintenance, or service functions. The discrepancy, and its bearing on the hypothesized 'inevitable' consequences of technical development were noted at the time, but it was not pursued further in the light of what seemed to be the more pressing need to elucidate the trend from union organization to revolutionary class consciousness.[1] Now that the sequence from the one to the other has been identified, however, the objection to considering other reservations about the Marxist hypothesis, arising from information about national differences in union structure, no longer has weight. If no more is done than to examine the evolution and consequences of industrial unionism in the American steel industry, at least this much must be investigated to determine how to account for a discordant fact. The danger of generalizing or in this instance of failing to revise a generalization, on the basis of a single case, is a common hazard in the social sciences, but it can be avoided to some extent by a judicious recourse to comparisons.

Some application of the technique of identity and contrast has, of course, already been made, although not across national boundaries but between industries inside Britain. In Chapter Nine the record of the mining industry was cited as an example

---

[1] See above, p. 86.

in some respects more consonant with the revised set of Marxist hypotheses about the intensity of class consciousness, than that of the steel industry. The miners had moved closer to a unified organization on the industrial pattern than the steelworkers, even before nationalization.[1] Their leaders were perhaps a little slow to support the establishment of the T.U.C. but they soon caught up, and they were well in the vanguard in taking political action and ensuring that they had member representation in the House of Commons. A very large number of mining M.P.'s, proportionately speaking, have been Cabinet Ministers in Labour Governments.[2] Yet, mining is not an industry that would have been chosen for study on the basis of the technical criteria used to select iron and steel. It is true that it was marked by Florence as a large industry in terms of the number of workers employed in medium-sized plants in 1930, but so were fourteen other industries, including iron and steel;[3] and as compared with the latter's 14·0 h.p. per worker, coal mines employed 3·8, that is, less than dyes and dyestuffs (5·6), cotton-spinning (5·6), grain milling (6·8), linoleum (4·4), paper (9·2), seed-crushing (6·5), railway carriage (4·0), sugar and glucose (5·4), to mention only the non-metal manufacturing industries.[4]

In attempting to account for the unexpected militancy of the miners, therefore, two aspects of their circumstances were accorded special attention. On the one hand, the class solidarity of the rank-and-file was explained by reference to community alienation, which was seen to be extreme in their case;[5] and on the other hand, the political consciousness of the miners' leaders was regarded as a reaction to the particularly intransigent opposition of the colliery owners to centralized collective bargaining.[6] A sharp contrast, indeed, was introduced here between the union members' and the union officers' attitudes to capitalism. The former, it was suggested, was in effect no

---

[1] See above, p. 125.
[2] See above, pp. 127.
[3] Florence, *Investment, Location and Size of Plant*, op. cit., Appendix II, p. 172.
[4] Ibid., Appendix IV, pp. 192–6.
[5] See above, pp. 129–31.
[6] See above, pp. 131–3.

more than trade union consciousness, perpetuated after nationalization because of the working miner's primary concern with everyday grievances in his employment;[1] whereas the latter was organizational consciousness directed towards the establishment of permanent machinery for dealing with such grievances in the context of running an industry, considered to be important, if not essential, to the community as a whole,[2] and hence was converted from protest unionism to administrative unionism,[3] once the unions were incorporated into the constitutional framework of the National Coal Board's subsidiary organs. Some further consideration was given to the general position of the trade unions generally in the Welfare State when industrial relations under private enterprise collectivism was discussed in Chapter Twelve, but the circumstances of rank-and-file members were little more than mentioned. Hence, it is open to question whether some aspects of the issue of alienation, thought to be relevant in the case of mining because of the technical nature of the industry and the location of coal seams, might be worthy of further attention against the background of the collectivization of the economy and the large and complex industrial organizations which this entails.

This problem has a special interest when it is considered in the light of the argument that 'many of the features which Marx identified with 'capitalism' were actually features of modern industry under any ism'.[4] From this point of view, the societies ushered in by Communist revolutions may be seen to present 'manifold patterns of alienation' similar to those in the later stages of capitalist societies.[5] To those sociologists for whom this industrial alienation is self-evident, the concept of an industrial society is to be preferred to any other when dealing with those parts of the world that have experienced an industrial revolution. This means that for such sociologists '*capitalism* merely signifies one form of industrial society',[6] and Communist

[1] See above, pp. 134–5.

[2] See above, pp. 135–7.

[3] See above, p. 134.

[4] Bertram D. Wolfe, *Marxism: One Hundred Years in the Life of a Doctrine*, Chapman and Hall, 1967, p. 346.

[5] B. F. Hoselitz, 'Karl Marx on Secular and Social Development', *Comparative Studies in Society and History*, Vol. 6, 1963–4, p. 153.

[6] Dahrendorf, *Class and Conflict*, op. cit., p. 40. Italics in the original.

and post-capitalist societies signify merely further forms. Of course, the industrial society concept can be made to fit into the categorization of the materialist conception of history, since Marx's ancient and feudal societies might be said to be agrarian, his Asiatic society hydraulic,[1] and his capitalist and socialist societies industrial, although capitalism might also be said to straddle the period of technological transition from agrarian to industrial, and perhaps also the transition from hydraulic to industrial, were it not for the complications introduced by the occurrence of Communist revolutions in some areas where hydro-agriculture predominates. However, the disadvantage of this approach, as an alternative to the regular Marxist analysis, is that it inevitably misses the significance of the differences between ancient and feudal, capitalist and post-capitalist societies, namely, the manner in which they extort surplus labour from the toilers. Because it overemphasizes the technological, it does not provide a satisfactory basis for the examination of class conflict in all societies, irrespective of whether they are agrarian, hydraulic, industrial, and so on.

Indeed, in so far as it is possible to identify 'dimensions' of alienation in industry, the distinction between capitalist and other forms of industrial system may well turn on the extent to which exploitation takes different shapes and leads to different kinds of alienation effects. For example, Blauner has claimed that 'alienation exists when workers are unable to control their immediate work processes, to develop a sense of purpose and function which connects their job to the over-all organization of production, to belong to integrated industrial communities, and when they fail to become involved in the activity of work as a mode of personal self-expression'.[2] On this basis he has been able to show that the *degree* of powerlessness, meaninglessness, integration and self-estrangement, vary considerably from one American industry to another, at least across the spectrum, printing, chemicals, textiles, and car manufacture. Most of these differences can be traced to the impact on the individual worker of the technical nature of the production process. In his book, to be sure, Blauner did not say whether the firms he con-

---

[1] The term is Wittfogel's, but the germ of the idea is taken from Marx. See Wittfogel, op. cit., pp. 2–5.

[2] Blauner, op. cit., p. 15.

sidered were joint-stock corporations or not, although it seems reasonable to suppose that they were all collectivist, as this term has been employed here, but he did emphasize in general that 'manual workers have little opportunity to control the major decisions of the enterprise. And . . . most employees do not seem to resent this aspect of powerlessness, which they also tend to accept as a 'given' of industry'.[1] At the same time, he noticed that a deliberate attempt to reduce powerlessness in this respect 'has been remarkably successful in a number of cases',[2] so that it is clearly possible for this dimension of alienation to be influenced by the degree to which the power system of the enterprise permits some worker participation in the processes of making decisions vital to his interests. Collective bargaining through joint industrial councils and shop-steward negotiation at shop floor level might possibly be seen as a case in point. Hence, the very success of the steel unions in obtaining recognition on a nation-wide basis could be interpreted as a causal factor in the reduction of alienation amongst steelworkers, whereas the failure of the mining unions to achieve the same results, except by nationalization, might equally be seen as contributory to alienation amongst miners. At this point, that is to say, it must be admitted that some further consideration is required of the whole question of industrial democracy and worker participation under different organizational structures and different social systems.

The influence of the mine-owners' obstinacy on miners' militancy might, therefore, be seen as part of the general alienation problem. On the other hand, it may also illustrate the very different point that they were pressed between the demands of the unions and competition overseas. The high labour costs of the industry[3] gave them little room to manœuvre, but how much room they had, as compared to the steel magnates, can only be examined by reference to the issues raised above under

[1] Ibid., p. 18.

[2] Ibid., footnote 7. The main reference is to worker participation in production committees, sponsored initially by the United Steelworkers of America, and adopted by a few firms in America. See Frederick G. Lesieur, ed., *The Scanlon Plan*, M.I.T. Press, 1958.

[3] According to Neuman, op. cit., Table 35, p. 344, Labour costs between 1871 and 1932 were never less than 60 per cent of total costs and were often greater than 70 per cent.

the general heading of imperialism. In this sense it may be argued that what might otherwise appear as discrete and separate topics in this Part of the book are really separate attacks on the same problem. Of course, there may well be other unsettled issues, not so clearly interrelated, and scattered through the pages of Part Two. With so many problems left undecided because of the paucity of evidence, this is inevitable. Nevertheless, imperialism, Communist revolutions, the course of collective bargaining in America, and industrial participation under voluntary collectivism and Communism, seem to be the *major* themes which the discussion so far has left further to be examined. Once these have been given some of the focussed attention they deserve, it may be possible to assess more accurately the validity of the proposals to revise the Marxist approach which are a consequence of British experience in iron and steel. The third part of this work is, accordingly, devoted to these questions.

14

IMPERIALISM AND THE ARISTOCRACY
OF LABOUR

'If it were necessary to give the briefest possible definition of imperialism', wrote Lenin in 1916, 'we should have to say that imperialism is the monopoly stage of capitalism'.[1] Historically speaking, he estimated this stage to have been reached only after Marx's death; for he dated the sequences as: '(1) 1860–70, the highest state, the apex of development of free competition; monopoly is in the barely discernible, embryonic stage, (2) after the crises of 1873, a lengthy period of development of cartels; but they are still the exception. They are not yet durable. They are still a transitory phenomenon. (3) The boom at the end of the nineteenth century and the crisis of 1900–03. Cartels became one of the foundations of the whole of economic life. Capitalism has been transformed into imperialism.[2] Marx, it should be understood, thought of cartels as temporary phenomena only, cases of 'exceptional co-operation in times of great stress and confusion;[3] and in so far as, like the joint stock company, they could be interpreted as 'the abolition of the capitalist mode of production within the capitalist mode of production itself', he saw them, apparently, as 'a self-dissolving contradiction, which *prima facie* represents a mere phase of transition to a new form of production'. Such a contradiction 'establishes a monopoly in certain spheres and thereby requires state interference'.[4] Hence, Lenin's characterization of mono-

---

[1] V. I. Lenin, *Imperialism, The Highest Stage*, op. cit., p. 266.
[2] Ibid., p. 202.
[3] Marx, *Capital*, Vol. III, op. cit., p. 118. This was written in 1865 and confirmed by Engels in a footnote, presumably written in 1894.
[4] Ibid., p. 429.

poly as a permanent feature of the capitalism of his day was a further aspect of his conviction that the critical stage in world history had been reached.

Moreover, although in some respects Lenin's imperialism doctrine was revisionist,—'an attempt to explain the stubborn fact that the revolution had not yet taken place in the most highly developed capitalist countries'[1]—in one respect, at least, it could be seen as no more than an extension of the main line of Marxist argument. The supremacy of competition in Marx's analysis of the dynamic of change within capitalism could not altogether obscure the possibility that monopoly might become an end-product of the process. 'The battle of competition', Marx wrote, 'is fought by cheapening commodities. The cheapness of commodities depends, *ceteris paribus*, on the productiveness of labour, and this again on the scale of production. Therefore, the larger capitalists beat the smaller.... Capital grows in one place to a huge mass in a single hand, because it has in another place been lost by many. This is centralization proper, as distinct from accumulation and concentration'.[2] For his part Engels added a footnote in 1890 to the effect that the latest English and American 'trusts' were already striving to attain this goal by uniting 'all the large-scale concerns in one branch of industry into one great joint-stock company with a practical monopoly'.[3] Such 'trusts have no other mission but to see to it that the little fish are swallowed by the big fish'.[4] To the extent, therefore, that 'capitalist production does not exist at all without foreign commerce',[5] monopoly capitalism in Lenin's analysis merely translated competition with foreign firms into imperialist domination over subject peoples.

For present purposes it is not necessary to consider all the ramifications of Lenin's treatment of imperialism. Nor is it necessary to examine in detail those arguments in support of his views which he propounded in debate with Social Democrats whom he castigated as advocates of 'imperialist econom-

---

[1] Alfred G. Meyer, *Leninism*, Praeger, 1957, p. 240.
[2] Marx, *Capital*, Vol. I, op. cit., p. 626.
[3] Ibid., p. 627, n. 1.
[4] Marx, *Capital*, Vol. III, op. cit., p. 118, n. 16.
[5] Marx, *Capital*, Vol. II, Foreign Languages Publishing House, 1957, p. 470.

ism'.[1] Rather should attention be directed towards clarifying the nature of that overseas commerce which his notion of imperialism entailed, and towards estimating its effect on the relationship between employers and employees within both the exploiting and the exploited nations, at least to the extent that it provides some kind of answer to the questions raised in the previous chapter.[2] How far, that is to say, was it the case that peaceful negotiations in the British iron and steel industry were a consequence of the ability of the employers to extort what Lenin called *super profits* by 'extra exploitation of the workers of the oppressed nations'?[3] To what degree were the workers in those nations unable to develop effective trade unions and so start along the road towards peaceful revolutionary class consciousness, as a result of this extra exploitation? In what sense were those peoples, who were driven to violent revolution as the only solution to their predicament, also victims of this kind of exploitation? Lenin, to be sure, did not approach the issue of imperialism in this fashion. For all that he made use of details about capitalist investment in single industries and indeed in single firms, as well as in whole states, he made no reference to comparable data about wages, but contented himself with general observations, such as 'the receipt of high monopoly profits by the capitalists in one of the numerous branches of industry, in one of the numerous countries, etc. makes it economically possible for them to bribe certain sections of the workers, and for a time a fairly considerable minority of them, and win them to the side of the *bourgeoisie* of a given industry or given nation against all the others'.[4] The implication was presumably meant to be that high wages in a single firm, an industry, or a nation, relative to other firms, industries or nations, were a by-product of monopolistic imperialism, but no evidence was provided to show even remotely how far this was true.

As a matter of fact, in so far as the British iron and steel

---

[1] See, for example, 'The Nascent Trend of Imperialist Economism', written in 1916, first published in 1929, and 'A Caricature of Marxism and Imperialist Economism', written in 1916, first published in 1924, both reproduced in Lenin, *Collected Works*, Vol. 23, op. cit., pp. 13–21, 28–76.

[2] See above, p. 210.

[3] Lenin, 'A Caricature of Marxism', op. cit., p. 55.

[4] Lenin, *Imperialism, The Highest Stage*, op. cit., p. 301.

industry is concerned, later data in support of Lenin's argument showed a clear failure on the part of the owners to achieve monopoly. Although there were some 'outstanding examples' of amalgamation in the 1920's and 1930's[1], ten separate firms still survived who shared 70–75 per cent of the industry's production between them, with the largest controlling only 16 per cent.[2] A generation later, the government proposed to nationalize fourteen companies who were identified as producing over 90 per cent of the United Kingdom's production of pig iron, crude steel, heavy steel products, sheets and tin plate,[3] and the four largest of these produced less than 50 per cent of the total ouptut. Indeed, in 1965 it still required eleven companies to account for some 72·7 per cent of the output; and in addition to the fourteen largest firms, scheduled for nationalization, there were six others with individual capacities of less than half a million tons, producing 7·3 per cent between them. The British Iron and Steel Federation, it is true, was talking at this time of the need for 'further concentration into bigger works and bigger company groupings',[4] but it seems clear that state action was more likely to achieve a unified industry than whatever tendencies towards monopoly existed amongst the capitalist—or rather, collectivist,—owners themselves.

This last point is of some importance, because the corporate revolution, with its control of joint-stock enterprise by the board of directors, has not only resulted in power being taken from capitalists as such, it has also opened the way to what Lenin called the 'personal link up'[5] between firms, through the device of interlocking directorships, and hence of their operating a co-ordinated policy without monopoly.[6] Thus in 1948 it was estimated that in the British Iron and Steel Industry 'the

---

[1] Varga and Mendelsohn, op. cit., pp. 37 and 39.
[2] Ibid., p. 279.
[3] 'The Steel Bill: A Summary', *Steel Review*, No. 43, July 1966, p. 3.
[4] 'Big Enough?', *Steel Review*, No. 44, October 1966, pp. 6–7.
[5] Lenin, *Imperialism, The Highest Stage*, op. cit., p. 221.
[6] Kemp, op. cit., p. 67, interprets Lenin's terminology as follows: 'It is clear that Lenin uses this term in contrast to the "free competition" of the earlier period of capitalism and not in the literal sense of the dominance of single sellers in particular industries.' He concludes, 'strictly, therefore, it corresponds to what modern economics terms "oligopoly"—a small number of sellers', ibid., p. 185, n. 9. Contemporary Marxist writers who prefer the

directors of the six main companies control 100 subsidiary companies and hold more than 600 seats on the boards of other companies inside and outside the steel industry. Within these firms there are many interlocking directorships, and the same names crop up over and over again with the smaller firms. At the very outside 100 men dominate the entire iron and steel industry and deploy outwards to link it with the rest of industry, the banks, financial houses and insurance companies.[1] Since that time it is likely that what have been called 'coalitions of interests'[2] in the industry have extended, rather than have curtailed, the range of the network. The basis of this assumption, of course, is the belief that interlocking directorships do not occur in a purely haphazard fashion. They are the result of 'at least a common interest in avoiding conflicts of interests'.[3] Moreover, these are interests which are so interpreted by the directors themselves. The decision of one board to invite a director from another to join it, is not one which the ordinary voting shareholder is called upon to make. So far as is known, interlocking arrangements are arrived at by negotiating between the boards concerned, and shareholding as such may play little or no part in the transaction. For example, in 1938 the boards of the United Steel Companies and John Summers and Sons discussed the latter's difficulties in installing a wide-strip mill. Eventually United Steel put over a million pounds into the venture and so acquired a one-sixth interest in Summer's shares. Two members of the United Steel board joined the board of John Summers. At the same time, although there was no question of Summers' acquiring United Steel stock, the managing director of Summers joined the United Steel board.[4]

---

term 'monopoly' to 'oligopoly' for referring to the situation described above, clearly abandon scientific accuracy for the pejorative impact the former word may be presumed to make on their readers.

[1] Wilfred Fienburgh and R. Evely, *Steel is Power: the Case for Nationalisation*, Gollancz, 1948, p. 39. For a chart showing how such interlocking networks are arranged, see Samuel Aaronovitch, *Monopoly*, Lawrence and Wishart, 1955, p. 32.

[2] Samuel Aaronovitch, *The Ruling Class*, Lawrence and Wishart, 1961, p. 89.

[3] Ibid., p. 79.

[4] Philip W. S. Andrews and E. Brunner, *Capital Development in Steel*, Blackwell, 1951, p. 206.

After the war United Steel invested a further £1,335,000 in John Summers,[1] and the latter's chairman joined his managing director on the board of United Steel. As the historians of this arrangement have pointed out, 'the relationship with Summers certainly did not depend upon whether United Steel held a lot of shares or not'.[2]

Thus the device of interlocking directorships succeeds in creating a form of unity in a situation of diversity, without going all the way to monopoly in a single organization; and it would seem to parallel on the employers' side, the coalitions which have evolved amongst British steel trade unions, apparently as an alternative to industrial unionism.[3] It is, that is to say, but another aspect of the collectivism of our time, and just as separate trade unions may be seen as continuing to exist because their members have some interests which conflict, as well as others which are common, so it may be that coalitions of employers are preferred to monopoly because the directors of industrial firms have interests which divide, as well as those which unite them. If there is any evidence to support Lenin's contentions, therefore, it must contain elements which clearly demonstrate how interlocking amongst boards may be exploited by some trade union leaders to benefit *their* members more than they could have achieved where untrammelled competition between firms prevails. Presumably, joint industrial councils, operating an institutionalized wage structure to the employees' advantage, would be such a case in point, since even without interlocking it might be argued that employers, who sit together across the table from trade unionists, have at least a common interest in avoiding a conflict of interest which their opponents might make use of disastrously; but this would surely only apply where interlocking permitted the employers to pass on the cost of higher wages to other industries or to countries other than those where institutionalized collective bargaining is the norm.

It is, to be sure, very difficult to find incontrovertible data to verify this notion. Indeed, one of the features of the device of interlocking is that its ramifications can become so intricate

---

[1] Ibid., p. 316.
[2] Ibid., p. 311.
[3] See above, p. 80.

that it is virtually impossible to determine whether any industry in a country is outside the network altogether. Moreover, if the concept of coalitions of interests is interpreted to cover not only interlocking directorships, but cartels and other bonds between businessmen cemented by loans, the network may easily become extended by implication to cover whole continents as well as nations merely. Lenin and his followers were, as a matter of fact, so impressed by what Hilferding described as finance capitalism,[1] that they sometimes wrote as if they believed industrial enterprises to have become entirely subservient to the credit houses and to the banks from whom they obtained loans. They also saw these financial networks to be world-wide in extension.[2] Thus, one of the consequences of speculating theoretically, without benefit of definite evidence on how businessmen actually operate in these circumstances, is that the 'theory' of imperialism can become so diluted as to lose all power of explanation. A world-wide network of interlocking interests, that is to say, if treated superficially, leads to the assertion that the whole of the working class is exploited simultaneously by a well-organized employing class, whence it is not at all evident how some sections of the proletartiat could be better off than others, save in terms of difference in skill, which occur in any case whether there is oversea investment or not.[3]

If the imperialism hypothesis is to have any meaning and make any contribution to accounting for a quiescent aristocracy of labour, it can only do so on the assumption that the employers are *not* well organized and unified, that coalitions of interests amongst them possess characteristics similar to those amongst nations in the international sphere—that they are unstable and transitory. The International Steel Cartel, for example, which existed from 1926 to 1939, may be said to have 'reached its prime' in 1938 when it included all the 'important

---

[1] Rudolf Hilferding, *Das Finanzkapital: eine Studie über die jungste Entwicklung des Kapitalismus* (Finance Capital: a study of the latest development of capitalism), Dietz, 1910.

[2] Lenin, *Imperialism, The Highest Stage*, op. cit., p. 220 et seq. Varga and Mendelsohn, op. cit., pp. 93 et seq. Note that the subtitle of Aaronovitch's *The Ruling Class*, op. cit., is 'a Study of British Finance Capital'.

[3] Contrast Kemp's emphasis on what he sees as important, namely, to shed 'the convention of seeing each capitalist state as a separate entity' and to consider imperialist capitalism 'as a world system', op. cit., Ch. 9, *passim*.

exporting producers of steel throughout the world and embraced the export markets of all the major steel commodities,'[1] but it went into liquidation for a time in 1931,[2] and it disintegrated completely on the outbreak of war in 1939.[3] Earlier cartels had had an even more precarious existence.[4] This does not mean that while they existed such coalitions had no influence. A relatively stable price policy was one of the aims of the I.S.C., and it is possible that exports of steel were controlled effectively in this respect, although a careful survey of the evidence is certainly not conclusive.[5] No doubt the steel directors whose firms supported the international cartel would have liked to have reduced the pressure on them for higher wages, by increasing their profits from some other source than exploiting their own workers, but the I.S.C. did not plan for a co-ordinated policy on labour matters, 'nor did any informal or tacit understanding in this respect exist'.[6]

There is, to be sure, no incontestable evidence which may be used to justify this last assertion; and, indeed, it is not at all clear how anyone will be able to find it now, unless some member of the I.S.C. has left behind him a personal and private record of tacit agreements with his colleagues. The argument from silence on the point can hardly be said to be conclusive. However, to the degree that the Marxist analysis of the basis of industrial conflict follows the correct lines, it is to be expected that firms in different countries would have found it extremely difficult, if not impossible, to co-ordinate their policies on wages, unless at the same time they had also invested capital in one another. Over and over again in *Capital* Marx warned his readers not to place too much weight on the relationship between money prices and money wages when considering the manner in which surplus labour is extorted from the workers. Capitalists always paid, *in real commodity terms*, what was necessary 'for the reproduction of the labour-power of the labourer

---

[1] Ervin Hexner, *The International Steel Cartel*, University of North Carolina Press, 1943, p. vii.

[2] Ibid., p. 81.

[3] Ibid., p. 91.

[4] Ibid., pp. 18–19.

[5] Ibid., Ch. 8, *passim*. See also George W. Stocking and M. W. Watkins, *Cartels in Action*, Twentieth Century Fund, 1946, Ch. 5, *passim*.

[6] Hexner, op. cit., p. 250.

himself'.[1] Always this varied 'according to the climatic and other physical conditions of the country' as well as in accordance with 'the degree of civilization of a country'.[2] What he called 'the thoughtless conception that the cost price of a commodity constitutes the actual value, and that surplus value springs from selling the product above its value'[3] may easily stand in the way of seeing that surplus labour can only be obtained by employers working labourers for longer than is necessary for them to reproduce themselves, and that therefore, although prices and money wages may for a time fluctuate about their real value, in the long run it is the relationship between necessary and surplus labour which determines the distribution of the products of that labour between the employers and their employees.

Hence the Leninist emphasis on the power of finance as such and on the power of cartels to determine prices, if not used with great caution, is likely to result in a major revision of the Marxist thesis so extreme as to amount to an almost complete reversion. To the extent that the intention here throughout has been to make only minor amendments unless these can be shown to be insufficient, it may be argued that all that may be legitimately inferred from the fact that manufacturers who bought British steel possibly paid inflated prices for it, is that some of the fruits of surplus labour which they were *already* exacting from their own employees were passed on to their suppliers and perhaps, therefore, to the British steelworkers. Certainly it may not be concluded that such high prices necessarily *caused* them to extort *more* surplus labour than they otherwise would have done.[4]

In the 1870's, of course, there was evidence that may be interpreted as indicating that British steel firms and their employees were benefiting in this way. At that time this country produced about 40 per cent of the total world output of pig-

---

[1] Marx, *Capital*, Vol. I, op. cit., p. 232.

[2] Ibid., p. 171.

[3] Marx, *Capital*, Vol. III, op. cit., p. 39.

[4] See K. Marx, *Capital*, Vol. III, op. cit., pp. 232-4, and p. 274. 'If a surplus value is realized in the sale of produced commodities, then this is only because it already existed in them.' Merchants' capital 'appropriates' a portion of the surplus which industrial capital appropriates directly as 'the unpaid labour of others'. Ibid., p. 288.

iron.[1] 60 per cent of this was exported, and in comparison the exports of her nearest rivals, Belgium, France, Germany and the United States were 'insignificant'.[2] The evidence also suggested that the wages of British steelworkers may have been higher than those obtained on the Continent, although they were lower than what was paid to steelworkers in America.[3] By the turn of the century, however, the British export trade was seriously threatened, at first by Germany, and then by America, formerly her two chief customers; and during the recession years, after 1903, the American steel firms 'adopted fully (not for the first time) the same policy as the German exporters, sales abroad at prices far below home prices and below total costs, with a view to disposing of stocks or keeping plant well occupied'.[4] Thus, world competition amongst steel companies, from time to time at least, buttressed often by tariff support from their governments, took the form of price reductions rather than price increases, and the British export trade appears to have suffered in consequence. In effect, this is rather what might be expected from Marx's economic writings, since he gave more weight over time to the importance of relative as compared with absolute surplus labour.[5] As technical developments permitted capitalists to increase their extortion of relative surplus labour, that is to say, those nations which were quick to seize upon their opportunities in these respects were able to undersell British steel manufacturers who were undoubtedly slow to exploit new inventions and processes.[6]

Where this experience is relevant to the imperialism thesis is in the fact that one result, apparently, of the increased competition from American and German steel firms was the reliance of British exporters on trade with countries of the British

---

[1] Burn, *Economic History*, op. cit., p. 19.

[2] Ibid., p. 20.

[3] Ibid., pp. 34–42, and Ch. 8, *passim*.

[4] Ibid., pp. 92–3.

[5] Marx, *Capital*, Vol. I, op. cit., Ch. XIII, *passim*.

[6] T. J. Onagh, 'Progress in Iron and Steel, 1870–1913', *Comparative Studies in Society and History*, Vol. III, 1960–1, pp. 216–30. For a more detailed treatment of the relationship between technical change and productiveness, see Peter W. Musgrave, *Technical Change, the Labour Force and Education, A Study of the British and German Iron and Steel Industries, 1860–1964*, Pergamon Press, 1967, *passim*.

Empire, although in this area even before 1914 'the penetrating power of German sellers was impressively shown'.[1] Nevertheless, right up to the outbreak of the Second World War Britain maintained the lead over her rivals in steel imports to the Empire; and indeed, one of the advantages which derived from membership of the I.S.C. was that the pressure of Continental competition in this market 'ceased to be immediately disturbing'.[2] By this time, of course, Britain was contributing only about 10 per cent to the total world output, a proportion that has fallen further in the post-war years.[3] Altogether the share of the United Kingdom in crude steel output has declined from 40 per cent in 1870 to less than 7 per cent in 1957, so that it might be concluded that one of the results of paying higher wages and charging relatively higher prices has been that other countries, for example, Australia, Canada, India and South Africa have been able to manufacture steel themselves and have increased their outputs disproportionately.[4] Imperialism might, therefore, be said in this sense to be eventually self-defeating, not, however, because these countries have gone in for violent revolution to get rid of their capitalists, but on the contrary, because they have developed their own steel industries on a capitalist and collectivist basis, often with government support.

The case of India is perhaps most instructive in this respect. The British forces under the East India Company, it may be argued, wrested power from the native rulers of a feudal, or feudal-type, economy in order to ensure that the Company's trading interests might be paramount; and until 1813 the Company held a monopoly over the trade which its servants often exploited in a spirit of plunder and brigandage. After 1813, and certainly after 1833 when the renewal of the East India Company's Charter involved its eventual demise, the administration of India was handed over largely to English civil servants who may well have seen their task primarily as to ensure that stable government existed so that English interests could flourish. Thus, it is said that 'United Kingdom manu-

[1] Burn, *Economic History*, op. cit., p. 332.
[2] Ibid., p. 482.
[3] Ibid., Table 6, p. 132.
[4] Burn, *The Steel Industry*, op. cit., Table 105, opposite p. 728.

facturers in the nineteenth century always resented the growth of competition in India. They regarded that country solely as a British possession, suitable for commercial exploitation, and they saw no reason why it should be allowed to compete with home industry'.[1] There was, of course, a long history of iron and steel making in India, going back for some 2,000 years. Yet, throughout the second half of the nineteenth century, while the industry was being revolutionized in Europe, Indian manufacturing firms held a precarious existence. Without government subsidies and help in other ways,[2] it does not seem likely that they would have survived.

Indeed, even with the more modern techniques and processes that may be said to have started to flourish in India with the founding of the Tata Iron and Steel Company in 1903, government assistance remained of considerable importance. In 1924, for example, when world competition between steel producers became very intense, a Steel Industry (Protection) Act) was passed which imposed duties on steel imports, and in 1925 bounties were paid as an additional protection for the industry.[3] The Tata Company, it should be understood, was wholly an Indian venture. 'While plant managers and leading assistants have been Europeans and Americans, no Europeans or Americans have been on the controlling board'.[4] Right from the beginning money was raised in India largely because the London money market was not prepared to assist. 'Whether this was to any extent due to the fact that the project was to be controlled by an Indian rather than by an Englishman is not clear'.[5] Thus, a government of English civil servants employed measures to protect an industry which might otherwise have succumbed to overseas competition and which soon began to compete with British Steel firms and even export pig-iron and steel bars to the

---

[1] Percival J. Griffiths, *The British Impact on India*, MacDonald, 1952, p. 442. See also J. Gallagher and R. Robinson, 'The Imperialism of Free Trade', *Economic History Review*, 2nd Series, Vol. VI, 1953, pp. 4–5.

[2] Daniel H. Buchanan, *The Development of Capitalist Enterprise in India*, Macmillan, 1934, pp. 278–81.

[3] Parakunnel J. Thomas, *India's Basic Industries*, Orient Longmans, 1948, pp. 5–6.

[4] Buchanan, op. cit., p. 287.

[5] Griffiths, op. cit., p. 447.

United Kindgom itself.[1] They carried out this policy in spite of the fact that the interests they were protecting seem to have been Indian rather than English.

Of course, it is true that protective tariffs were directed mainly at cheap steel from the European mainland. In 1934, for example, the Indian Tariff Board decided that 'protection was required only against the low prices of untested steel which came mainly from the Continent'.[2] No protection was imposed upon English tested steel, because it was accepted that the average import price was a 'fair' selling price. Nevertheless, that this was not an uncomplicated case of Imperial preference is apparent in the fact that steel bars, and black and galvanized steel sheets imported from the United Kingdom were subject to duty.[3] To the extent that Indian users of British steel paid relatively high prices for it, it may be argued that some element of the high wages of steel workers in Britain was derived from exploitation of the Indian working class, but it can hardly be claimed that this was the result of a policy pursued with single-minded ruthlessness. What seems, indeed, to have motivated government officials was a lesson learned during the First World War, that India had both 'potential and actual significance, as a base of supplies for the British army in the event of a world war';[4] and one effect of this, it has been argued, was that they became 'caught in the cross fire between the rising pressure in India for a vigorous policy of state aid to industry and the same old pressures in Great Britain for the complementary type of economy'.[5]

This might be interpreted, from a Leninist point of view, as a consequence of the Indian proletariat's response to exploitation by the owners of the factories. After all, strike experience in India before independence was 'fantastically high, by far the

---

[1] Gilbert E. H. Hubbard, *Eastern Industrialization and its Effect on the West*, Oxford University Press, 1935, pp. 282–3.

[2] Thomas, op. cit., p. 7.

[3] Ibid., p. 8.

[4] Nuru Islam, *Foreign Capital, and Economic Development, Japan, India and Canada*, Tuttle (Tokyo), 1960, p. 54.

[5] H. B. Lamb, 'India: A Colonial Setting' in Harold F. Williamson and J. A. Buttnik, eds., *Economic Development: Principles and Patterns*, Prentice-Hall, 1954, pp. 500–1.

highest in the world'.[1] Yet, there is also evidence which supports the view that 'the independence of India summed up mainly a national not a social revolution'.[2] Native capitalist employers saw British control as an obstacle to industrialization[3] and the Congress movement as an instrument which might obtain for them 'political and economic concessions',[4] so that the way was opened in the 1930's for Gandhi to make this into 'a multi-class and mass'[5] movement for independence. This suggests that possibly an important element in industrial unrest was civil disobedience, inspired by Gandhi and his followers, and aimed at dispelling not so much the capitalists as the foreigner. At most, therefore, all that can be said is that, possibly because of British imperialism, the Indian steel industry was slow to grow under native capitalist auspices, so that after independence the new state decided to establish its own steel works *alongside* those of private enterprise.[6] It is true that strike intensity remains high, although having fallen from the pre-independence peaks,[7] but it is certainly also clear that the outcome of imperialism has been neither a proletarian, nor a Communist revolution in India. All that seems to have happened apparently is that one kind of 'state capitalism' has been substituted for another.

A warning about the term 'state capitalism' is in order here. As used, for example, of the industrialization of Russia during the late nineteenth century, what is meant is a deliberate policy, implemented by government officials, for encouraging private capitalists to invest money in industrial enterprises, such as the building of railways. It should be understood that although, unlike traditional Marxist writing on politics, such a conception of state capitalism implies that the capitalists are never the

---

[1] Arthur M. Ross and P. T. Hartman, *Changing Patterns of Industrial Conflict*, Wiley, 1960, p. 131. See Appendix for statistical details of strike action.

[2] Hiranyappa Venkatasubbiah, *Indian Economy since Independence*, Asia Publishing House, 2nd edition, revised, 1961, p. 7 and Ch. 1, *passim*.

[3] Akshayakumar R. Desai, *Social Background of Indian Nationalism*, 3rd edition, Popular Press, 1959, p. 283.

[4] Ibid., p. 187.

[5] Ibid., p. 320.

[6] Baditha Rao, *Survey of Indian Industries*, Oxford University Press, 1957, Ch. 1, *passim*.

[7] Ross and Hartman, op. cit., p. 131.

masters but always the servants of the state,[1] private enterprise is one means merely, even if sometimes it is the most influential means, whereby the government of a country seeks to attain its political ends. The concept should, therefore, not be confused with what is entailed by another usage of the term, prompted perhaps by the 'pangs of conscience' of those who have become disillusioned by the Communist system' and have equated 'its evils with those of capitalism'.[2] Except for a very short period between 1921 and 1928,[3] post-revolutionary Russia, which has inspired this usage, has never been state capitalist. Private enterprise where it exists, as in the case of some handicrafts,[4] survives rather because its elimination is reckoned not to be worth the trouble, than because it is government policy to make use of it for its own purposes. State capitalism, as understood to refer to pre-revolutionary Russia and to India before and after independence, has some of the features which have been referred to above in the examination of the Welfare State,[5] namely that government officials interfere as *they* see fit into the workings of the economic system even if, as is often the case, they are aware that their interference will be to the disadvantage of certain of their country's employers.

Of course, it is also the case historically that such interference as state capitalism employs has occurred largely during the period of transition from capitalism to collectivism, so that in this sense the term state *capitalism* is perhaps misleading. Nevertheless the concept has the merit of directing attention to the fact that in some societies, such as England and America, commercial and industrial enterprises were established and flourished without benefit of direct state assistance or even encouragement, whereas in others government policies and

---

[1] Theodore H. von Laue, *Sergei Witte and the Industrialisation of Russia*, Columbia University Press, 1963, pp. 77 and 304.

[2] Milovan Djilas, *The New Class*, Unwin Books, 1966, p. 156. See also A. Sherman, 'Tito—A Reluctant Revisionist' in Leopold Labedz, ed., *Revisionism: Essays on the History of Marxist Ideas*, Allen and Unwin, 1902, pp. 259–61.

[3] Alexandr Baykov, *The Development of the Soviet Economic System*, Cambridge University Press, 1947, Ch. 7, *passim*.

[4] Philippe J. Bernard, *Planning in the Soviet Union*, trans. by J. Nove, Pergamon, 1966, p. 21.

[5] See above, pp. 181–2.

administration have played an important part in at least shortening the period of their development. It is in this sense that it is proper to talk of state capitalism in India, even if after independence joint-companies grew substantially in size and numbers,[1] as also did nationalized enterprises under collective boards.[2] It is in this sense, too, that it is proper to talk of state capitalism in Tsarist Russia, since it seems reasonably clear that 'the development of large-scale industry in Russia was based first of all on the desire of the Government to emancipate the country from dependence on foreign supplies of manufactured goods. The aim was to render Russia an entirely self-sufficing and independent entity, which would remain apart from the countries of the West'.[3] To this end also they tried to encourage foreign capitalists to invest in Russian industry. In so far as they were successful, therefore, it may be argued that the payment of super-profits on foreign capital was one of the reasons why the Russian workers were prompted to violent revolution, especially if it is further argued that it was 'the dependence of Russian capitalism upon the finance capital of the West European powers'[4] which plunged Russia into the disasters of the First World War;[5] but this is an issue which may be postponed to the next chapter. The main point to notice here is that the Russian government was throughout the major actor in these developments in a sense which does not apply to the part played by the state in Britain.

At the same time, an examination of Russo-British relations ensures that one question can be answered by data beyond dispute. British investment in Russia had little contribution to make to the support of an aristocracy of labour at home. In December, 1913, for example, Russia's share in long-term publicly issued, British capital investments abroad accounted for less than 3 per cent of the total—that is, less than the investments in Brazil (3·9 per cent), Argentina (8·5 per cent),

[1] Venkatasubbiah, op. cit., pp. 148–51.

[2] Ibid., Ch. 5, *passim.*

[3] Margaret S. Miller, *The Economic Development of Russia, 1905–1914,* King and Sons, 1962, p. 219.

[4] Petr I. Lyashchenko, *History of the National Economy in Russia to the 1917 Revolution,* trans. by L. M. Hemen, Macmillan, 1949, p. 780.

[5] Ibid., p. 716.

India and Ceylon (10·1 per cent), Australia and New Zealand (11·1 per cent), Canada and Newfoundland (13·7 per cent), and the United States (20·0 per cent).[1] Indeed, English capitalists seem to have been reluctant to invest in Russia after the Crimean War. In the 1880's when they were providing the funds for railroad building in the United States, Canada, India, Ceylon and Argentina,[2] in spite of the Russian government's eagerness to float new loans for railway development, 'British investors took virtually no share of them'.[3] However true it may be that overseas investment made it possible for British employers to pacify the trade unions, it was at the expense of the nationals in countries other than those where Communist revolutions have in fact occurred. Other imperialist nations may have had their part to play in these events, but from the primary fact of investment *per se* at any rate, British imperialism has certainly not fulfilled the purpose which Lenin seems to have expected of it.

It should be emphasized here that territorial expansion, from Lenin's point of view, is prompted by the special interests of rentiers with overseas investments to protect or extend. From this point of view the British empire was a consequence, not a cause of capitalist expansion. Yet, the trend of investments from 1913 to 1930 was away from the rest of the world and into the Empire. Thus by 1930, 58·7 per cent of the British total of foreign investments were made in Empire countries, as compared with 47·3 per cent in 1913.[4] It is tempting to see this as a product of the British government's wartime policy, especially with respect to the U.S.A. which more than anywhere had been favoured as a source of exploitation by Britain before 1914. During the war American investments were sold under government order to pay for supplies and armaments,[5] so that from contributing 20·0 per cent of the whole in 1913, investments in the U.S.A. had fallen to 5·4 per cent by 1930. Yet the Finance

---

[1] Figures calculated from Herbert Feis, *Europe: The World's Banker, 1870–1914*, Yale University Press, 1930, Table, p. 23. The comparable Russian figure was in fact 2·9 per cent.

[2] Ibid., pp. 19–20.

[3] Ibid., p. 230.

[4] Royal Institute of International Affairs, *The Problem of International Investment*, Oxford University Press, 1937, p. 142.

[5] Edward V. Morgan, *Studies in British Financial Policy 1914–25*, Macmillan, 1952, pp. 326–31.

Act of 1919,[1] and Imperial preference in the inter-war years also had their impact on directing overseas investments towards empire countries. Moreover, to the degree that the Second World War was paid for *inter alia* by an even more drastic sale of oversea investments than in 1914–18, it seems reasonably clear that not only has Britain received an ever-decreasing income from overseas investments during the twentieth century but foreigners have found it increasingly profitable to invest money here.[2] Varga's point that the loss of overseas territories has not affected the level of living in Britain because of the more rapid growth of output due to technical progress in the post-war years'[3] thus emphasises the fact that investors have found it more profitable to support home industries in this later period; but it plays havoc with the classical Leninist notion of imperialism. As Marx put it, 'if capital is sent abroad, this is not done because it absolutely could not be applied at home, but because it can be employed at a high rate of profit in a foreign country'.[4] If, therefore, home investment has become more profitable than foreign investment, the drive towards imperialism must necessarily have slackened. What then becomes of the notion that imperialism is the final stage of capitalism? It is true that Varga also argued that the loss of actual territory had not affected Britain's imperial status since British capitalists still continued to own much of the industry in her erstwhile colonial possessions, but however much this may be important for events in those lands, its significance for events in Britain *has* been reduced, simply because it no longer plays the part in the national income that it did before the First World War, and even before the second.

Much the same kind of conclusion emerges from even a brief examination of British overseas trade. In 1899 about 32·5 per cent of the world's exports in manufactured goods were from the

---

[1] Sidney Pollard, *The Development of the British Economy 1914–1950*, Arnold, 1962, p. 196.

[2] T. Balogh, 'The International Aspect' in George D. N. Worswick and P. H. Ady, eds., *The British Economy 1945–1950*, Clarendon Press, 1952, p. 478. John H. Dunning, *American Investment in British Manufacturing Industry*, Allen and Unwin, 1958, Ch. 1, *passim*.

[3] Evgenii Varga, *Twentieth Century Capitalism*, Lawrence and Wishart, n.d., p. 100.

[4] Marx, *Capital*, Vol. III, op. cit., p. 251.

United Kingdom. By 1929 this proportion had fallen to 23·6 per cent. It stood at about 22·1 per cent in 1938 and had fallen to 17·3 per cent by 1959.[1] Whereas in 1910–13 some 96·6 per cent of the national income in Britain came from overseas trade, by 1927–29 it had fallen to 83·0 per cent and by 1930–33 to 61·2 per cent, that is, lower than it had been in 1860–69.[2] At that time, of course, it could be claimed that the income from overseas investments (invisible imports) rescued the British people from the effects of the loss of overseas trade, but by 1946 this was no longer so and they were 'beginning to become aware of a problem which had first begun to emerge some sixty years of more ago'[3]. It is not too much to claim that British economic history since the end of the Second World War has been dominated by this problem. Yet industrial unrest, as exemplified by strike action, has declined over the period rather than increased. All the evidence points to the very great possibility that traditional capitalist society has been superseded by a different kind of social system.

Altogether, then, the notion that an aristocracy of labour is a product of imperialism has very little to commend it. Possibly, indeed, the very brevity of Lenin's briefest possible definition— the monopoly stage of capitalism—has become a barrier in the way of understanding what is happening in countries like Holland and Britain which once had large overseas empires and are now relying more and more on the home economy. The conquest of foreign lands and the investment of capital in foreign industries are not associated in quite the simple manner that Lenin thought, if indeed historically they are associated at all. In many respects it is easy to sympathize with Mayo who largely dismissed the whole topic with the words, 'countries such as the Scandinavian, without empires, had shown a high standard of living . . . colonial powers, such as Portugal, showed a much lower standard of living . . . the bulk of the world's trade is not with colonial and 'backward' territories at all'.[4] Even a sup-

[1] Sidney J. Wells, *British Export Performance*, Cambridge University Press, 1964, Tables 1.1 and 1.2, p. 15.

[2] Werner Schlote, *British Overseas Trade*, Blackwell, 1962, Table 10, p. 49.

[3] William A. Lewis, *Economic Survey, 1919–1939*, Allen and Unwin, 1949, p. 79.

[4] Henry B. Mayo, *Democracy and Marxism*, Oxford University Press, 1955, p. 89.

porter of the imperialism thesis has found himself constrained to point to the anomaly that countries like Sweden which have had no overseas empires have nevertheless 'produced a reformist labour movement of the kind which Lenin ascribed to the effects of imperialism'[1]—all of which suggests that discussions of this topic have been carried on without a careful examination of the facts. Certainly, so far as Britain is concerned, the nature and impact of her imperial possessions, her overseas investments, and her overseas trade, demonstrate how complicated a problem Lenin was introducing when he seized on Hobson's work on the subject as a way out of the Marxist dilemma. This chapter may not, of course, be read as a refutation of every aspect of the imperialism but it surely throws doubts upon the value of it for the purpose it is intended to serve. The validity of analysing British industrial relations in terms of the peaceful institutionalization of collective bargaining is in no way threatened by the introduction of the notion of imperialism as a *deus ex machina*. If anything, the course of England's development since the 1880's can only have been made more difficult because of her declining importance as a world power, rather than have been facilitated by her growing imperial strength. In this respect the analysis of the Second Part of this book may fairly be said to have been confirmed, or at least certainly not refuted, by an attempt to examine empirically what is implied by the Leninist thesis.

---

[1] Kemp, op. cit., p. 81.

15

VIOLENT COMMUNIST REVOLUTIONS

'No misinterpretation of Marx is more grotesque', Hobsbawm has written, 'than the one which suggest that he expected a revolution exclusively from the advanced industrial countries of the West'.[1] The reference here is to the possibility of 'a European revolution in Russia', which Hobsbawm infers from some remarks by Marx on the historical significance of the Russian village community[2] and from a letter by him on the war with Turkey and its likely effect on a country which, he thought, 'has long been standing on the threshold of an upheaval'.[3] For his part, Lenin did not see any revolutionary prospects in the village community. 'Despite the theories that have prevailed here during the past half-century', he wrote, 'the Russian community peasantry are not antagonists of capitalism, but, on the contrary, are its deepest and most durable foundation'.[4] He therefore turned instead to the historical mission of a Russian proletariat produced by immanent developments of capitalism, both in agriculture and in industry, and looked to the emergence of class consciousness on the classical model

[1] E. J. Hobsbawm, 'Introduction' to his edition of Karl Marx, *Pre-Capitalist Economic Formations*, Lawrence and Wishart, 1964, p. 49.

[2] Ibid., pp. 49–50 and references cited. For a different interpretation see Edward H. Carr, *The Bolshevik Revolution, 1917–1923*, Vol. 2, Penguin Books, 1966, pp. 384–8.

[3] Letter from Marx to F. A. Sorge, 27th September 1877, in Marx and Engels, *Selected Correspondence*, op. cit., p. 374.

[4] Lenin, *The Development of Capitalism*, op. cit., p. 173. See also Vladimir I. Lenin, *The Heritage We Renounce*, in Vladimir I. Lenin, *Collected Works*, Vol. 2, Foreign Languages Publishing House, 1963, pp. 517–20.

derived from Marx's analysis of English society.[1] To the degree,
however, that Russia's entry into the First World War may be
seen as crucial to the events of 1917, and to the degree that the
decisions in 1914 may be held to have been a result of that
country's dependence on the Western powers,[2] Lenin's imperialism thesis may possibly be necessary to explain the preci-
pitation of Communist revolution in this and in other parts of
the world—despite, that is to say, its inability to account for
events in Britain. Although it cannot easily be shown that overseas trade and investments materially benefited the English
working class and hence created a quiescent labour movement
in this country, it might nevertheless be the case that Communist
revolutions elsewhere were brought about by such a form of
imperialism.

For example, although British investments in Russia amounted
to no more than 2·9 per cent of the British total in 1913, they
accounted for some 14 per cent of the Russian total of foreign
debt, or to 25 per cent if only industrial investments are considered.[3] Althogether, indeed, about one third of corporate
capital in Russia was owned by foreigners in 1914, and this had
grown steadily from 28 per cent in 1900. 'In rate of growth',
estimated Lyashchenko, 'foreign capital increased faster than
did internal accumulation'.[4] The Russian Empire, that is to say,
entered its industrial phase in 'a position of semi-colonial dependency on Western European capitalism'.[5] As a nation it was far
from imperialist in Lenin's sense of the term. 'Only with some
of the more backward neighbouring centres, which in agreement with the Western powers, were her 'spheres of influence'
(Persia, partly Turkey and Manchuria), did Russian capital play
the active, if small, role of exporter. Because of its subordinate
position, Russian finance capital even in such cases did not, in
fact, act independently but rather as an 'agent' or partner of
foreign capital in the division of Turkey, Persia and China. In
any event, Russia was far from having become a 'rentier-state'

[1] See above, pp. 152–3.
[2] See above, p. 233.
[3] Leo Pasvolsky and H. G. Mowlton, *Russian Debts and Russian Reconstruction*, McGraw-Hill, 1924, pp. 21–2.
[4] Op. cit., p. 716.
[5] Ibid., p. 564.

as were France and England, to whom, on the contrary, she also paid millions of roubles in interest on industrial investments and state loans.[1]

One consequence of this, apparently, was that capitalist industry in Russia passed fairly quickly through phases which in Britain had taken far longer to traverse.[2] Russian industry was large-scale industry. For example, by 1910 53·5 per cent of industrial workers in Russia were employed in establishments of more than 500 workers, a figure which Lyashchenko compared with 33 per cent for the United States of America. As he understood it, foreign investment 'was attracted chiefly in the form of big corporate capital introducing a highly advanced production technique'.[3] This resulted in a very uneven development. A whole series of major industries were either completely or almost completely non-existent in Russia.[4] Nevertheless, to the extent that the Marxist analysis of the growth of class consciousness is correct, it would seem that the conditions existed for the development of a militant labour movement in those areas where large-scale establishments were common. Lyashchenko, indeed, provided some evidence in support of this claim. Lockouts, unemployment and a marked deterioration in labour conditions at the turn of the century resulted in an increase in 'direct participation of workers in political demonstrations. . . . Strikes became more frequent, assuming a militant political character and spreading into all branches of economy. . . . Leading the strike movement was the vanguard of the working class —the metalworkers, who were the best organized and politically most mature'.[5]

However, in all this the most noticeable feature was the spontaneity, or at least the apparent spontaneity of the workers' militancy. Trade unions were illegal in Russia until 1906, so that there was no long tradition behind the movement. Some trade union machinery existed in embryo, of course, and one

---

[1] Ibid., pp. 641–2. The figures for indebtedness to French investors were 80 per cent of total Russian foreign debt, and 32 per cent of industrial securities. Pasvolsky and Moulton, op. cit., pp. 21–2.

[2] Seton-Watson, *The Russian Empire*, Clarendon Press, 1967, p. 322.

[3] Lyaschenko, op. cit., pp. 669–70.

[4] Ibid., p. 673.

[5] Ibid., pp. 656 et seq.

account of the movement dates it from 'the secret associations which were formed around 1890 to gather strike funds so as to prepare and support direct action for better conditions'.[1] The leaders of these secret societies were regularly subject to police persecution, so that only those workers who were prepared to risk the possibility of a prison sentence or exile were likely to join and become active in trade unions at this time; and as Deutscher has emphasized, 'those who were already so politically-minded were, naturally enough, more attracted by political organization'.[2]

This situation, although far from identical with that of the trade union movement in England before 1850,[3] had more in common with it than it did with English experience afterwards. Those aspects of trade union organization and collective bargaining with employers which eventually led to social disillusionment and hence to the formation of a workers' political party to solve their economic problems through welfare policies and the nationalization of key industries, never appeared in Russia, and were hardly beginning to appear by 1914. Thus the explanation for the Revolution of 1917, if it is to be couched in Marxist terms at all, must be made largely by reference to the impact of imperialist investment on the Russian economy, especially in so far as this was a cause of Russia's entry into the First World War. Since by 1917 the total of English, French and Belgian capital accounted for 69·5 per cent of the total foreign capital employed in the industrialization of the country, whereas the contribution of German and Austrian capital amounted to only 20·1 per cent, a Marxist may perhaps be expected to assume that 'this fact alone helped to predetermine the side on which Russia eventually participated'.[4] During the military crises of the war, moreover, the dependency of Russia on the financial capital of the Western powers may be interpreted, from this point of view, as developing into 'absolute financial, technological and military subjugation for the benefit

---

[1] *The Trade Union Situation in the U.S.S.R.*, International Labour Office, 1960, p. 24.

[2] Isaac Deutscher, *Soviet Trade Unions*, Royal Institute of International Affairs, 1950, p. 1.

[3] For some of these differences, see above, pp. 151–2.

[4] Lyaschenko, op. cit., p. 716.

of alien interests, and into needless sacrifice of millions of lives and the complete disruption of the country in the interests of the Western powers'.[1] Presumably, this may be understood as implying that the Russian proletariat turned against its capitalist masters because the workers saw no alternative to their misery but to take over the running of industry themselves.

To some extent the action of workers in taking possession of the factories in which they worked is direct evidence of this. At first, their demands were for an eight-hour day and for higher wages, and although some employers came to terms with the factory committees, which the unrest of these years produced, more often than not they responded to the workers' demands by declaring lock-outs or closing down their factories.[2] Compromise with even conciliatory owners was, moreover, short-lived. 'The employer was not willing to conduct his business merely in order that he should teach it to his workpeople. . . . The workers for their part were filled with a hatred for Capitalism and were unwilling to remain voluntarily as objects for exploitation.' Workers were accordingly appointed by their fellow workers to manage the factories.[3]

In terms of Marx's comparison of corporate with co-operative enterprise, referred to above,[4] the Russian industrial workers' action seems to have been directed towards a 'positive' solution of the conflict between labour and capital; and although it has been claimed that the immediate effect was parochial rather than patriotic in the degree to which 'every factory committee, aspired to have the last and final say on all matters affecting the factory, its output, its stock of raw materials, its conditions of work, etc., and paid little or no attention to the needs of industry as a whole',[5] there is evidence that the factory committees were conceived by those who set them up as the basis of what might become a network of 'cells' rather than sovereign industrial units. As early as May 30, 1917, for example, more

[1] Ibid., p. 780.
[2] Carr, op. cit., p. 63.
[3] Yuri Larin and L. Kritsmann, *Economic Life and Economic Development in Soviet Russia from 1917 to 1920* (in Russian, 1921), quoted from the German translation in Arthur Rosenberg, *A History of Bolshevism*, translated by I. F. Morrow, Oxford University Press, 1934, pp. 111–12.
[4] See p. 173.
[5] Deutscher, op. cit., p. 17.

than 400 representatives of the factory and works' committees of the Petrograd region met in conference to discuss the issue of workers' control of industry. Between this meeting and October, 1917, four more conferences were held; and on the eve of the October revolution 'a larger and more representative assembly' which declared itself to be the 'first Russian conference of factory committees' met to create 'a central organization of factory committees'.[1]

Into the ultimate fate of this movement, and its conflict with the trade unions, on the one hand, and with the Bolshevik Party, on the other, it is not necessary for present purposes to go. Nor is it necessary to consider the extent to which it was the Anarchists rather than the Marxists who inspired the thinking behind the syndicalist notions which the workers appear in some measure to have held. The main point to notice is that the 'spontaneous' efforts of the industrial workers were classless in intention in that they were directed towards substituting management by elected representatives in place of management by a class of exploiting owners over whose power of making decisions the employees previously had had no control. This intention appears not to have been shared by the peasants who in distributing the former landowners' estates among themselves thought primarily in terms of the right of the worker to use his land as he thought fit, or, where it was redistributed parochially according to traditional Russian notions of the *MIR* organization, thought in terms of some conception of equality rather than of collective agricultural action.[2] The peasants saw themselves, that is to say, as having created a rural society of small proprietors producing for their own needs, who if they had a surplus, might dispose of it as they thought fit. Some, indeed, regarded themselves as small capitalists who might legitimately employ landless men to work on their behalf for wages.

It is important to notice, moreover, that the action of both the industrial workers and the peasants in dispossessing capitalists and landowners seems to have been possible in 1917 only because the army turned against the government. 'The revolution was victorious', asserted the official Bolshevik view, 'because its vanguard was the working class which headed the

[1] Carr, op. cit., pp. 66–9.
[2] Deutscher, op. cit., p. 17.

243

movement of millions of peasants clad in soldiers' uniform demanding 'peace, bread and liberty'.[1] In Petrograd in the early spring of 1917, for example, the workers went on strike, the police moved in and started to fire on the workers and the troops fired on the police.[2] This contrasts very forcibly with the abortive rising of 1905 when in spite of some mutinies in the army and navy, the military stood by the government.[3] As Maynard put it, 'between 1914 and 1917, the army had learned to distrust, if not its military leaders, at least the Government behind them, and, in the months preceding the Revolution, discipline was seriously shaken, of which wholesale desertions, bad treatment of horses, of equipment, even of weapons, were symptoms . . . disease was rife, there was frequent shortage of food, and there was no confidence in the success of the war whether among officers or men'.[4] This is not to say that the army *made* the revolution, for all that the mutinies played an important, and in some respects crucial, part. The point is that the government of the Czar had collapsed in all its major functions by 1917, largely as a result of its military, strategic failures in the war; and this collapse made it possible for a war-weary population to create workers' committees and Soviets of Workers' and Soldiers' Deputies because the resources at the government's disposal were insufficient to repress these organizations.[5]

The explanation of the Russian revolution in imperialist terms, that is to say, requires acceptance of the truth of the two major propositions, firstly, that entry into the First World War on the part of the Russian government was a *direct* result of its indebtedness to foreign capitalists, rather than a consequence of some other facet of government policy, and secondly, that its wartime experiences so weakened the system of internal social control by the government that strikes and organized attempts of the *proletariat* to get rid of its capitalist masters could not be defeated by the power of the police and the armed forces, because these agencies no longer had confidence in their masters.

[1] *A History of the Communist Party of the Soviet Union*, edited by a Commission of the C.C. of the C.P.S.U., Foreign Languages Publishing House, 1950, p. 217.

[2] Ibid., pp. 215–17.

[3] Ibid., pp. 97–101.

[4] John Maynard, *Russia in Flux before October*, Gollancz, 1941, p. 275.

[5] Robert V. Daniels, *Red October*, Secker and Warburg, 1967, p. 13.

Taken together as hypotheses to account for Communist revolutions elsewhere, these propositions imply that *as a matter of fact* the *condition* for revolution is the class conflict between the native proletariat and foreign imperialist capitalists, the precipitating factor is an obligation on the part of the native government to these foreigners of such a nature that it embarks upon military, or presumably equally costly adventures, and the *decisive factor* is its failure to maintain control over the social means of coercion whenever these adventures lead to the virtual collapse of the economy.[1] Of course, it is possible to account for Communist revolutions since 1917 in terms other than these, but the analysis of the Russian revolution presented above implies that any other explanation requires a drastic departure from the Marxist-Leninist framework of ideas.

At the same time, it is not at all clear that the facts about such revolutions fit easily into that framework. In China up to 1937, for example, most industrial development had been in response to foreign investment, mainly British and Japanese,[2] but there was not much of it and it was largely concentrated on the eastern seaboard so that any class conflict in the form of strikes was highly localized. It is possible that 'the Chinese people by and large considered foreign capital in China as dominating and oppressive, not merely because of its large share in the various sectors of the Chinese economy, but because of the special background against which it was possible for foreign capital to grow to such mammoth proportions. It grew under special protections and privileges provided by the various unequal treaties'.[3] Yet when the revolution eventually occurred

[1] For the importance of a rather different emphasis on 'a short period of sharp decline' following 'a prolonged period of objective economic and social development' as the precipitating factor in all violent revolutions see J. C. Davies, 'Toward a Theory of Revolution', *American Sociological Review*, Vol. 27, 1962, pp. 5–19.

[2] Chi-Ming Hou, *Foreign Investment and Economic Development in China, 1840–1937*, Harvard University Press, 1965, Table 18, p. 81. In terms of investments generally Japan had increased her share from 0·1 per cent in 1902 to 40 per cent in 1936, largely at the expense of Russia whose share had declined from 31·3 per cent to nil over the period. The British share was 33 per cent and 35 per cent on the two occasions, ibid., Table 4, p. 17.

[3] Yu-Kwei Cheng, *Foreign Trade and the Industrial Development of China*, University Press of Washington, 1956, p. 41. For details of the 'mammoth proportions' see Table 15, p. 40.

the urban proletariat apparently 'waited inertly and passively for the peasant troops to occupy the cities'.[1]

Moreover, the warfare in which the Chinese government was involved from 1937 onwards can hardly be claimed to have been precipitated by its indebtedness to the foreign capitalists of the seaboard. Rather was it a war of defence against Japanese military aggression, a major consequence of which was that the Chinese government followed a state-capitalist policy of aiding private Chinese firms to move their factories to new sites outside the Japanese area of control and to develop new plants in that of 'free China'. After 1937, too, there was a 'spectacular growth of government-owned industries'[2] and an impressive development of industrial co-operative societies.[3] Indeed the most characteristic feature of the period from 1937 to the eventual defeat of Japan at the end of the Second World War, was that the spirit of nationalist resistance for the first time in modern China gave the government, in coalition with the Communists, a more or less unified control over that part of the country which was not occupied by the troops of the foreigner, and encouraged it to foster industrialization in the modern manner. Before this time, that is to say, there had occurred a long period of what has been called 'a rigmarole of transient power politics'[4] and 'almost un-diluted militarism'[5] which had flared up from time to time into armed combat between the warlords in one local area and those in another. The central government had, moreover, been ideologically unable to develop industry.[6]

In this respect the rise of Communists to power was facilitated by the fact that they had already had some military successes in the countryside, even before the Japanese invasion.

[1] Benjamin I. Schwartz, *Chinese Communism and the Rise of Mao*, Harvard University Press, 1951, p. 197. For information that the Communist forces were largely peasant in origin see Samuel B. Griffith, *The Chinese People's Liberation Army*, Weidenfield and Nicholson, 1967, pp. 5, 320, n. 7, and p. 329, n. 24.

[2] Cheng, op. cit., p. 108.

[3] Harley F. MacNair, ed., *China*, University of California Press, 1941, pp. 184–5.

[4] Ibid., p. 145.

[5] Ibid., p. 152.

[6] Albert Fuerwerker, *China's Early Industrialization*, Harvard University Press, 1958, p. 48.

These were amongst a peasantry, ready for action against absentee owners and against landlords who 'in reaction to the Japanese occupation . . . moved out of the countryside and into the towns, leaving the peasants to their own devices'.[1] It is for this reason that some observers have regarded the Chinese uprising as conditioned by agrarian rather than industrial conditions, by land hunger rather than by capitalist exploitation, and it is possible to point to the important part played by the peasantry in the Russian revolution as an indication that Communist revolutions, the world over, have never been anything but agrarian revolutions. In support of this thesis it may also be emphasized that whenever Communists came to power in Europe with the collapse of Hitler Germany, there was a striking lack of an organized proletariat; and in the inter-war years it was precisely those countries where industrialism had hardly taken root that Communist Parties obtained the highest votes.[2]

It is not the task of the present chapter, as it happens, to provide an alternative explanation for the advent of successful Communist revolutions in countries where industrialization has been meagre; although it should perhaps be noted that an important part has been played in such revolutions by a spirit of simple nationalism, a desire to expel the foreigner and to create home industry by collective action on the part of the élite which controls the state,[3] and which is able to appeal to a mass following in this respect. Nor is it necessary to do more than to notice that the revolutionary élite in such countries has not been composed of either proletarian or peasant leaders primarily, but of alienated professionals—doctors, lawyers and schoolteachers— people who, it may be claimed, become influential because they are the only ones who are able to introduce the industrial ideas of developed nations to countries which otherwise would resist industrialization because it spells imperialist exploitation.[4]

There is, to be sure, a problem here that after 1917 an impor-

[1] Barrington Moore, Jr., *Social Origins of Dictatorship and Democracy*, Lane, 1967, p. 223.
[2] Richard B. Burks, *The Dynamics of Communism in Eastern Europe*, Princeton University Press, 1961, *passim*.
[3] Kerr, *et al.*, *Industrialism and Industrial Man*, op. cit., pp. 59–62, 66–70.
[4] Burks, op. cit., p. 186. See also Lasswell, *et al.*, op. cit., Chs. 3 and 6.

tant ingredient in Communist revolutions has been the success of the previous one.[1] As Seton-Watson has put it, 'the existence of an intelligentsia both ideally and personally frustrated, of a peasantry suffering from over-population and land-hunger, of an exploited and bewildered unskilled working class, and of national humiliation or colonial subjection, give Communists their opportunity. But they do not necessarily ensure Communist victory. In such conditions revolutionary movements of some sort are almost certain to appear, but they need not be Communist, or even 'left'. They may take the form of fascism, anti-semitism or some kind of religious traditionalism. What form they will take, will depend on the intellectual climate in which the intelligentsia, which will provide the revolutionary leadership, has grown up. In present times, it will depend largely on the national attitude to Russia or China or their enemies'.[2] Alternatively, Lenin's *Imperialism* may be thought of as the theoretical alternative for 'less developed areas' of the *Communist Manifesto* for 'advanced countries',[3] but no matter how the subject is examined, it clearly requires such marked departures from the Leninist revision of Marx, with which this enquiry into the postponement of revolution in advanced capitalist societies began, that the link with the second part of this study becomes very tenuous indeed.

The question, therefore, of whether social revolution, carried through by violence and coercion, is the 'normal' pattern of history in the transition from capitalism,[4] must be answered with so many qualifications as to imply a negative. The Communist revolutions of the twentieth century, with the possible exception of the first, were a prelude to industrialization for the most part, rather than a response to it. Lenin and Stalin, indeed, have been represented as having 'arrived at a completely new meaning of socialism; not an ideal system based on established industry and stressing the even distribution of economic value

[1] Note Brinton's argument that the history of revolutions from the British to the Russian suggests 'a development of conscious revolutionary technique'. Crane Brinton, *The Anatomy of Revolution*, Revised and Expanded Edition, Vintage Books, 1965, p. 259.

[2] H. Seton-Watson, *The Pattern of Communist Revolution*, Methuen, 2nd edition, 1960, p. 340.

[3] Kemp, op. cit., p. 67.

[4] See above, p. 211.

and political power throughout the population, but a system for accomplishing industrialization and overcoming backwardness'.[1] In this respect Communist revolutions may fairly be said to usher in a society which is an *alternative* to capitalism and not a *consequence* of it, at least when considered internally. The type of social order they have produced may thus be said to be 'not a stage beyond capitalism but a substitute for it—a means by which the nations which did not share in the Industrial Revolution can imitate its technical achievements; a means to achieve rapid accumulation under a different set of rules of the game'.[2] In terms of the Marxist approach to industrial relations, that is to say, the peaceful sequence of events, described in the Second Part of this volume, is most likely to have been the 'normal' one, and the achievements of the Communist governments, which have come to power elsewhere, have largely been based on lessons drawn by them from the experiences of capitalist employers and their organized employees in the later stages of capitalism. This does not mean that the countries where Communist revolutions have occurred might not have followed the same pattern as in Britain, had there been no overseas investment by capitalists to initiate the process of change; but it does mean that some copying has occurred and that this has largely taken the form of creating collectivist organizations without a capitalist element. In this sense it may be argued that all industrial societies are collectivist now.

---

[1] Robert V. Daniels, *The Conscience of the Revolution: Communist Opposition in Soviet Russia*, Harvard University Press, 1960, p. 408.

[2] Joan Robinson, 'Marx, Marshall and Keynes' (1955), reprinted in her *Collected Economic Papers*, Vol. 2, Blackwell, 1960, p. 15.

16

THE CASE OF AMERICA

The division of societies into two types—(1)those where violent revolutions have occurred and in which the transition from pre-capitalism to collectivism has proceeded without there first developing both a *ruling* class of native capitalist and an organized labour movement of the industrial proletariat; and (2), those where class conflict between capitalists and workers has been the precondition for the gradual emergence of a new class of exploiters—should not be so maintained as to obscure the possibility that *within* each type further subdivisions may occur, produced by factors which may be loosely regarded as national or cultural. As Marx put it in a rather different context, the necessary wants of labourers vary from place to place according to 'a historical and moral element', namely, 'the degree of civilization of a country' or 'more particularly the conditions under which, and consequently on the habits and degree of comfort in which, the class of free labourers has been formed'.[1] Differences in other respects in the relationship between employers and employees in different countries might thus legitimately be thought to depend on similar historical and moral elements.

In turning therefore to consider whether the analysis of the peaceful process of development in industrial relations and collective bargaining, as set out in Part Two, is confirmed or contradicted by events outside Britain, some attention must be paid to the problem of distinguishing between what is uniquely British, and what is common to all those countries where

---

[1] Marx, *Capital*, Vol. 1, op. cit., p. 171.

violent Communist revolutions have not occurred. Of course, it is not possible in the confines of a study such as this to conduct a cross-cultural series of comparisons which would suffice for such a purpose. Instead, one example only has been chosen, that of America, and this partly for reasons already given above[1] and partly because American experience has long been seen as not altogether typical of industrial capitalism. Marx himself, for example, wrote of the American labour movement of the second half of the nineteenth century that it was 'paralysed so long as slavery disfigured a part of the Republic' and that the eight hours agitation was in this sense 'the first fruit of the Civil War'.[2] In like fashion Sombart explained the lack of socialism in America at the turn of the century as due to the 'chances for the worker over there to rise out of his class, which were greater than for the workers in old Europe',[3] and he pointed to the fact that the number of farms in America had increased fourfold between 1850 and 1900, as evidence for his claim that the 'free land' of the West provided the possibility for 'a flight into freedom' on a scale greater than in any country.[4] It may be suspected in consequence that the advent of a labour movement along the lines described in the Second Part of this book would have been postponed at least until the land was more or less settled from the Atlantic to the Pacific seaboards.

As against this, however, must be set the countervailing influence on American development which was exercised by immigrants from the Old World; for 'it was British immigrants, in the American trades in which they worked, who both formed the nucleus of the skilled working class which first turned to unionism and also infused into the new labour movement the essence of British trade unionism'.[5] Indeed, two British unions, the Amalgamated Society of Engineers and the Amalgamated Society of Carpenters and Joiners, were in a sense transplanted overseas when they set up branches in America in 1861 and

[1] See p. 212.

[2] Marx, *Capital*, Vol. I, op. cit., p. 301.

[3] Werner Sombart, *Warum gibt es in den Vereinigten Staaten keines Sozialismus?* (Why is there no socialism in the United States?), Mohr, 1906, p. 135.

[4] Ibid., p. 137.

[5] Rowland T. Berthoff, *British Immigrants in Industrial America*, Harvard University Press, 1953, p. 88.

1867,[1] although this method of developing trades unionism in America was not followed in other industries. What seems rather to have happened was that British immigrants to the New World were more likely than other immigrants to stay in their old trades,[2] and often, because of their prior experience of trade union organization, to become the initiators of collective action and to rise to the leadership of native American unions.[3]

Nevertheless, their task was in many respects harder than it had been at home. The Eastern European peasant immigrants, in particular, with 'their habit of silent submission, their amenability to discipline and their willingness to work long hours and overtime without a murmur' which made them 'a better slave than the American'[4] were regarded by union activists as poor material to organize. Such immigrants consitituted, from the employers' point of view, a 'floating supply of labour'[5] who would join a firm at a time of prosperity and leave it at the first sign of depression or as soon as they had gained whatever savings they were working for. Peaceful relations between employers and the unskilled workers in, for example, the steel industry were altogether commonplace as a result, in spite of conditions which elsewhere in the world might well have led to strikes and other forms of unrest.

Of course, this does not mean that the industry was strike free. Between 1876, when the Amalgamated Association of Iron and Steelworkers of America was formed, and 1885 this union authorized as many as 93 strikes of which it won 28,[6] but its membership was largely limited to skilled men who could not rely on the immigrant labourers to walk out with them. Employers were quick to seize upon the fact that by introducing improved machinery they could take on 'green' labour, train it

---

[1] Ibid., p. 89. Yearley dates these events as 1862 and 1868 respectively. See Clifton K. Yearley, *Britons in American Labour*, John Hopkins Press, 1957, p. 188.

[2] Berthoff, op. cit., p. 23.

[3] Ibid., pp. 91–5; Yearley, op. cit., pp. 85–6.

[4] The Pittsburgh *Leader* (1912?), quoted in David Brody, *Steelworkers in America: the Non union Era*, Harvard University Press, 1966, p. 135.

[5] A. H. Young, 'Employing Men for a Steel Mill', *Iron Age*, 1916, quoted in Brody, op. cit., p. 109.

[6] Philip Taft, *Organised Labor in American History*, Harper and Row, 1964, p. 137.

in about eight weeks, and ignore entirely the union's demands. As compared with British experience, where union recognition and the establishment of viable collective-bargaining machinery is what characterized development from the 1870's onwards, American history demonstrated the attitude of the steel employers hardening over time, so that as the new century opened they began to take more aggressive, and even openly violent, action against the union members in their empoyment.

One of the main consequences of these differences between industrial relations in the United States and in Britain was that when the American steelworkers began effectively to become organized in the late 1930's, the form espoused was that of the single union for all the workers in the industry. Although up to this time there had been three unions with some claim to organize steelworkers—the International Union of Mine, Mill and Smelter Workers, the Steel and Metal Workers' Industrial Union, and the Amalgamated Association of Iron, Steel and Tin Workers—the combined membership of the three organizations represented a very small proportion of the total labour force. The Amalgamated was by far the largest of the three. Yet it had less than 10,000 members in 1935,[1] at a time when the industry employed 479,000 wage workers.[2] The drive to organize new members, indeed, came in large part from outside the existing unions, from the United Mine Workers in particular, some of whose members were employed in mines owned by steel companies. As their president John Lewis put it, 'the steel companies are going to push us around with a great deal more ferocity if they recognize they are free from organization in their own industry. It resolves itself down to the point that unless we carry the fight to the steel companies they are going to carry the fight to the organizations that are hanging on the fringe of the industry like the United Mine Workers'.[3]

In the event, the Committee for Industrial Organization of which Lewis was a member, formed a Steel Workers' Organizing Committee, which with funds from the C.I.O. and a loan from the United Mine Workers, began a vigorous recruiting campaign

[1] Walter Galenson, *The C.I.O. Challenge to the A.F.L.*, Harvard University Press, 1960, p. 75.
[2] Ibid., p. 87.
[3] Quoted in ibid., p. 77.

in 1936. By 1942 when the S.W.O.C. joined forces with the Amalgamated to form the United Steel Workers of America, it had about half a million fee-paying members and had signed agreements with 903 steel firms.[1] The Amalgamated, to be sure, had had two representatives on the S.W.O.C. from the beginning and had permitted an arrangement whereby its members could be transferred to the S.W.O.C. wherever there was no collective agreement between a lodge and an employer.[2] In this sense the eventual merger of the two bodies was little more than a formal termination to a distinction which had been nominal for most purposes over the previous six years.[3] Paradoxically, it seems that the steel employers made possible the creation of a powerful industrial union through their action a generation earlier in taking advantage of the mobility of unskilled workers to weaken the solidarity of steel workers at that time.

Some consideration of the C.I.O. is relevant at this point. Up to 1935 the central organization of trade unions in America had been the American Federation of Labour, a body which had been formed in 1886 for purposes, similar in many respects to those of the Trades Union Congress in Britain, but with one very important difference. Before this there had been attempts to form a federation of trade unions, such as the National Labour Union (1866–72), the Industrial Congress and Industrial Brotherhood (1872–5)[4] and the Federation of Organized Trades and Labour Unions of the United States and Canada (1881–1886),[5] but they were all short lived. In contrast, there had developed from a craft union of garment cutters in 1869 a new type of organization, the Noble Order of the Knights of Labour, which set out to enroll into a single trade union all manual workers, regardless of occupation and irrespective of whether there already existed a union for their trade. By the 1880's the Knights of Labour was a powerful body which was quite prepared to establish a union in a firm, alongside an existing one, would invade the jurisdiction of a well-established labour organization and generally was seen as interfering with

[1] Ibid., p. 119.
[2] Ibid., p. 86.
[3] Taft, op. cit., p. 521.
[4] Ibid., Ch. 5, *passim*.
[5] Ibid., Ch. 7, *passim*.

the trade activities of many unions[1] It was, indeed, the complaint of these other unions against such encroachments upon their autonomy which gave the impetus to the founding of the A.F. of L., while at the same time the very organizing success of the Knights of Labour resulted in the new federation assuming the task of establishing new local unions of workers where they did not already exist, and of organizing national unions where the locals had little contact with one another.

Thus, although at the outset the A.F. of L. had some of the political bias of the British T.U.C. in that its preamble recognized the existence of conflict 'between the oppressors and the oppressed of all countries, a struggle between the Capitalist and the Labourer, which grows in intensity from year to year, and will work disastrous results for the toiling millions, if they are not combined for material protection and benefit',[2] and that its first meeting urged 'a most generous support to the independent political movement of the working man',[3] purely trade union organizational matters largely dominated its interests and activities throughout its history. Moreover, the leadership of the A.F. of L. was substantially provided by the craft unions who saw themselves as having interests to protect against the claims of the anti-craft structure of the Knights of Labour and against the unskilled workers once the Knights had ceased to be a threat. The Committee of Industrial Organization, in consequence, was a challenge issued to the A.F. of L. from amongst those of its members who were 'concerned with the organization of unorganized workers in mass production and other industries'.[4] The emphasis, that is to say, was on industrial unionism *versus* craft unionism, and the very success of the C.I.O. and its subsidiaries in extending the coverage of union membership into areas traditionally regulated by the A.F. of L. did much to give American unionism an industrial character almost entirely different from the heterogeneous nature of British union organization.

[1] Philip Taft, *The A.F. of L. in the Time of Gompers*, Harper, 1957, Ch. 2, *passim*.

[2] Quoted in Taft, *The A.F. of L. in the Time of Gompers*, op. cit., p. 61, n. 20.

[3] Quoted, ibid., p. 37.

[4] From the Minutes of the Meeting of the C.I.O., 9th November 1935, quoted in Philip Taft, *The A.F. of L. from the Death of Gompers to the Merger*, Harper, 1959, p. 145.

The success of the C.I.O., it should be emphasized, did not rest on the superiority of industrial unionism as an organizing principle in the American context. What seems to have been much more important was the impetus behind the development of trades unionism as a whole which came from the manual workers' reactions to the depressions of the inter-war years. Their experiences of unemployment and economic insecurity, it has been said, 'dug deep into the consciousness of workers; confidence in employers had generally disappeared; grievances were abundant'. Hence there was a 'spontaneous' growth of 'new' unions, unions for the first time amongst 'factory workers, service workers, and other groups which had previously been outside union ranks,'[1] unions which turned to the C.I.O. rather than to the A.F. of L. for support. The general lack of confidence in employers was also responsible for positive action by the Federal authorities to raise many of the restrictions placed upon the workers to organize by the courts under anti-trust legislation and other statutes, as well as under the common law of the land. The National Labour Board which was set up by the Wagner Act of 1935, in spite of many setbacks, seems to have been instrumental in consolidating the effect of this reaction to economic depression. 'By 1947 the openly anti-union activities which had formerly been common in major corporations as well as in less well-established concerns had largely been eliminated from common practice in industrialized areas and to some extent in others. The labour spy, 'yellow-dog contracts', espionage, discrimination, violence against organizers, and bitter violence on both sides in organizing strikes were no longer usual. . . . To a large extent collective bargaining had been accepted. Some employers accepted it as permanent; others by force of the law and the compulsion of events, but hoping that it was only temporary. Some still fought it actively. But the difference was highly significant between the bitterly fought and violent postwar strikes of 1918–19 and the peaceful though determined strikes over wage issues in 1945–46 with no apparent effort by employers to smash the unions'.[2] The

[1] M. Derber, 'Growth and Expansion' in Milton Derber and E. Young, eds., *Labor and the New Deal*, University of Wisconsin Press, 1957, p. 9.

[2] Harry A. Millis and E. C. Brown, *From the Wagner Act to Taft-Hartley*, University of Chicago Press, 1950, p. 253.

establishment of collective bargaining in America, that is to say, owed much to governments of politicians without a single trade union representative amongst them.

Of course, there is some evidence that the conflict between the A.F. of L. and the C.I.O. was one of conservatism versus reform, not only in an industrial but in a political sense. The debate was between union leaders who thought almost exclusively of trade unionism in terms of collective bargaining and of strengthening their members' position through the development of business-like organizations and those who saw their members as having broader social needs than these, requiring political action for legislative purposes.[1] Of course, the conservative leaders of the A.F. of L. were not altogether indifferent to the need for state action to deal with the serious and widespread unemployment of the 1930's and they had supported the National Industrial Recovery Act of 1933 which was one of the first measures introduced by the New Deal administration. Nevertheless, they seem to have been chary of state interference in particular and of political action in general, asserting that the Labour's Non-Partisan League, formed in 1936 to rally support behind Roosevelt, was a C.I.O. political machine, to which member unions should not give support.[2]

The eventual merger of the A.F. of L. with the C.I.O. in 1955 may be seen, therefore, as in part a consequence of the gradual abandonment of its traditional non-partisanship in politics by the A.F. of L., in response to the unfavourable labour legislation and the administration of such legislation in the post-war years. The merger, indeed, was interpreted at the time as an indication that the Labour movement planned in future to be more active in politics, especially by attempting to influence the Democratic Party,[3] to which the majority of union members' votes had been given for at least the previous fifteen years.[4] Its Committee on Political Education, however, like earlier bodies

[1] James O. Morris, *Conflict within the A.F. of L.*, Cornell, 1958, Ch. 10, *passim*.

[2] Galenson, op. cit., pp. 607–8.

[3] E. E. Witte, 'the New Federation & Political Action', *Industrial and Labor Relations Review*, Vol. 9, 1956, pp. 406–18.

[4] See the Table in Seymour M. Lipset, *Political Man*, Heineman, 1960, p. 286.

within the C.I.O. and the A.F. of L. has apparently been more concerned with pressure-group tactics, supporting even friendly Republican candidates occasionally, than with independent political action.[1] In this regard there is little sign that any but a handful of union leaders are conscious of the need to create a Labour Party of their own.[2]

Why should this be? One possibly important factor, stressed by Perlman[3], derives from the nature of the American political constitution. Not only Congress, but each of the forty-eight States, has the power to legislate on labour matters. In all forty-nine power is divided between an executive body and two houses responsible for legislation. A Labour Party would thus have to fight on a greatly extended front, already firmly contested by two major political parties, and the alternative of working through one of these would not seem unreasonable, granted that the task facing the union leaders, had they set out to create a political machine to fight elections in the 1950's, would have been of much greater magnitude than that tackled by English trade unionists at the end of the nineteenth century. One English observer, indeed, has concluded that the effective differences between America and Britain now are more apparent than real in spite of their historical roots. 'Both American parties attract a far wider area of support than their most important groups, business and labour. But in this respect so do the two British parties. Moreover, probably one third of the members of the British trade unions vote Conservative. . . . The Labour Party has, in practice, abandoned socialism and the Conservatives have embraced the welfare state, although neither party likes to admit its conversion and both claim they have not departed from their pristine positions. . . . In all this there is much that is familiar in the American political scene'.[4]

On the other hand, it must also be emphasized that American trade union leaders demonstrate a striking lack of class-con-

---

[1] Valdimer O. Key, *Politics, Parties and Pressure Groups*, 4th edition, Crowell, 1958, Ch. 3.

[2] William H. Miernyk, *Trade Unions in the Age of Affluence*, Random House, 1965, Ch. 7.

[3] Selig Perlman, *A History of Trade Unionism in the United States*, Macmillan, 1923, pp. 286-7.

[4] Benjamin C. Roberts, *Trade Unions in a Free Society: Studies in the Organisation of Labour in Britain and the U.S.A.*, Hutchinson, 1959.

sciousness, as a Marxist understands it. The Mission of the International Labour Office which went to America in 1959 to examine freedom of association there, reported that it was 'struck in its discussions with union leaders by the almost total absence of any questioning of the bases of the American economic and social system. Unlike many labour movements in Europe and elsewhere, the trade unions in the United States do not appear even to advocate, any major change in the system in which they operate, in spite of the many bitter battles that have occurred between unions and capital'.[1] It is difficult at first sight to understand why this should be, why the American trade union leaders should not show the same kind of characteristics as those which, it was claimed above,[2] justify the union leaders in Britain being regarded as a revolutionary élite, American trade unions are, after all, powerful bodies. In 1963 two of them had more than a million members each, and five others had over half a million each. All seven of these as well as six smaller ones had enrolled at least 80 per cent of the workers in those industries which they organized.[3] Their presidents in this respect might well be termed men of power.

They were also men in receipt of relatively middle-class incomes. For example, 42 of them, surveyed by *Fortune* in 1957, were in receipt of annual salaries of 15,000 dollars or more, rising to as high as 60,000 dollars in one case. The median salary of 75 union presidents was about 16,500 dollars,[4] at a time when the median for the most favoured group of manual workers—male craftsmen, foremen and 'kindred workers'—was 6,000 dollars[5]. Yet the union leaders had not become part of the establishment to the degree that was true of the British trade union élite. Of the 117 major appointments made by President Roosevelt in his early New Deal days only one went to a trade unionist, as compared with nineteen to businessmen. Later Presidents have improved on this but not substantially so.

---

[1] *The Trade Union Situation in the United States*, International Labour Office, 1960, p. 26.

[2] See Ch. 10, *passim*.

[3] John E. Maher, *Labour and the Economy*, Allyn and Bacon, 1965, Table 5-1, p. 72.

[4] *Fortune*, July 1957, summarized in Maher, op. cit., p. 86.

[5] Ibid., p. 271.

Thus, President Eisenhower gave three appointments to trade unionists, and 65 to businessmen out of 180 posts,[1] while President Kennedy who apparently most favoured the trade unions, found room for only 5 in 199 appointments, although since he also reduced the number going to businessmen to 12[2], the relative acceptance of trade unionists into the councils of state in the 1960's as compared with the 1930's parallels on the American side of the Atlantic what has been happening on the British. Nevertheless, to the extent that the analysis of trade union leaders in the first part of this study is correct, American trade unionists might have been expected to react to their situation of status inconsistency by positive demands for changes in the American way of life; and this does not seem to have occurred.

Of course, their failure to demand such classical socialist measures as the social ownership of the major industries in their country should not be interpreted as a complete rejection of everything that the trade union in Britain stands for. As one study has emphasized, at the same time as the organized labour movement has adhered to 'a firm belief in private capitalism and individual freedom . . . unions have generally advocated *collective* improvements for the workers, including both improvements to be won directly from employers and those to be provided by extensive governmental actions in the areas of social security and medical care, progressive (versus regressive) tax systems, free education, regulation of business, public works programmes, fiscal policies to maintain full employment, and similar measures to provide for the security and welfare of the common man'.[3] Yet, as compared with the *promise* of political action which the merger of the A.F. of L. with the C.I.O. was seen to offer in the 1950's, the political realities of the subsequent years demonstrated the union leaders to be anything but militant in their attitude to the government. In the economic recession of 1957–8, for example, when American unemployment rose to 7 per cent, the unions were said to have offered 'nothing but token resistance to the administration's decision that

---

[1] Seymour E. Harris, *The Economics of the Political Parties*, Macmillan, 1962, Table I, p. 22.

[2] Ibid., Table 2, p. 25.

[3] Arthur Kornhauser, *et al.*, *When Labour Votes: a Study of Auto Workers*, University Books, 1956, p. 283. Italics in the original.

potential inflation deserved more consideration than actual joblessness'.[1] Although, indeed, it may have been true that the 'labour leaders were polite in public, but privately bitter'[2] it also seems true that throughout the whole of the Kennedy period 'labour accepted the imposition of guidelines on wage increases and official frowns on use of the strike weapon with only muted complaints'.[3]

Nothing of this alters the fact that the trade union leader, if not a member of the power élite is nevertheless in America, as in Britain, a 'public figure' like the politician and the businessman,[4] inspite of the failure of trade unions to form 'a power-block independent of corporation and state but operating on and against them'.[5] Hence, when he is asked to serve on government bodies along with prominent industrial leaders, much the same kind of consequence is reported as in the British case.[6] Relations between them become cordial and affairs of state are conducted on 'a first-name basis'.[7] This parallels on the political side the change in relations between union leaders and employers which has occurred on the industrial side since the 1930's. What have been termed 'maturing union-management relations' are a continuous feature of the post-depression, post-war years. Although the National Association of Manufacturers in America has consistently condemned the unions, the practice of individual firms, it has been said, 'seems to have disregarded national association pronouncements'.[8] In 1955, for example, 93 of the 171 companies represented on the directorate of the N.A.M. had agreements with A.F.L.–C.I.O. unions, 83 per cent of them with union security clauses, at a time when the N.A.M. was

[1] N. Chamberlain, 'The Corporation and the Trade Union' in Edward S. Mason, ed., *The Corporation in Modern Society*, Harvard University Press, 1959, p. 125.

[2] Hobart Rowen, *The Free Enterprisers: Kennedy, Johnson and the Business Establishment*, Pulnam's Sons, 1964, p. 43.

[3] Ibid., p. 17.

[4] Mills, *The New Men of Power*, op. cit., pp. 13 et seq.

[5] Mills, *The Power Elite*, op. cit., p. 262.

[6] See above, pp. 149–50.

[7] J. Stieber, 'The President's Committee on Labour Management Policy', *Industrial Relations*, Vol. 15, 1966, p. 17.

[8] Richard A. Lester, *As Unions Mature: An Analysis of the Evolution of American Unionism*, Princetown University Press, 1958, p. 41.

resolutely opposed to such clauses.[1] As the International Labour Office Mission put it in 1960, 'in the United States good relations have been built up between employers and workers over a large part of the industrial field. Although it is the strikes and grievances which attract most publicity, more problems are settled by agreement than through conflict. The primary characteristic of labour management relations is not strife but bargaining'.[2] In this regard it is instructive to notice that accounts of the more hostile line taken by American employers in the 1960's do not attribute the rejection of collective bargaining to the situation. On the contrary, it is asserted that the way in which management has taken the initiative is by meeting the unions 'at the bargaining table with a set of counter-proposals'.[3] Thus, what all this suggests is that, inspite of the obvious differences in the style and content of collective bargaining on both sides of the Atlantic, American trade union leaders have willy-nilly found themselves engaged in tactics which have helped to usher in the era of collectivism, for all that they have rejected traditionally European socialist politics and have eschewed state intervention through public ownership as a means of solving their members' economic problems.

From this point of view, 'business' unionism—'the dominant ideology of the American labour movement which perceives unions as fighting for more money rather than for any programme of social reconstruction[4]'—should be examined rather less in terms of the degree to which trade union leaders have accepted the same social standards as employers and rather more in terms of the effect their pursuit of economic advantages for their members may be presumed to have had on the organization of industry. For example, Ulman has argued that it would be difficult to find more 'impressive evidence of American unionists' continued commitment to the method of collective bargaining than that afforded by the dramatic growth, since the end of the Second World War, of those elements of wage-earner income which have been labelled—with increasing inaccuracy—as 'fringe benefits'. These included items which were reflected

---

[1] Ibid., p. 159, n. 7.
[2] *The Trade Union Situation in the United States*, op. cit., p. 108.
[3] Miernyk, op. cit., p. 116.
[4] Seymour M. Lipset, *The First New Nation*, Heinemann, 1964, p. 187.

in current earnings per hour worked, such as paid vacations, holidays, sick leave, and absences from the job by union shop representatives or for jury or National Guard duty or voting purposes; they also included paid time for travel, clothes change, wash-up, lunch, rest, etc. Other fringe items can be regarded as deferred pay and consisted principally in employer payments into employee pension and supplementary unemployment benefit plans, on the one hand, and so called 'health and welfare fund' on the other. The latter insured wage earners against death, disability, and non-occupational sickness and accidents, and many provided medical or surgical services in kind or on a non-profit, pre-payment basis'.[1]

Although it is not possible to make a detailed and systematic study of this development over time, it is worth noting that an American Chamber of Commerce survey reported an increase in such 'fringe' benefits, exclusive of what was required by law, from 12·1 per cent of the payroll in 1947 to 20·5 per cent in 1957.[2] Of course, it would be a mistake to regard these as equivalent to the kinds of services provided under the notion of the 'Welfare State' in the British context, as only about 40 per cent of workers in America were covered at that time; but in so far as what was achieved in the period was a direct result of collective bargaining, it is clear that some of the incentive to agitate publicly for social change was weakened by the very fact that employers made such concessions.

Or, again, a number of writers have held that the purely economic militancy, which seems to characterize business unionism, is 'one of the major factors contributing to the pattern of innovation which characterizes the economy'.[3] The success of unions in pressing for wage and fringe increases, that is to say, is seen as forcing employers to increase their capital expenditure on labour-saving equipment and so to raise productivity. While it is possible to counter this argument with evidence that

[1] L. Ulman, 'Unionism and Collective Bargaining in the Modern Period' in Seymour E. Harris, ed., *American Economic History*, McGraw-Hill, 1961, pp. 436–7.

[2] *Fringe Benefits*, Washington, 1958, Table 18, p. 28, referred to in Ulman, op. cit., pp. 437 and 459, p. 39.

[3] Lipset, *The First New Nation*, op. cit., p. 197, and the references in note 26, p. 198.

wage increases tend rather to raised prices and inflation[1] and hence to conclude that this is 'a strange doctrine and . . . part of the mythology of technological change',[2] it is nevertheless true that, whatever the cause, the *increase* in the productivity of labour in the United States since the end of the Second World War has been greater than 'the *total* output obtained per hour of work in most regions of the earth'.[3] To the extent, therefore, that successful collective bargaining, along with competition and other presumed advantages, may possibly have been one of the factors inducing employers to mechanize, the rapid increase in the capital-labour ratio is likely to have provided an impetus to the growth of large-scale production and hence have hastened on the trend towards collectivism in the private sector of the economy. Thus, while it is clear that the degree of concentration in America is far short of monopoly, it is also clear that a relatively large section of the working population in industry is employed by a very small number of firms.[4]

At the same time, the corporate revolution in America, first identified as such by Berle and Means in the inter-war years,[5] may now be said to be 'close to complete'.[6] Whereas 12 of the 200 largest non-financial corporations in 1929 were still privately owned, none were so owned in 1963. Whereas 89 in 1929 were subject to what Berle and Means called 'management' control, that is, control by a self-perpetuating oligarchy of directors, by 1963 the number had risen to 169.[7] Of course this American experience merely confirms the general argument of Chapter Eleven above, namely, that the movement towards a collectivist society proceeds irrespective of government action.[8] Whether trade unions press for public ownership

[1] Maher, op. cit., Ch. 15, *passim.*

[2] Ibid., p. 394.

[3] S. Fabricant, 'Basic Facts on Productivity Change', an introduction to John W. Kendrick, *Productivity Trends in the United States*, Princetown University Press, 1961, p. xxxvii.

[4] Edward S. Mason, *Economic Concentration and the Monopoly Problem*, Harvard University Press, 1957, Ch. 1, *passim.*

[5] See above, pp. 95–6.

[6] R. J. Larner, 'Ownership and Control in the 200 largest nonfinancial corporations, 1929 and 1963', *The American Economic Review*, Vol. 56, Part I, 1966, p. 787.

[7] Ibid., Table I, p. 781.

[8] See above, pp. 170–3.

of the means of production and welfare state measures, as in
Britain, or confine themselves to militant collective bargaining,
as in the United States, the general trend in the economy is very
much the same—away from capitalist exploitation towards a
new social form in which employment is in large units, controlled
by men of considerable economic power, and determining the
prices of the products by administrative *fiat* rather than by
reference to the ebb and flow of costs. The steel industry in
America, indeed, seems an excellent case in point; for, the steel
firms have uniform prices for basic steel and steel products,
which follow those set by United States Steel. Thus, it has been
argued, 'U.S. Steel has, in a fashion that has become almost
standardized, raised prices whenever there is a wage boost, but
without setting a norm for return to be earned as part of the
standard cost. Unless the comments of other firms in the industry
are discounted, U.S. Steel is sitting on the lid of the steel price
pot'.[1]

In this connection it is interesting to notice a feature of difference in British and American experience at this level which
nevertheless confirms the essential validity of the argument. The
income of executives in the United States contains an element
of some magnitude which is lacking in equivalent British incomes. This arises from the opportunity which American corporate executives have to purchase the stock of their companies
at favourable prices.[2] The whole point of such stock 'options',
it should be understood, is to permit the employee to sell the
stock when prices rise. There is no question here of increasing
his voting power as against those of other shareholders. Thus,
whereas under the classical concept of capitalism it is the ownership of property which gives the employer power to extort
surplus labour from employees, under the American collectivist
system it is the executive's position in the firm which gives him
power to obtain property as a source of *extra* income, just as it is
this position which enables him to charge to the company's
accounts personal expenses which are difficult to estimate but

[1] Abraham D. H. Kaplan, *et al.*, *Pricing in Big Business: A Case Approach*,
Brookings Institution, 1958, p. 275.

[2] Merrett, *Executive Remuneration*, op. cit., pp. 56–7. For details, see
Leonard R. Burgess, *Top Executive Pay Package*, Free Press of Glencoe, 1963,
Ch. 4.

which are nevertheless part of his income and often considerable.[1]

At the same time, this practice of making stock ownership part of the remuneration of executives has the effect of maintaining certain of the features of capitalist profit-making and dividend distribution, and hence of perpetuating the impression that the American economy has not gone so far along the road to collectivism as the British—an impression which is also perpetuated in another way by the wider dispersion of stock ownership throughout the community over there than in this country. Yet, that this latter is largely illusory as a sign of 'People's Capitalism' has been challenged by reference to the smaller percentage of the American population owning stock in 1956 than in 1930;[2] and stock holding by institutions rather than by individuals has been increasing steadily in both countries. It is to be expected, therefore, that the difference in collectivism between the two economies is one of degree rather than of substance, and if this is taken together with the marked similarities in the two systems of collective bargaining, it is difficult to avoid the conclusion that the cultural differences which emerge, when America is contrasted with Britain, demonstrate variations merely on a general theme. In this sense it is possible to use an amended Marxist analysis for the analysis of both systems. However, it should also be clear from this brief account of the American case, that detailed analysis requires a much closer attention to the sources of difference than has been possible here. At least as close a scrutiny of the American coal and steel unions as was given in the Second Part of this study to those in Britain would be required if the arguments of this book are to be maintained. All that this chapter has shown is that no *major* departures from the previously used analytical framework are required to account for the obvious differences which exist.

[1] Burgess, op. cit., Ch. 5, *passim*, see also Gabriel Kolko, *Wealth and Power in America*, Thomas and Hudson, 1962, pp. 16–20.

[2] V. Perlo, ' "People's Capitalism" and "Stock Ownership" ', *The American Economic Review*, Vol. 68, 1958, p. 336.

17

RANK-AND-FILE PARTICIPATION

The essence of Marx's attitude towards the factory worker of his day was compassion. Some of the most memorable passages in *Capital* are bitter in their denunciation of conditions of work so appalling as to dehumanize human beings. His alienation thesis may in this sense be said to have been derived from his agony—the agony of an intellectual—at the spectacle of fellow men and women becoming 'crippled monstrosities',[1] unable to gain satisfaction from their labour and rendered incapable of contributing to the progressive development of mankind. Marx's conception of a classless society, in consequence, contained within it the notion that it would provide the optimum opportunity 'for the free development, intellectual and social, of the individual'.[2] Of course, Marx's materialism made it inevitable that he would emphasize the overriding need, even in such a society, to continue the struggle with the natural environment for the satisfaction of physical wants. Indeed, he went further than materialism, crudely understood, by pointing out that the advance of civilization actually extended the 'realm of necessity' by increasing those wants *at the same* time as it made their satisfaction continuously easier by extending the powers of production. Altogether then, in Marx's view, man's capacity to escape from the restraints of his biological heritage is very limited, and it is only beyond the realm of necessary labour that there 'begins that development of human energy which is an end in itself, the true realm of freedom, which, however, can blossom forth only with this realm of necessity as its

[1] K. Marx, *Capital*, Vol. I, op. cit., p. 360.
[2] Ibid., p. 530; see also ibid., p. 592.

basis. The shortening of the working day is its basic prerequisite'.[1]

Nevertheless, Marx also believed that within the realm of necessity itself the passing of capitalism would be accompanied by modifications in the nature of work which would make it more bearable to the worker. Technical changes within the factory, as early as the 1860's, were compelling 'society, under penalty of death, to replace the detail-worker . . . crippled by life-long repetition of one and the same trivial operation and thus reduced to the mere fragment of a man, by the fully developed individual, fit for a variety of labours, ready to face any change of production, and to whom the different social functions he performs are but so many modes of giving free scope to his own natural and acquired powers'. The establishment of technical and agricultural schools, he thought, was a step already taken 'spontaneously' in this direction. The provision in the English Factory Acts for elementary education to be provided for apprentices alongside work in the factories was another, although it would not be until the working class obtained power, 'as inevitably it must,' that 'technical instruction, both theoretical and practical, will take its proper place in the working-class schools'.[2] It is perhaps not altogether clear what Marx had in mind here, but his reference to both theoretical and practical instruction would seem to give some support to Braybrooke's argument that he was demanding that every individual should be given the opportunity to develop and to exercize not only many skills, but manual and intellectual skills alike.[3]

Moreover, and this is perhaps the more important facet of his conception of the future society, Marx thought of freedom in the work itself—that limited freedom possible in the realm of necessity—as consisting in 'the associated producers, rationally regulating their interchange with Nature, bringing it under their common control, instead of being ruled by it as by the blind forces of Nature, and achieving this with the least expenditure of energy and under conditions most favourable to,

---

[1] Marx, *Capital*, Vol. III, op. cit., pp. 799–800.

[2] Marx, *Capital*, Vol. I, op. cit., p. 488.

[3] David Braybrooke, 'Diagnosis and Remedy in Marx's Doctrine of Alienation', *Social Research*, Vol. 25, 1958, p. 337.

and worthy of, their human nature'.[1] Obviously, this type of association most exemplified for Marx in the producers' co-operatives of his day, was structurally very different from capitalist enterprise in which the employer decided the form and extent of his employees' 'interchange with Nature' and required them to put in more than 'the least expenditure of energy' in order that he might extort surplus labour from their efforts. For present purposes, therefore, what is relevant to consider is not the advent of the classless society as such but whether, as capitalism is superseded by collectivism, workers have become more involved in the 'rational' regulation and 'common control' of their work. Have there been spontaneous developments within the enterprise which have resulted in employees becoming to some degree, at least, participants along with managers and the new ruling class of industry in the processes which dominate so much of their lives?

There should be no confusion about this point. A fully class-less society, by definition, could contain no individuals who could make such decisions without first being empowered to by those to whom the decisions apply and without being regularly held accountable for these decisions. Some surplus labour would inevitably be a feature of such a society to cover 're-placement of the means of production used up . . . expansion of production . . . accidents, dislocations caused by national calamities, etc. . . . The general costs of administration not belonging to production . . . the common satisfaction of needs such as schools, health services, etc. . . . funds for those unable to work, etc'.[2] Although there is no record of how Marx himself envisaged that such provisions would be decided, it seems un-likely that he had anything in mind other than some kind of democratic procedure. Indeed, enthused at one time by the Paris Commune of 1870, he wrote as if he believed his ideal would be attained through the self-government of the various associations of producers which would constitute the operating units of the post-capitalist economy. Clearly such a society would require to regulate national production 'upon a common plan' and at this time Marx seems to have thought that this

[1] Marx, *Capital*, Vol. III, op. cit., p. 800.
[2] Karl Marx, *Critique of the Gotha Program* in Marx and Engels, *Selected Works*, op. cit., Vol. 2, pp. 20–1.

could be achieved through some kind of federation of associations, what he termed 'united co-operative societies'.[1]

This notion, of course, was compatible with his long-standing conviction that the state was destined to wither away, but the controversy in the First International with Bakunin[2] suggests that this interpretation is perhaps too facile. However, whatever form might eventually be taken by the national organization of associated producers, it can hardly be doubted that some kind of democratic participation in the decision-making process within the post-capitalist factory was a pre-requisite for Marx, partly because he believed that the dignity of the labourer as a human being required it, and partly because without it there could be no guarantee that alienation would come to an end. The classless alternative to capitalism—under which the worker looks at 'the social nature of his labour, and at the combination with the labour of others for a common purpose, as he would at an alien power',[3]—could only be self-determination in the factories —that is, some form of industrial democracy.

At the present time, to be sure, the term 'industrial democracy' is employed with so many different meanings, ranging, as W. H. Scott has pointed out, 'from proposals for outright workers' control of industry to the establishment of advisory and non-union canteen committees' that it is verily 'in danger of becoming a shibboleth, so vague and ambiguous as to have little or no general meaning'.[4] Nevertheless, the mere fact that

---

[1] Karl Marx, 'Address of the General Council of the International Working Man's Association on the Civil War in France, 1871' in Marx and Engels, *Selected Works*, op. cit., Vol. 1, p. 474.

[2] Franz Mehring, *Karl Marx: the Story of His Life*, translated by E. Fitzgerald, Bodley Head, 1936, Ch. 14. George D. H. Cole, *A History of Socialist Thought Vol. 2, Marxism and Anarchism, 1850–1890*, Macmillan, 1954, pp. 117 et seq.

[3] Marx, *Capital*, Vol. III, op. cit., p. 85. Presumably, the reference in this passage to 'factories owned by the labourers themselves, as in Rochdale' in which such alienation was unknown, was to the Rochdale District Co-operative Corn Mill Society, rather than to the distributive co-operative, the Rochdale Equitable Pioneers' Society. See George J. Holyoake, *Self-Help by the People: The History of Co-operation In Rochdale*, Part II, 1857–1877, Trubner, 1878, Ch. 7.

[4] William H. Scott, *Industrial Democracy: a Revaluation*, Liverpool University Press, 1955, p. 7.

the expression has such wide currency suggests that a change has occurred in the circumstances of the rank-and-file worker, as compared with those of his grandfather and great-grandfather, which is of some significance. From being hands merely, workers have come to be perceived, and treated, as social animals whose share in the work process is influenced, if not conditioned, by the nature and quality of the relations they have with one another and with their industrial superiors. In ideological terms this change may be said to have taken place in accompaniment with the rise to importance of what is now known as the 'human relations school of managment'—'human relations' being a collectivist conception which has been defined as 'the integration of people into a work situation in a way that motivates them to work together productively, co-operatively, and with economic, psychological, and social satisfaction.[1]

Possibly, some notion on the part of employers, especially in America, that there were advantages in appealing to, and dealing with, individual workers rather than with their trade unions, gave some impetus to this development;[2] but the internal re-organization of modern industry in response to technical and other innovations which have continuously introduced new tasks and new occupations into firms, together with the steady growth in the number of people employed by them, would seem to have created the same type of circumstances everywhere, irrespective of whether trade unions are partners in collective bargaining arrangements or not. As an extreme case of the kinds of situation facing modern management the 'world government' of the Standard Oil Company of New Jersey indicates the magnitude of the organizational problems to be faced. Standard Oil employs well over 100,000 employees. It has 77 subsidiaries in the United States alone, 37 in Canada, 24 in Great Britain, and a further 137 scattered elsewhere

---

[1] Keith Davis, *Human Relations in Business*, McGraw-Hill, 1957, p. 4. Davis dates what he calls 'the age of human relations' as 'beginning about 1945, near the end of World War II', ibid., p. 7. Compare Loren Baritz, *The Servants of Power*, Wiley Science Edition, 1965, p. 142. 'It was the experience of World War II that finally convinced a significant number of America's managers that they needed help to solve the human problems of industry.'

[2] Reinhard Bendix, *Work and Authority*, op. cit., p. 287.

throughout the world.[1] Clearly the fourteen 'working' members which constitute its board of directors cannot control such an empire without considerable delegation of authority and they cannot do even this directly. They must operate, that is to say, by means of remote control, using for the most part written and other symbolic devices for communicating with those who are empowered to take decisions on the board's behalf. Of course, being 'multi-national',[2] the firm is faced with many problems of communications with customers, government officials and other people in the various countries where its operating units are located; but even internally the difficulties which threaten the transmission of commands from above to below and of information below to above are numerous. The 'integration' of more than 100,000 employees into a single working unit, so that they work together 'harmoniously' is a task which pioneer factory capitalists who could, if they choose, know every one of their employers personally, never had to face.

The whole history of the invention of social science techniques to aid modern managers to increase production and lower costs may thus be seen in this connection as deriving in large part from the bewilderment, not only of the directors of modern enterprises but of their managerial subordinates, at the complex problems of communication at second, third and fourth hand and more remotely. In particular they are regularly confronted with a marked contrast between their conception of the organization as a tightly-built, going concern, over which they have undisputed powers of direction, and their every-day experience of indications that some of the rank-and-file workers somewhere have failed to become 'good' organization men as they would like to have them. This is often their most persistent business worry. In the words of a Standard Oil executive in September 1954, 'the biggest competitive advantage that Esso can gain lies in continuing to build initiative, co-operation, and

[1] Paul A. Baran and Paul M. Sweezy, *Monopoly Capital*, Penguin Books, 1968, Table 6, p. 194. Statistics for 1962.

[2] D. Lilienthal, 'The Multinational Corporation' in Melvin Anshen and G. L. Bach, eds., *Management and Corporations*, 19—, McGraw-Hill, 1960, p. 119. Such corporations are those 'which have their home in one country but which operate and live under laws and customs of other countries as well'.

the will to work within our people'.[1] This will to work, or
rather the evidence of a certain unwillingness in this regard as
manifested in absenteeism, 'malingering', labour-turnover,
restrictive practices, wild-cat strikes, etc., had prompted
managements, even enthusiastically from time to time, to
employ professional experts in time-and-motion study, in-
telligence and other testing for employee selection, rating
scales for fixing remuneration and determining promotions,
personnel counselling, and the conduct of attitude surveys
on likes and dislikes at work[2]—all designed to make the large-
scale factory into an effective social system for achieving the
aims and purposes, ostensibly of all who work in it. Yet, industrial sociologists continue to be impressed by the signs of
rejection which rank-and-file workers continue to show. In this
sense they would probably agree with Blauner that 'alienation
is not a consequence of capitalism *per se* but of employment in
large-scale organizations and impersonal bureaucracies that
pervade all industrial societies'.[3]

It should be understood that human relations policies are
not the only ones which have been found to be relatively unsuccessful in promoting solidarity with the company. In
Britain some firms have sought to inculcate a sense of loyalty
amongst the rank-and-file by introducing schemes of joint consulation, designed to give employees a modicum of participation
in the running of the plant. These have largely taken the form
of works' committees, composed of delegates appointed from
amongst managers and representatives elected by workers, set
up to discuss 'matters of common concern which are outside
the scope of the negotiating machinery'.[4] During both World
Wars, indeed, the government actively encouraged such committees, expressly for the improvement of productivity and the
more effective use of the labour force in the war effort. After
both World Wars it seem to have hoped that private employers
would continue the practice. For the newly nationalized in-

[1] Quoted in Baritz, op. cit., p. 169.
[2] For examples of Standard Oil's acceptance of such techniques more or
less as they arose, from the 1920's onwards, see Baritz, op. cit., p. 48 (rating
scales), p. 151 (attitude surveys), and p. 164 (counselling).
[3] Blauner, op. cit., p. 3.
[4] Ministry of Labour, *Industrial Relations Handbook*, op. cit., p. 126.

dustries after the Second World War, moreover, an elaborate system was written into the legislation.[1] It has, however, as Clegg has pointed out, been 'much easier to write of joint consultation's subsequent history as a failure than to discover its successes'.[2] In mining, for example, its effect on raising productivity and reducing strikes and absenteeism has been minimal.[3] Even the apparent aims of the system have not been realized. The notion of employee participation through joint consultation, that is to say, entails the dynamic conceptions that management originates consultation, the staff representatives respond to such moves with suggestions, and management subsequently follows with action along lines *mutually agreed upon*. In practice, if a careful study of a nationalized industry in 1956 and 1957 is any guide, management begins by originating action, not consultation. The staff representatives thereupon raise questions on the action or air complaints at the next available committee meeting. At this meeting management delegates either agree to reshape the action or to refer the matter, as a 'difference' which has to be decided at a higher organizational level.[4] On the whole, as a form of industrial democracy, joint consultation may thus be said to have failed largely because 'management has not made it work';[5] and workers' representatives who have been reported as showing a very real interest in their responsibilities under the system, have also been reported as remaining unconvinced of their firm's willingness to use it as a viable means of consultation.[6]

It is true that they have also been reported to be rather critical of their constituent electors' lukewarm acceptance of the system as a possible means of access to management which might be made to work;[7] but the contrast between what now

[1] *The Framework of Joint Consultation*, Action Society Trust, 1952.
[2] Hugh A. Clegg, *A New Approach to Industrial Democracy*, op. cit., p. 36.
[3] Ibid., pp. 36–7.
[4] F. Fuerstenberg, 'The Dynamics of Joint Consultation', *British Journal of Sociology*, Vol. 10, 1959, p. 211.
[5] Clegg, op. cit., p. 41.
[6] William H. Scott, *Industrial Leadership and Joint Consultation*, University Press of Liverpool, 1952, Ch. 6, *passim*. Banks, *Industrial Participation*, op. cit., pp. 53–4.
[7] Scott, *Industrial Leadership*, op. cit., Chs. 3 and 4. National Institute of Industrial Psychology, *Joint Consultation in British Industry*, Staples, 1952, p. 211.

appears to have been a marked decline in the effective practice of joint consultation since the end of the Second World War and the growing numbers of shop stewards,[1] suggests that the rank-and-file workers prefer their representatives to be concerned with issues of collective bargaining rather than with 'lavatories, canteens, and the iniquities of foremen'.[2] It is also likely, as the Trades Union Congress argued in its *Evidence* to the Royal Commission on Trade Unions and Employers' Associations, that the formal machinery of collective bargaining is already beginning to encompass the content of jobs as well as pay and working conditions, and that the latter are already being extended to such matters as safety, training and redundancy.[3] What evidence there is on these points, indeed, indicates not only that the range of the shop stewards' responsibilities has been growing but that in their relations with managers, 'a relatively high degree of mutual toleration among the parties, based on an understanding of differences in their respective positions and roles in the process of workshop relations', has emerged.[4] The process of 'humanising' work, that is to say, seems to have entailed the recognition of the shop-floor representative as a person who speaks responsibly and with authority for his fellow workers.[5] The frequency with which shop stewards are apparently seen by managers as likely people for promotion to supervising posts within the factory,[6] may be interpreted as a device on their part for depriving the rank-and-file of an effective mouthpiece; but experience since the war would surely have taught them by now that as one shop-floor leader goes, another is soon found to take his place. The alternative interpretation, therefore, that the shop stewards' knowledge of rank-and-file attitudes is positively valuable to management, would seem to be more reasonable. In this respect, the institutionalization of collective bargaining at the shop-floor level, like the pursuance of a human-relations policy, may be seen as a response to

---

[1] McCarthy and Parker, op. cit., p. 15.

[2] George S. Walpole, *Management and Men: a Study of the Theory and Practice of Joint Consultation at all Levels*, Cape, 1944, p. 94.

[3] *Trade Unionism*, op. cit., p. 100.

[4] McCarthy and Parker, op. cit., p. 67.

[5] Ibid., pp. 30–3.

[6] Clegg, Killick and Adams, op. cit., pp. 174–7.

the complexities of running a modern, large-scale, and largely bureaucratic enterprise.

A word on the concept of bureaucracy is in order here. In its original sociological formulation, the term was applied by Max Weber to a particular type of administration. 'The development of the modern form of the organization of corporate groups in all fields', he wrote, 'is nothing less than identical with the development and continued spread of bureucratic administration. This is true of church and state, of armies, political parties, economic enterprises, organizations to promote all kinds of causes, private associations, clubs, and many others'.[1] The explanation for this development, he thought, lay in the necessity for large-scale organizations to escape from 'dilettantism' in the administration of their affairs. What they required was 'stable, strict, intensive, and calculable administration',[2] and this was most adequately provided by a carefully selected, properly qualified, and continuously functioning bureaucratic staff, the members of which might be referred to as 'officials' irrespective of whether the organization they served was 'devoted to political, religious, economic—in particular, capitalistic—or other ends'.[3]

Subsequent analysis of bureaucracy by sociologists has tended to concentrate in large part on the degree to which, as a matter of fact, administrative personnel perform their roles in the way Weber indicated and especially to emphasize the unintended consequences of the growth in importance of such officials.[4] Where attention has been drawn to other personnel in large-scale organizations, the focus has been on the distinction between the 'line' and the 'staff', between 'bureaucrats' and 'professionals', another important and growing body of employees who are also carefully selected, properly qualified, and

---

[1] Max Weber, *The Theory of Social and Economic Organisation*, op. cit., p. 301.

[2] Ibid., p. 310.

[3] Ibid., p. 304. All this is from Weber's *Wirtschaft und Gesellschaft* (Economy and Society), Part I. A more elaborate treatment of the topic is given in Part III, translated as 'Bureaucracy' in Weber, *Essays in Sociology*, op. cit., Ch. 8.

[4] See, for example, the collection of papers in Robert K. Merton, *et al.*, eds., *Reader in Bureaucracy*, The Free Press, 1952.

continuously functioning.[1] To some extent, this concentration on the middle and upper reaches of the industrial hierarchy has obscured the fact that, in passing, Weber referred to two other categories of people involved in the activities of large-scale organizations, *in addition to* the administrative staff, and presumably, therefore, not part of the bureaucracy as such. These were what he referred to as employees[2] and workers' on the one hand,[3] and those 'at the top of a bureaucratic organization . . . an element which is at least not purely bureaucratic,'[4] on the other. In the present context, these would be the rank-and-file workers, both manual and clerical, and the members of the board of control of the enterprise, together with those top executives who sit regularly with the board to decide broad issues of policy, to allocate resources, to determine priorities, and to lay down the principles on which the division of the product will be carried out.

The most obvious feature of large-scale enterprise, of course, is that these two non-bureaucratic elements have no contact with each other, save through the mediation of the administrative hierarchy. Hence the claim of the representatives of rank-and-file employees for some voice in decision making is likely to be seen by the bureaucrats as *both* an attempt to go over their heads directly to the seats of power, *and* a challenge to their definition of what is administratively viable. From the bureaucratic point of view, promotion from one level of responsibility and authority to a higher one properly depends upon the acquisition of further qualifications, through formal education and training, or through demonstrated capacity in the job. It is true that the latter is sometimes equated simply with seniority but in such cases, seniority itself is regarded as a valuable form of experience. In any case, promotion is based always on the judgement of a bureaucrat's superiors that advancement has

[1] For an excellent survey and discussion, see the introduction by Amitai Etzioni, *Modern Organizations*, Prentice-Hall, 1964, Ch. 8.

[2] In the original German, *Angestellten*, a term which is almost impossible to translate. It refers to employees receiving a salary or a *fixed* wage; in a bank or office, a clerk; in a shop, a shop assistant. *Der Angestelltenverband* is translated as the Union of (German) Salaried Employees. Trevor Jones, ed., *Harrap's Standard German and English Dictionary*, Vol. 1, Harrap, 1963, p. 85.

[3] Weber, *Theory*, op. cit., pp. 304, 310.

[4] Ibid., p. 308.

been earned.[1] There is, obviously, no room here for the notion that the responsibilities and authority of a *representative*, elected by his peers, should be determined by them and them alone. Shop stewards, or joint-consultation representatives for that matter are 'entitled' to just as much responsibility and authority as managers deem it administratively reasonable for them to have; and the consequence of this point of view is that the rank-and-file employees can increase their share of power in this situation, only to the extent that through strike action or by militant collective bargaining they can wrest concessions from managements. This is the sense in which it is correct to talk of unions as representing a challenge to management power, a challenge which is resisted by the administrators and their spokesmen on the grounds that 'it is undoubtedly management's duty to manage; and management's proper function must be preserved'.[2] In the British context, such an ideology is referred to as 'managerial prerogative', a doctrine which holds 'that matters not settled in collective agreements should be decided by managers, although managers can if they wish consult with their employees, or representatives of their employees, before taking their decisions'.[3] In the British context, too, managerial prerogative covers the working of overtime, the recruitment and dismissal of workers, the manning of machines, the pace of work, and the introduction of new machines and new jobs.[4]

All this is important in the present context, because it helps to clarify a confusion which sometimes obscures discussions about workers' participation, when a parallel is drawn between the intentional oligarchy of bureaucratic management and the unintended results of what is often seen as the oligarchic tendencies of administration in trade unions. Some reference to

[1] R. Dubin, 'Technical Characteristics of a Bureaucracy' in Robert Dubin, ed., *Human Relations in Administration*, 2nd edition, Prentice-Hall, 1961, pp. 142–7.

[2] Peter F. Drucker, *The New Society*, Heinemann, 1951, p. 273. Ch. 35 of this book deals with the shop steward's role as seen from this point of view.

[3] *Report of the Royal Commission on Trades Unions and Employers' Associations*, op. cit., p. 24.

[4] Ibid., p. 25. See also pp. 105–6 where the Royal Commission attributes most unofficial strikes to disputes over managerial decisions, executed in the light of this prerogative.

Michels' 'iron law of oligarchy' has already been made above.[1] Here the main point to notice is not the argument that the elected leaders wish to stay in office and the rank-and-file members do not wish to participate in union politics,[2] but that in their dealings with managements and the departments of state, trade unions have perforce been obliged to create an administrative system, run on bureaucratic lines, which controls the formal means of communication within the union *on behalf* of the leadership.

To the extent that such a system is as a matter of fact officered by specially selected, properly qualified, and continuously functioning personnel, elements of bureaucracy, as described earlier, are likely to have permeated into the administration of trade union affairs. The questions to be answered, therefore, are whether unions now appoint rather than elect individuals to fill administrative posts, and if so, what proportion of such posts are filled by selection from above rather than by election from the same level, and whether this proportion has been increasing over time. It should be emphasized, of course, that the basis of the distinction here is between those who make the decision when offices are filled, a man's superiors in the hierarchy or his peers. When a trade union officer continues in office for a long period, either because there are no other candidates nominated for election, or because he is consistently returned at the top of the poll, the effect on the office *itself* is not to convert it from one filled by a representative to one filled by an appointee, however much this particular individual acquires oligarchic characteristics in his dealings with fellow unionists. The office still remains open to be won by election at some time, whereas bureaucratic posts, correctly understood, are never open in this sense.

It should also be emphasized that within a trade union the classification of offices as voluntary and part-time or as full-time is not a classification of them as filled by elected as compared with selected personnel, although as a general rule appointees are full-time. The correct terminological distinction between representative and bureaucratic posts, that is to say, is between those filled by union *officers* and those filled by their

---

[1] Pp. 84–5.
[2] Lipset, *et al.*, op. cit., pp. 10–13.

administrative *staff*;[1] and it is of some interest in this context to notice that trade unions are sometimes held to be at fault to oblige their elected officers to undertake routine and other auxiliary administrative chores, for which they could employ specialist personnel. As Roberts has commented, 'the resistance of most union executives to increasing the size of administrative staffs, arises to some extent from a genuine fear of the danger of building up a large bureaucracy. And there is always the consciousness that in this aspect of administration the active members will be vigilant and suspicious'.[2]

Thus, although the question about the possibility that there has occurred a growth in the proportion of bureaucratic employment in trade unions cannot be answered at all accurately, and although it does not seem unreasonable to suppose that there has been some increase over the years, the general impression which remains is that the union ideology has a built-in opposition to bureaucratization *per se*. This, together with information about the defeat in elections of several sitting union presidents in America, to say nothing of a long history of closely fought elections for the post of general secretary in at least one British union,[3] serves to introduce some caution about applying the 'iron law' too readily. As Gouldner has put it,'even as Michels himself saw, if oligarchical waves repeatedly wash away the bridge of democracy, this eternal recurrence can happen only because men doggedly rebuild them after each inundation. Michels chose to dwell on only one aspect of this process, neglecting to consider the other side. There cannot be an iron law of oligarchy, however, unless there is an iron law of democracy'.[4]

The correct procedure to follow in an examination of the difficulties in the way of participation by the rank-and-file members of a trade union, therefore, is not to confuse their situation with that of the rank-and-file employees in large-scale

[1] Clegg, Killick and Adams, op. cit., pp. 19–20 and Ch. 7, *passim*.

[2] Roberts, *Trade Union Government*, op. cit., p. 309.

[3] J. D. Edelstein, 'Democracy in a National Union: The British A.E.U.', *Industrial Relations*, Vol. 4, 1965, pp. 105–25.

[4] A. W. Gouldner, 'Metaphysical Pathos and the Theory of Bureaucracy', *American Political Science Review*, Vol. 49, 1955, reprinted in part in Amitai Etzioni, ed., *Complex Organisations: A Sociological Reader*, Holt, Rinehart and Winston, 1962, p. 80.

enterprise, but rather to examine the institutional and psychological problems of federalized democracy.[1] The geographical dispersion of union members, for example, which tends to result in the responsibility for decision-making being concentrated above the level of the local leaders,[2] may be regarded as a type of organizational imperative which leads to an administrative device with the unintended result that, to be effective, democratic pressure must be directed higher up the union hierarchy than is the case where the membership is not so dispersed. This means that trade unions may be expected to differ in their practices of democratic control, according to characteristically different modes of organization which they invent to meet the special circumstances of their members. This parallels on the side of democratic participation what happens in collective bargaining, where shop stewards seek to by-pass supervisors and lower ranks of management when they discover that these are virtually powerless to make the kinds of decision which a dispute is about.

Of course, nothing of this should be taken to imply that trade unions are not faced with certain oligarchic tendencies, such as an elected official deliberately, or often largely unconsciously, manipulating the system of communication within a union to his own advantage, or to further the aims of an outside organization.[3] Nor need it be denied that, in being able to develop public-speaking and other *political* skills to a degree denied to rank-and-file members who spend their lives in routine manual or clerical work, full-time trade union leaders are able to concentrate power in their own hands. These are, indeed, features of large-scale organization which trade unions have in common with industrial enterprises. Nevertheless, such oligarchical similarities should not be so over-emphasized as to obscure the differences in direct opportunity to participate which divide the two systems—differences which arise from the democratic ideology of trade unionism on the one hand and the oligarchic ideology of business management on the other—or,

[1] J. D. Edelstein, 'An Organizational Theory of Union Democracy', *American Sociological Review*, Vol. 22, 1967, pp. 19–31.

[2] E. E. Raphael, 'Power Structure and Membership Dispersal in Unions', *American Journal of Sociology*, Vol. 71, 1965, pp. 271–84.

[3] Cecil H. Rolph, *All Those in Favour*, Deutsch, 1962.

rather, since bureaucratic managerialism contains the notion that it is a system of control not merely by the few but by those who are selected because they are believed to be best qualified to administer, the contrast is between a democratic and an aristocratic ideology.

More precisely understood, in fact, the bureaucratic ideology, because it is based not upon birth but upon attainment, upon the acquisition of scarce skills learned through formal education, is a particular form of the aristocratic idea. Bureaucrats, and for that matter, the professionals in industrial organizations constitute what has been called a 'meritocracy',[1] that is, a system of administration in which power is proportionate to the level of formal education attained. The ideology of contemporary industrial enterprises justifies on meritocratic grounds a structure of authority in which those with the best academic qualifications may rise to the top where they are entitled to make decisions about the allocation of resources, because the rank-and-file and those on the intermediate levels of authority are deemed to have insufficient knowledge and to lack the necessary skills to decide such issues for themselves. In this respect, collectivism demonstrates that it is a class society, like capitalism, feudalism and despotism before it; for, from the notion of merit flows also the belief that the top administrators are similarly entitled to determine the structure of rewards which pertains to the system of authority. The great body of bureaucrats, to be sure, do not make decisions of this kind. They merely carry out instructions which come to them from above, but as Weber pointed out,[2] the bureaucratic office entails the concept of 'career' in that it offers to its incumbents the opportunity to move 'from the lower, less important, and lower paid to the higher positions', and it is a mark of the status consciousness[3] of what might be termed the petty-administration, that they see themselves, correctly for the most part, as *not* having interests in common with the rank-and-file employees but as possessing ruling-class potential. Some of them will certainly rise to become top decision-makers one day.

[1] Michael Young, *The Rise of the Meritocracy, 1870–2033*, Thames and Hudson, 1958.
[2] Weber, *Essays*, op. cit., p. 203.
[3] See above, p. 162.

It is also a feature of the meritocratic idea, as contrasted with aristocracy in its classical form, that the system of authority which it justifies is essentially open. Any rank-and-file worker can enter the hierarchy, if he takes the trouble to obtain the necessary qualifications; or, since it is recognized that nowadays the first step on the ladder to the top is almost wholly confined to those who have obtained a degree by going straight from school to university, the argument is that any rank-and-file worker could have entered the contest, if he had taken the trouble while at school to work for his examinations. Hence, the fact that an individual is merely a rank-and-file worker may be interpreted, from this point of view, as indicative of his essential lack of merit, a belief that becomes the more intensified, the more educational reformers succeed in increasing the chances for able children of working-class parents to mount the educational ladder. Given the fairly close association between the hierarchies of authority and income and the hierarchy of educational qualifications, the slogan, 'equality of opportunity in education,' formulated in the latter days of capitalism, has become converted into that of 'equality of opportunity to become unequal' as the dominant economic form becomes collectivist; and this applies whether the industrial system is one of autonomy from or subjection to the close supervision of state planning.

The example of Russia is illuminating in this respect. As was indicated above[1] the grass-roots democracy of the industrial soviets in the early days of the revolution was short-lived.[2] Factory managers soon came to be appointed from above and the principle of administration known as 'unity of management' was laid down as a *sine qua non* of Communist industry. This principle conceives of a system of industrial production 'in which there is direct subordination of all workers to the single will of the manager and in which each worker is fully responsible for the business entrusted to him and is subordinate to one definite person—the one-man chief'. To the Russians the rationale for such unity of management is self-evident. 'Modern large-scale production cannot be conducted without a director.

---

[1] See above, pp. 242–3.

[2] Margaret Dewar, *Labour Policy in the USSR., 1917–1928*, Royal Institute of International Affairs, 1956, Ch. 1, *passim.*

Because of its peculiarities, large-scale machine industry requires the strictest unity of will directing the joint work of the group (hundreds, thousands, and tens of thousands of persons). This unity can be attained only by subordinating the will of all worker personnel to the will of one director.'[1] The principle also obviously entails the notion of a hierarchy of authority. 'Every production unit (brigade, division, shop, enterprise, trust, and ministry) has a director, who is fully responsible for his section of the work, and who enjoys unlimited rights in this section. Every director receives his tasks from a higher director, and is directly subordinate only to that higher director'.[2] Such directors are appointed, not elected, to their posts; and it has long been a feature of the industrialization of Russia that the political leaders have demanded that directors, so appointed, should possess the requisite technological and managerial skills to administer an integrated production system. Thus, by the middle of the 1930's, a closer relationship between formal educational level and the hierarchy of managerial authority had already begun to emerge from the chaotic management of the earlier days of the revolution.[3] By the 1950's it was even more clearly apparent, and an American observer could comment that there was by then 'a much larger group of managers with formal college training in Russian industry than in American'.[4]

The great expansion of professional training in Russia since the 1920's, indeed, has provided disproportionately more people who have completed courses of higher education for industrial and agricultural occupations than for the other professions in the country. Whereas the general ratio of growth between 1929 and 1954 was 7·1 per cent for professionals as a whole, that for industry had been 13·3 per cent and for agriculture 15·2 per cent.[5] This paralleled, on the managerial side, the rise in educational level generally; for, while in 1918 about 36 per cent of industrial workers were illiterate, by 1939 over

[1] A. Arakelian, *Industrial Management in the U.S.S.R.*, translated by E. L. Raymond, Public Affairs Press, 1950, p. 87.

[2] Ibid., p. 85.

[3] David Granick, *Management of the Industrial Firm in the USSR.*, Columbia University Press, 1954, pp. 42–4.

[4] David Granick, *The Red Executive*, Macmillan, 1960, p. 63.

[5] Nicholas Dewitt, *Soviet Professional Manpower*, National Science Foundation, 1955, Table 6, p. 239.

8 per cent of them had had at least a secondary education, and by 1964 nearly 40 per cent had been so educated.[1] It is, of course, true that the Russians put a very great emphasis on their rank-and-file workers obtaining educational qualifications even while at work, so that the possibility of vertical mobility within the enterprise remains open to them;[2] but so long as the vertical principle of authority holds, the number of persons of senior position, appointed to their posts, must be smaller than the number of persons below them in authority and responsibility, with the result that there is *necessarily* a limit to the amount of mobility possible.

It is also not at all unlikely that the bulk of graduates who enter industry as foremen, assistant foremen, shop dispatchers or shop economists[3] come disproportionately from the families of what in Russia are referred to as members of the 'intelligentsia'.[4] Certainly there is some evidence for the existence of institutional restrictions on mobility in the past,[5] and certainly a study of secondary school leavers in Novosiborsk in 1962 showed that 'children of the intelligentsia were twice as likely as lower-class children to continue their education',[6] although there was very little difference between both kinds of children in their desire for non-manual occupations.[7] As in Britain and

---

[1] G. L. Smirnov, 'The Rate of Growth of the Soviet working class and changes in its composition with respect to occupation and skill', in Gennadii P. Osipov, ed., *Industry and Labour in the U.S.S.R.*, Tavistock Publications, 1966, p. 33.

[2] S. T. Guryanov, 'Vertical mobility of employees in an enterprise', in Osipov, ed., op. cit., pp. 126–9.

[3] Granick, *The Red Executive*, op. cit., pp. 93–7.

[4] I.e. 'bureaucratic, managerial, and administrative personnel, intellectuals, white-collar workers, technical and supervisory personnel'. Dewitt, op. cit., p. 245.

[5] A. Inkeles, 'Social Stratification and Mobility in the Soviet Union, 1940–1950', *American Sociological Review*, Vol. 15, 1950, pp. 463–79.

[6] J. Azrael, 'Bringing up the Soviet Man: Dilemmas and Progress', *Problems of Communism*, Vol. 17, May–June 1968, p. 25. The reference is to V. N. Shubkin, 'Youth Enters Life', *Voprosy Filosofi* (Questions of Philosophy), May 1965. See also the treatment of this and other material in M. Matthews, 'Class Bias in Russian Education', *New Society*, 19th December 1968, pp. 911–13.

[7] V. N. Shubkin, 'Social Mobility and Choice of Occupation', in Osipov, ed., op. cit., Table 3, p. 193. For comparable data on earlier generation

America, it seems, the meritocratic ideology has an important part to play in the recruitment of managerial personnel into Russian industry.

Nevertheless, the similarities between the two systems should not be read as evidence for a hypothesis of cultural convergence towards some kind of 'fully industrialized society' which 'the industrialization process inherently tends to create'.[1] The difference between the largely oligopolistic and pluralist industrial systems in those collectivist societies which have developed out of capitalism and the almost entirely monopolistic systems of those which have emerged from the violent revolutions of essentially peasant economies, shows itself most clearly in the way the ruling class is recruited and maintained. At the top of the various bureaucratic hierarchies which constitute the industrial enterprises of non-Communist countries sits a Board of Control whose sole concern is with the operation of the enterprise, and increasingly recruitment to the Board, even where the industry is state owned, is from senior personnel in the administrative levels below that of the Board. In Russia, by contrast, the operation of an enterprise is the concern of the director whose responsibility is to a hierarchy of more senior authorities, the tasks of which become increasingly political as the hierarchy is ascended. Thus the distinction between what is purely industrial or even purely economic and what is purely political is regularly blurred in such a society, and recruitment to the top can begin up either the industrial or the political ladder,[2] although at the very top the political dominates.[3]

Even at the level of the enterprise, of course, the political

---

collected from Russian *émigrés* in Western Europe, see Alex Inkeles and R. A. Bauer, *The Soviet Citizen*, Harvard University Press, 1959, Table 13, p. 81.

[1] Kerr, *et al.*, *Industrialization*, op. cit., p. 33. See also A. A. Feldman and W. E. Moore, 'Industrialization and Industrialism, Convergence or Differentiation', *Transactions of the Fifth World Congress of Sociology*, International Sociological Association, Vol. 2, 1962.

[2] J. A. Armstrong, 'Party Bifurcation and Elite Interests', *Soviet Studies*, Vol. 17, 1965–6, pp. 417–30.

[3] Jeremy R. Azrael, *Managerial Power and Soviet Politics*, Harvard University Press, 1966,

system intrudes in part, because there is always a branch of the Communist Party in every enterprise, and where the size of the branch warrants it, the Party secretary is a full-time official. This does not mean that the enterprise director is necessarily subject to the dictates of the local official, but clearly, those directors who are ambitious to rise in the industrial hierarchy will seek to be in a favourable position to win support from the relevant Party Committee whenever vacancies occur. Thus an element of election enters into the selection process, which is entirely absent from the bureaucracies of non-Communist systems where political scrutiny of the internal workings of industrial enterprises is unknown; and the abolition of the Ministerial system for the organization of Russian industry and its replacement by a territorial system in 1957,[1] would seem to have strengthened the electoral element.

From the point of view of rank-and-file participation, of course, such democracy as the existence of the Communist Party introduces into industry has little or no effect on the relationship between the individual worker as such and the enterprise director. It is only as member of the Party that a manual worker can exercise some influence over his 'boss' and then only if he is elected to office in the Party well above that of its 'Primary' Organizations.[2] The question of freedom to join the Party is not at issue here. Indeed, the Constitution is quite clear that 'any working person who is a Soviet citizen not exploiting anyone else's labour, accepting the Programme and Statutes of the Party, taking active part in effecting them, working in one of the Party organizations and carrying out all the decisions of the Party may became a member of the Communist Party of the Soviet Union . . . Workers, peasants and intelligentsia who are politically aware, active, and devoted to the Communist cause are accepted as Party Members,'[3] and although there is no alternative Party for them to join if they do

---

[1] Alec Nove, *The Soviet Economy: an Introduction*, Allen and Unwin, 2nd edition, 1965, pp. 67–75.

[2] 'Statutes of the Communist Party of the Soviet Union', in Boris Meissner, *The Communist Party of the Soviet Union*, edited with a chapter on the Twentieth Party Congress by J. S. Reshetar, Atlantic Press, 1957, pp. 169–72.

[3] Ibid., pp. 153–4 and 156.

not accept the Communist Party Programme and Statutes, there is no special reason to believe that rank-and-file members of the Party contain less than a proportionate share of industrial workers, for all that peasants may well be under-represented,[1] and that representatives to higher bodies from the Primary Organizations may come disproportionately from the better educated members of the Party.[2]

Once admitted to a Primary Organization, however, a Party Member's task is, among other things, the 'mobilization of the masses . . . to fulfil the production plan, strengthen labour discipline and develop socialist competition' and to 'struggle against laxity and thriftlessness in management of enterprises'.[3] It is in this sense, and in this sense alone, that Primary Organizations possess 'the right to supervise the work of the management of the enterprises'.[4] Thus, the Russian emphasis on productivity and the strengthening of labour discipline to achieve it,[5] together with the payment of bonuses to directors who fulfil and over-fulfil the targets laid down for their enterprises,[6] emphasise that it is a major task of the director to increase the amount of surplus labour he can extort from his workers and a major task of the Party members to ensure that he does this.

This is not to deny that the overfulfilment of targets also results in an increase in the rank-and-file worker's earnings, because of the widespread employment of piece-rate systems and output norms,[7] often to the disadvantage of white-collar workers, civil servants, teachers, and others on fixed salaries;[8]

[1] Ibid., p. 67. Some attempt to bring about more proportionate representation has occurred since 1956. See E. C. Brown, 'Interests and Rights of Soviet Industrial Workers and the Resolution of Conflicts', *Industrial and Labour Relations Review*, Vol. 16, 1962–3, p. 256, n. 8.

[2] Meissner, op. cit., pp. 67–8.

[3] Ibid., p. 170.

[4] Ibid., p. 171. A footnote to the word 'supervise' reads: 'The Russian word "Kontrol" does not imply "management", but "supervision", or "check-up", depending on context—Trans.'

[5] P. Barton, 'The Current State of the Soviet Worker', *Problems of Communism*, Vol. 9, No. 4, July, August 1960, pp. 18–27. See also the discussion on this article in No. 6, November, December 1960, pp. 40–6.

[6] Granick, *Red Executive*, op. cit., pp. 130–4.

[7] Lief Björk, *Wages, Prices and Social Legislation in the Soviet Union*, trans. by M. A. Michael, B. Dobson, 1953, Ch. 5, *passim*.

[8] Nove, *The Soviet Economy*, op. cit., p. 243.

but such an admission in no way detracts from the argument that
the Russian economy is run on collectivist principles, as described above,[1] with the salaries of top officials and industrial administrators being fixed by themselves in advance as a first charge
on the product, while wages are treated as a variable cost. Indeed
the class nature of the system is to be seen in the fact that the
rank-and-file Russian workers have no power to determine
their leaders' incomes, if indeed they know what they get, whereas the latter not only decide how the hierarchy of incomes will
in general be structured, subject to rewards for extra effort,
but can pay themselves bonuses and maintain expense accounts,
if not what Khrushchev once called 'lavish bonuses' and 'excessive
expense accounts'.[2] From this point of view the rank-and-file participation of Russian workers in trade union administration within the factory, in works committees, Party branches and so forth,
may be seen as little more than a State collectivist parallel to
joint industrial council and human relations devices in private
enterprise collectivism in non-Communist countries; namely
means by which to obtain the integrated labour force necessary
for modern large-scale production. Signs of strain in the form of
labour disputes about managerial prerogative[3] and strikes and
labour turnover arising from workers' dissatisfaction with their
level of living[4] may similarly be interpreted as indications of how
difficult it is for industrial managers to achieve the integration
desired.

Altogether, then, Marx's belief that with the passing of
capitalism, changes would occur in the organization of work
which would bring it under the common control of associated
producers has not been confirmed by events. Instead, the
producers have become associated with managerial personnel
in collective enterprise over which the managers exercise
authority on behalf of directors who form the new ruling class
of industry. This does not mean that the demand for workers'
control, which was raised in the later days of capitalism, has
died. From time to time, largely unnoticed by the great bulk of

[1] See above, pp. 178–9.
[2] R. A. Feldmesser, 'Equality and Inequality under Khrushchev', *Problems of Communism*, Vol. 9, March–April 1960, p. 34.
[3] E. C. Brown, op. cit., pp. 254–6.
[4] Ibid., pp. 271–2.

the population, rank-and-file workers, shop-stewards and intellectuals seek for an alternative to their present discontents in a more democratic order in industry.[1] Yet, it is a striking feature of the contemporary version of this demand, in this country at least, that participation by workers and their trade union representatives is conceived as a form of partnership with the managerial bureaucracy and not as a substitute for it.[2] Possibly the type of technological and organizational knowledge required to produce goods on the scale which obtains in America and Russia, and indeed in all modern industrial societies generally, is accepted as incompatible with the kind of workers' co-operative democracy which Marx' notion of the end of alienation entailed. The division of labour and the specialization of skills in man co-ordination have gone too far. Of course, as this chapter has shown, the very magnitude of the social problems involved in large-scale collective co-ordination has resulted in some participation by workers with managers in the conduct of day-to-day production affairs; but this is a far cry from the conception of human freedom from restraints imposed by a ruling class, apparently arbitrarily, which informed the Marxist vision of the classless society of the post-capitalist era.

[1] M. B. Brown, 'The Search for Workers' Control', *New Society*, 11th April 1968, pp. 256–7.
[2] See particularly the model for workers' control in a nationalized industry put forward by the Sheffield Steel Group in Kenneth Coates, ed., *Can the Workers Run Industry?*, Sphere Books, 1968, p. 149.

18

THE NECESSITY FOR COLLECTIVISM

What would have happened in Russia in October, 1917, if the Prime Minister, Kerensky, had not decided that the Bolsheviks were about to start an armed insurrection and had not ordered a detachment of cadets to close down the Bolshevik newspapers?[1] Would the Congress of Soviets have met without insurrection? Would Russia have remained 'for the time being on the course of peaceful political compromise'? Would 'the basic political cleavage of Bolsheviks and anti-Bolsheviks . . . not have been so sharp'? and would there not have occurred the 'opportunity for one-party Bolshevik rule' and 'a militarized dictatorship of revolutionary extremism'?[2] Of course, such questions are unanswerable in the sense that they do not demand knowledge but counter-to-fact speculation. Nevertheless, the frequent regularity of their posing suggests that social scientists and historians are uneasy lest their concern for the accuracy of the historical record be misinterpreted for the implication that human beings are powerless before the inexorable forces of destiny. The Marxists, in particular, have laid themselves open to the charge that the materialist conception of social change leaves no room for individual men and women to make decisions and to take actions which will influence the course of events and seriously modify the direction of affairs. The very phases of Marxist parlance—'the inescapable circumstances in which people have had, and still have, to act', circumstances which are 'necessary, inevitable, unavoidable'[3]—seem

---

[1] Daniels, *Red October*, op. cit., pp. 132–3.

[2] Ibid., pp. 217–18.

[3] Maurice Cornforth, *The Open Philosophy and the Open Society*, Lawrence and Wishart, 1968, p. 155.

to indicate that 'scientific socialism' is not so much a set of hypothetical propositions of sociological import, as a body of prophetic utterances about the future, fore-telling events which human beings 'can do nothing to prevent'.[1] Yet, Marx himself was careful to assert that 'men make their own history' even if 'they do not make it *just* as they please';[2] and Plekhanov found it necessary to add 'and, therefore, the activities of individuals cannot help being important in history'.[3]

The Marxist terms, 'inevitability', 'necessity', and so on, therefore, in spite of their apparently absolute finality, should be interpreted as strictly referring to events which are relative and conditional. They are meant to be *sine qua non* expressions of what must be done by human beings to prevent possibilities materialising or to bring about occurrences which otherwise would not materialise. As Cornforth has put it, 'the word "necessary" has the sense of "impossible without" or "impossible unless". Thus the class struggle necessarily leads to the dictatorship of the proletariat because that is the only way it can finish, and because the class aim of emancipation from exploitation is impossible to realise without establishing first a system of political power to abolish exploitation'.[4] It does not matter for present purposes that the application of the phrase, 'dictatorship of the proletariat' to Communist societies is misplaced,[5] because as a matter of fact the systems of political power which they have established there have not abolished exploitation but merely changed its nature. What is important

---

[1] Popper, *Poverty*, p. 43. The whole of this section on the distinction between technological and prophetic predictions (pp. 41–9) should be read in conjunction with Cornforth's treatment of historical prediction, probability and intent (op. cit., pp. 137–51), especially since the latter's work is subtitled: 'a reply to Dr. Karl Popper's refutation of Marxism'.

[2] Marx, *Eighteenth Brumaire*, op. cit., p. 225. Italics *not* in the original.

[3] George Plekhanov, *The Role of the Individual in History*, International Publishers, 1940, p. 23. In the light of this statement, in italics in the original, it is not altogether clear why Daniels should regard Plekhanov as an 'ultra-determinist'. R. V. Daniels, 'Marxian Theories of Historical Dynamics', in Werner, J. Cahnman and A. Boskoff, eds., *Sociology and History*, Free Press of Glencoe, 1964, p. 79. See, however, Sidney Hook, *The Hero in History*, Beacon Press, 1955, pp. 82–101.

[4] Cornforth, op. cit., p. 157.

[5] Compare Cornforth on the U.S.S.R., op. cit., pp. 366–83, with what has been written above, pp. 283–6.

is the realization that the phrase, 'necessity *for* collectivism' at the head of this chapter, and in some respects, the phrase 'inevitability of collectivism' the author's original title of this work, are intended to imply a position with respect to sociology which is taken by Marxists in their scientific, as opposed to their messianic moments—a position which has been retained here, not only because this is intended as an essay in the sociological critique of the Marxist analysis and not a philosophical refutation of it, but also because the author believes that sociology, whether it is considered a science or not, is possible only on the basis that valid generalizations about the behaviour of large numbers of people are possible.

Such a belief, to be sure, does not involve attempts to answer questions of the form 'what would have happened if . . . ?'[1] Rather is it based on the observation that, although individuals sometimes behave in an unusual, unexpected and in other ways remarkable fashion, regularities in behaviour have been commonly noted and recorded again and again throughout the course of history. Especially where knowledge is concerned, the propensity of most people to learn something from their own mistakes and from the mistakes of others, as well as to absorb what is taught to them, is more in evidence than their deliberate refusal to make use of information which they have once applied. Popper, indeed, has tried to show that '*for strictly logical reasons, it is impossible for us to predict the future course of history*', because this course 'is strongly influenced by the growth of human knowledge' and 'we cannot predict, by rational or scientific methods, the future growth of our scientific knowledge'.[2] Yet even Popper has asserted with respect to *existing* knowledge that, for example, 'a return to pre-Marxian social science is inconceivable'.[3] It is the discernment that people do not easily relinquish knowledge, together with the further observation that knowledge becomes diffused rather than concentrated over time, that makes it possible for sociologists to formulate certain types of prediction about social change, in

---

[1] On the logical justification for asking such questions, see Hook, op. cit., Ch. 7, *passim*.

[2] Popper, *Poverty*, op. cit., pp. v–vi. Italics in the original.

[3] Karl Popper, *The Open Society and its Enemies*, Vol. 2, Routledge, 1945, p. 78.

spite of their not knowing what *new* knowledge might also become available during the period covered by the prediction.

In Marx's case, moreover, it was the application of knowledge about productive forces by growing numbers of people, which was seen as the driving force behind history,[1] and there has been nothing in this account so far which might be regarded as demanding an amendment of this hypothesis, for all that some other attack on the problem of social change might have emphasized a different set of factors as crucial, such as the growth in population. Thus, the influence of Lenin's *Imperialism*, which has been said to play a 'theoretical role' in less developed areas of the world, comparable to *The Communist Manifesto* and to *Capital* 'in the advanced countries',[2] has arisen in large part from its intense appeal to nationalist sentiments; for, Lenin argued that imperialist countries grew wealthy at the expense of their colonies and dependants, and that the latter could not expect much of the future until they threw off the yoke. Indeed, unlike the *Communist Manifesto* of 1848, this far more effective political pamphlet of 1917 seemed profoundly unconvinced of the possibility that the workers of the world might unite. The proletariat, or at least the better-paid parts of it, in imperialist lands had from Lenin's point of view become opportunist and permeated by the imperialist ideology.[3] The rationale for revolutionary activity, designed to throw over imperialist rule by means of violent nationalist upheaval, was thus not an appeal to working-class, world solidarity but the argument that 'moribund' capitalism prevented the subject nations from developing their economic resources; and the most striking feature of nationalist movements, inspired by Lenin's words, has been their wholehearted acceptance of the technical and organization processes used at home by their former oppressors —the industrial means of production—while at the same time largely rejecting their capitalist form.

The task of what has been called 'the ideology of delayed industrialization',[4] that is to say, has been to decide between

[1] See above, p. 24.

[2] Kemp, op. cit., p. 67.

[3] Lenin, *Imperialism: the Highest Form of Capitalism*, op. cit., pp. 281–5, 301–2.

[4] M. Matossian, 'Ideologies of Delayed Industrialisation: Some Tensions

what to copy and what to ignore, although there is no single example of any nationalist revolution in the twentieth century in which the people of the new nations have chosen to have nothing to do with the factory system of production at all. For them the leap into the twentieth century has entailed the subservience of agriculture to industry, and hand craftsmanship to mass, batch and process production. The transition from dependence and poverty to a more abundant epoch has been seen as not only desirable but impossible, save by way of industrialization; and if these nations have chosen the Russian rather than the American form of collectivism as the model to follow, this is largely because they have believed, in their haste to enjoy the benefits of affluence, that the most effective means for accumulating large masses of industrial capital quickly and for deploying a massive and disciplined labour force is a centralized economic system under the direct control of the state. For all that the sentiments of patriotism and nationalism may be held to be crucial in nerving people to sacrifice themselves, if necessary, for the freedom of their countries from imperial subjugation, the driving force behind their willingness to fight may equally be held to be the consciousness that the foreigners' investments and trade have deprived them of desirable worldly goods. Such violent revolution as occurs may therefore be held to be a consequence of inexorable necessity only if it is also held that anti-imperialist doctrines based upon a desire for withheld opportunities are inexorable, or at least, inevitable, and this implies the further assumption that such opportunities will continue to be both demanded by the dependent populations and withheld by the imperialist foreigners.

The significance of the technological and organizational means for obtaining *desired* economic ends may also be observed in a further reference to the problem of rank-and-file participation, discussed at some length in the previous chapter. In the 1950's the Yugoslavian Communists found themselve critically involved with a reconsideration of the nature of the state in modern society as a result of their ideological struggle against

---

and Ambiguities', in John H. Kautsky, ed., *Political Change in Under-developed Countries*, Wiley, 1963, pp. 252–64.

the demands of the Communist Party in Russia.[1] One of the domestic reforms which they introduced in an attempt to induce some reality into the notion of the withering away of the administrative bureaucracy was a reorganization of the industrial enterprise, so that the technical director who before 1953 was 'a state official appointed and dismissed by his superiors, working under their orders, and answerable to them alone for his actions',[2] became appointed first by a committee composed of representatives from the Workers' Council of the enterprise he was to direct and representatives of the People's Committee of the commune in which it was located, and then after 1963 apparently by the Workers' Council alone.[3] It was also decided that as an employee of the undertaking he would be responsible to the Workers' Council for the implementation of *its* decisions. Thus, the rank-and-file workers, through their elected representatives, may be said to have been provided with the opportunity actively to participate in the organization of their working lives, especially as the composition of such Councils must, by law, reflect the numerical ratio between production workers and other workers in the enterprise,[4] and their Boards of Management must have at least three quarters of their members directly engaged in the essential economic activity of the undertaking.[5]

Yet, subsequent studies have shown that such participation is largely exercised by the better educated sections of the work force and that the director and his managerial colleagues, by virtue of their superiority in debate and in knowledge of the economics and technology of modern production, have continued to wield a disproportionate amount of authority in spite

---

[1] Djilas, op. cit., pp. 86–99. T. P. Svennevig, 'The Ideology of the Yugoslav Heretics', *Social Research*, Vol. 27, 1960, pp. 39–48. George W. Hoffman and F. W. Neal, *Yugoslavia and the New Communism*, Twentieth Century Fund, 1962, pp. 150–1, 163–7.

[2] *Workers' Management in Yugoslavia*, International Labour Office, 1962, p. 100.

[3] Phyllis Autry, *Yugoslavia*, Thames and Hudson, 1965, p. 146. See, however, Paul Blumberg, *Industrial Democracy: The Sociology of Participation*, Constable, 1968, pp. 204–5, where the Workers' Council is recorded as still only 'participating in the selection of the director'.

[4] *Workers' Management*, op. cit., pp. 75–6.

[5] Ibid., p. 85. Blumberg, op. cit., pp. 217–19.

of the change in the law.[1] This does not mean that there is not a considerable amount of rank-and-file participation in the running of the plant in Yugoslavia,[2]—surely much greater than anywhere else in the world! Nor does it mean that there is not more control over plant directors there than is the case in other countries. Indeed, some have been dismissed from their posts by decision of the Council;[3] but what the influence of the senior personnel in management indicates, is that the formal opportunity to participate is limited by the requirements of large-scale, economic enterprises when this is run on principles of business efficiency, because the people who understand it most are those with higher qualifications, those who fill the superior posts in the administrative hierarchy. The director and his executive colleagues—the production manager, the chief accountant, the chief of personnel, and the commercial manager —are all *appointed*, it should be emphasized. Vacancies are advertised in newspapers and the 'qualification and experience of applicants as prescribed by the undertaking's rules'[4] are specified. There is no question here of the workers in the enterprise *electing* one of their own number for a period to be director or 'chairman' of production. The Yugoslavian factories are not 'primitive' democracies in the sense that some of the early French producer co-operatives and the Israeli productive *kibbutzim* were democracies.[5] The great bulk of Yugoslavian workers will continue to perform manual work under the in-struction of others *for the whole of their working lives* and thus remain a class of life-long industrial servants. The degree to which productivity and output are first priorities in Yugoslavia, as elsewhere, is the degree to which meritocracy must necessarily enter into the organization of production, even in a system which has been deliberately designed to weaken the power of the oligarchy.

[1] D. S. Riddell, 'Social self-government: the background of theory and practice in Yugoslav socialism', *British Journal of Sociology*, Vol. 19, 1968, pp. 60–9 and the authorities cited.

[2] *Workers' Management*, op. cit., Table E, p. 303. Autry, op. cit., p. 157.

[3] John T. Dunlop, *Industrial Relations Systems*, Holt, 1958, p. 290. Blumberg, op. cit., p. 205.

[4] I.L.O., *Workers' Management*, op. cit., p. 102, n. 2.

[5] I. Sobel, 'Management In Israel', in Frederick Harbison and C. A. Myers, *Management in the Industrial World*, McGraw-Hill, 1959, pp. 191–2.

A comparison of rank-and-file participation in private enter-prise and state collectivist industry[1] with that prevailing in Yugoslavia, that is to say, yields the conclusion that the im-peratives of modern factory production entail a *necessity* for a society with very strong leanings towards meritocratically controlled collectivities, and although it is true that the Workers' Councils in Yugoslavia seem to have considerable control over their own finances and surpluses, the differential system of incomes which continues to be associated with the managerial and political hierarchies—surely a first charge on resources? —raises the possibility that there may be an element of exploi-tation in the employment of manual labour in that country. It is also open to question whether, since this is a case of indus-trialization and democratization from above, the Workers' Council system in Yugoslavia would have been continued in its present form, had there not occurred a marked increase in out-put after 1953.[2] Thus, this particular example of rank-and-file participation serves to illustrate the point that the nature of the class system in any society, although not a simple product of the material forces of production,[3] is sufficiently influenced by them seriously to limit the choices open to mankind at any point of time. In this sense there appears to be an element of the inexorable about the social responses to technological advance.

At the same time, in spite of the similarities which the tech-nical and organizational imperatives of collectivism impose on all countries, there are nevertheless what Dunlop has called 'significant differences' between them in the kinds of relation-ships which employers, managers and employees in their factories experience. In particular he has drawn attention to 'the timing of the national, political, and industrial "revolutions" in a country relative to the rise of the labour movement',[4] a factor which has also been underlined in the present study. Marx's emphasis on the circumstances in which change occurs, 'circumstances, directly encountered, given and transmitted

[1] See above, pp. 282–8.
[2] Albert Waterston, *Planning in Yugoslavia*, John Hopkins Press, 1962, pp. 85–6. Blumberg, op. cit., p. 222.
[3] See above, pp. 25–7.
[4] Dunlop, op. cit., p. 313.

from the past',[1] may therefore be interpreted by reference to what sociologists regularly, if somewhat vaguely, refer to as culture or tradition—the sum total of the social characteristics of a people which is transmitted from generation to generation and which colours what they can learn from the mistakes of people in other societies. Of course, in asserting this the sociologist must be careful to avoid committing the fallacy of cultural determinism.[2] There is no special merit in discarding Marx's economic determination *in toto* for the conviction that it is the values of a society which condition the kinds of economic, political and social systems its citizens will accept, especially where this still leaves unexplained why it is they continue to retain the values, culture and traditions that they have. The comparison of the British, American, Russian and Yugoslavian systems by reference to unspecified and incomplete references to the 'culture patterns' of these societies implies an abandonment of the more substantial basis of Marxist hypothesizing for 'explanations' perilously close to *ignotum per ignotius*. Clearly what is needed is an empirically viable formulation of hypotheses which will help to explain why it is that different forms of collectivism are possible alongside remarkably similar systems of technology and organization for the production of goods and services. The problems of delayed industrialization— what to copy, what to retain, what to discard—might thus be set in this way against the background of education and upbringing in a society in an attempt to estimate compatibilities and incompatibilities between the economic and technical means employed by societies to achieve what their people are taught to regard as desirable ends.

To follow this further here would take the present enquiry far beyond its original scope. What has been attempted has had rather more modest implications, namely to estimate how far the Marxist framework of ideas could be used for the purpose of interpreting what has been happening to the relationships between employers and employees in a single industry in Britain; and the contrasts and comparisons drawn between these and what appears to have occurred elsewhere in the

[1] See above, p. 30.
[2] J. Blake and K. Davis, 'Norms, Values and Sanctions', in Robert E. L. Faris, ed., *Handbook of Modern Sociology*, Rand McNally, 1964, pp. 461–4.

world, were selected deliberately to sharpen and refine the implications from the analysis of this single case. At many points, of course, other more radical departures from the Marxist framework of ideas might have been preferred as alternative explanations of the *specific* events under review; but such amendments as have as a matter of fact been proposed here have been those deemed necessary for the primary task and not for the secondary issues *per se*. Thus it has not been the purpose of the Third Part to provide amendments to the original framework of ideas in order to provide an interpretation of what has been happening in Russia, India, China, America and Yugoslavia since the end of the nineteenth century. Nor for this reason should the failure to discuss industrial relations and social change in Germany and Japan be necessarily regarded as a handicap.

In the light of this disclaimer, what may fruitfully be added now to the appraisal in Chapter Thirteen? Probably the most important, single, theoretical issue that was raised, it will be recalled, was whether the course of development in Britain, described in Part Two, was 'normal', dependent upon the endogenous impact of technological change on the class structure of capitalism to convert it into collectivism, or whether it was an 'abnormal' consequence of imperialist exploitation of oversea peoples which made possible a peaceful transition from one society to the next through hastening on the spread of the device of joint-stock enterprise amongst employers and of militant trade unions amongst employees, with institutionalized bargaining, culminating in Joint Industrial Councils, as the collective link between them.[1] The conclusion of Chapter Fourteen was that, at best, only a very tenuous association could be shown to exist between industrial relations in the iron and steel industry and overseas trade and investment. Thus, British experience may be better explained *sui generis*, a conclusion which is enhanced by reference to the development of collective bargaining in Sweden, where institutionalization not very different from that which has occurred in Britain,[2] has ensued in an economy without an overseas empire and with overseas investments and trade not remarkably more important than

[1] See above, pp. 210–12.
[2] R. A. Lester, 'Reflections on Collective Bargaining in Britain and Sweden', *Industrial and Labor Relations Review*, Vol. 10, 1957, pp. 375–401.

in the British case. Of course, there are differences between the English and Swedish systems of collective bargaining. For example, the Swedish Employers' Confederation has apparently more control over the conduct of industrial disputes by its members than has its counterpart in Britain;[1] and bargaining between unions and employers is rather more 'guided' by the Confederation of Trade Unions, the Swedish alternative to the T.U.C.[2] but the Swedish extra standardization and centralization of the bargaining process merely serve here to emphasize the point that for all that there are cultural differences between the two societies which have influenced their industrial relations' systems, the similarities between them have arisen because the course of collectivization seems to have responded to broadly the same technical and organizational changes, albeit at a different rate.[3]

Throughout the discussion in Part Two, to be sure, the focus of attention was directed on the whole towards the trade unions, and in particular, towards their 'revolutionary' leaders and the part they have played in the transition from capitalism. Indeed, the logic of the Marxist analysis of industrial relations with its emphasis on the historical 'mission' of the working class, virtually compels this preoccupation. Nevertheless, it is not inappropriate to consider also that élite of the capitalist class who for their part carried through a 'revolution from above' by converting capitalist private enterprise into voluntary collectivism by means of their oligarchic, and in some respects, technocratic[4] control of both shareholders and employees. Is it reasonable to claim that this new ruling class emerged out of the class struggle between capitalists and the proletariat, much as in the way it might be said that the class of capitalists emerged out of the struggle between feudal lords and their serfs? The issue of political struggle between feudal lord and capitalist in the earlier period should not be misunderstood. After all, Marxist

[1] Thomas L. Johnstone, *Collective Bargaining in Sweden*, Allen and Unwin, 1962, Ch. 2.

[2] Ibid., Chs. 1 and 14, *The Trade Union Situation in Sweden*, International Labour Office, 1961, Ch. 3.

[3] Harbison and Myers, op. cit., Chs. 15 and 16.

[4] John K. Galbraith, *The New Industrial State*, Hamilton, 1967, Ch. 6, *passim*.

scholars are divided amonst themselves as to whether or not the English Civil War should be regarded as an earlier example of a successful attempt to overthrow the feudal state machine in the name of capitalism, in roughly the same fashion as they regularly so interpret the French Revolution;[1] and it cannot be decided by simple analogy that there should be a similar violent struggle between capitalists and collectivists at the present time, for all that the advance of collectivism generally during the national emergencies of the two World Wars suggests that such a struggle may have passed unnoticed in the general turmoil of these years.

In his treatment of the genesis of capitalism Marx appears to have been concerned rather to stress the gradual transformation of the class of serfs into a class of wage workers, and in this sense seems to have implied a similar gradual transformation of the feudal lords into capitalist employers.[2] Why not, therefore, look now for a parallel metamorphosis of capitalist into collectivist? The main difficulty here lies in the fact that it is not very apparent that the wage-working proletariat has been converted into some new kind of producer of surplus labour, although some attempt was made in Chapter Eleven to indicate that the manner in which surplus labour is nowadays extorted from the primary producer is characteristically different from what it was under classical capitalism.[3] The feudal lord, it might be said, became a capitalist the better to exploit his lands and labour by making the latter legally free, whereas the capitalist has become a collectivist the better to exploit capital and labour through the massive organization of productive capacity. In the process 'the worship of individualism has given way to a positive cult of team-work and group action'.[4] Directors of modern enterprises, that is to say, see themselves as members of 'a team whose collective responsibility is to direct the business in the interests of all affected by its well-being'.[5] For them 'the

---

[1] Paul M. Sweezy, *et al.*, *The Transition from Feudalism to Capitalism*, reprinted from *Science and Society, 1950–1953*, Fore Publications, 1954.

[2] Marx, *Capital*, Vol. I, op. cit., pp. 717–44.

[3] See above, pp. 178–9.

[4] Charles A. R. Crosland, *The Future of Socialism*, Abridged and Revised Edition, Cape, 1964, pp. 31–2. Galbraith, op. cit., p. 70.

[5] *Standard Boardroom Practice*, prepared by a special committee under the chairmanship of Sir Edwin Herbert, Institute of Directors, 1961, p. 55.

company—and this includes the *future* of the company—comes first every time'.[1] Thus, although the Institute of Directors in Britain has expressed itself very much in the language of capitalism, describing for example, the 'long-term interests of the shareholders and the future prosperity of the company' as identical,[2] the relative frequency of government committees of enquiry between 1906 and 1959, set up to investigate the powers of directors and the rights of shareholders,[3] suggests that since the turn of the century there has been some conflict of interests here to match on this side of the Atlantic what has been called 'the debate' about the control of corporate power in America.[4] At the same time, the greater importance of stock options in the working director's remuneration over there[5] indicates that the victory of collectivism over capitalism in the private sphere has proceeded much further in this country than in the United States.

Of course, the transition to collectivism in countries which have experienced violent Communist revolutions, has not involved frictions and debates of this sort. As was pointed out in Chapter Fifteen, far from industrialization being the driving factor in social change by intensifying class conflict between capitalists and the proletariat, what has been of rather more importance in these areas has been the circumstances of the great bulk of a population living on the land and the relationship the governments of those countries have had with those where capitalism has flourished. The conflict between peasants and landlords, which reached a climax with the collapse of the machinery of state during wartime, opened the way to a successful attack on the government by patriotic élites inspired by the conviction that industrialization would lift their homeland into the ranks of independent and even wealthy and powerful nations. Nor is it altogether true in these countries that, as Moore has argued, 'by themselves the peasants have never been able to accomplish a revolution. . . . The peasants have to have leaders

---

[1] Ibid., p. 13. Italics in the original.
[2] Ibid., pp. 13–14.
[3] Grove, op. cit., pp. 173–8.
[4] Richard Eells, *The Government of Corporations*, Free Press of Glencoe, 1962, p. 19.
[5] See above, pp. 265–6.

from the other classes'.[1] For all that the Bolshevik leaders in 1917 were 'brilliant young intellectuals from a middle-class background',[2] nearly half of the Chinese leadership in 1945 consisted of the sons of peasants, albeit often wealthy peasants, and another fifth came from the land-owning families.[3] The striking facts about these people were that neither trade union leaders not capitalist entrepreneurs were prominent amongst them and that they eschewed capitalism and its institutions as mechanisms for attaining their economic and political ends.

Once in power, that is to say, they strove to introduce a social and industrial revolution from above by copying the technical and organizational achievements of voluntary collectivist societies, but largely without recourse to private enterprise. In this respect later revolutions took the Russian as prototype; and since the Russian economy was one which had passed straight from state capitalism to state collectivism, it was apparently regarded as demonstrating with its rapid industrialization that if speed were an important consideration, public coercion was more effective than leaving matters to the discretion of private organizations and laissez-faire collectivism, for achieving massive economic change. At the same time, to the degree that 'despotism' was a feature of the political organizations of the pre-industrial and pre-revolutionary societies where Communist revolutions have occurred, to that degree their post-revolutionary, post-industrial economies have been monopolistic and totalitarian in their collectivist forms.[4]

The fact that state collectivist societies share certain features in common with voluntary collectivist societies, such as bureaucracy and meritocracy,[5] in spite of their not having passed through a phase of having been ruled by a capitalist class, raises the question of whether Marx was at fault in asserting that 'even when a society has got upon the right track for the discovery of the natural laws of its movement . . . it can neither

[1] Moore, op. cit., p. 479.

[2] G. K. Schueller, 'The Politburo', in Lasswell and Lerner, eds., op. cit., p. 140.

[3] R. C. North and I. de Sola Pool, 'Kuomintang and Chinese Communist Elites', in Lasswell ed., op. cit., Table 2, p. 378.

[4] Wittfogel, op. cit., pp. 436–43.

[5] See above, pp. 276–9, 282–6.

clear by bold leaps, nor remove by legal enactments, the obstacles offered by the successive phases of its normal development'.[1] Certainly the normal development of transition from capitalism, described in Part Two of this book, cannot in any sense be regarded as 'inevitable' for Russia and China, or for any of those societies where the state itself conducts the economy along collectivist lines. Nor is there any clear evidence of a convergence between the state collectivist and the voluntary collectivist societies,[2] which would suggest that the state collectivist is an 'inevitable' form which the post-capitalist societies will eventually adopt. Although both types show marked variations within their genus, Yugoslavian Communism is nevertheless rather more like Russian Communism than it is similar to the British Welfare State. The role of the political party in economic life is what divides the genera; and only a rather stubborn and essentially chiliastic expectation of an eventual, political victory for the Communist Party in voluntary collectivist societies can blind the observer to the fact that these are alternative and *not* successive forms of social system. On the present showing, that is to say, some changes are required in the Marxist framework of ideas as set out in Chapter Two, to account not only for those cultural differences which give character to each member of the species but also for these political differences which characterize the two genera. In this sense it does not appear methodologically sound to attempt to reduce each social system to its technological and economic base; for, industrialism, factory production and collective control to the advantage of those who head the collectivities are features common to all these societies.

At a different level it may also be remarked that certain aspects of the social structure other than the purely economic appear to be significant in differentiating the species within the genus. Thus, there is some evidence to show that a major factor in the American situation which hindered the trade union leaders there from forming political organizations on the model of the British Labour Party has been the legislative pluralism of the States in the Union.[3] Of course, as was pointed out in this

[1] Marx, *Capital*, Vol. I, op. cit., p. 10.
[2] See above, pp. 286–9.
[3] See above, pp. 258.

context, in some respects their failure to enter the political arena may alternatively be seen as a reflection of the striking lack of class consciousness in the European sense of that term, although when American unionism is examined from the angle of its consequences rather than from that of its ideology, much of this objection loses its appeal.[2] In more theoretical language, that is to say, it is apparent that the Marxist emphasis on the overriding significance of the economic structure for conditioning the course of industrial relations, requires amendment to permit of the influence of other structural features of a society which may be economically relevant in certain circumstances. What these circumstances are is clearly beyond the scope of this book, but it may be suggested that a more thorough comparison of events in the transition from capitalism to collectivism in Britain and America, with special reference to the development of collective bargaining in the two countries, would be a fruitful next step in the amendment of the Marxist framework of ideas for sociological purposes. Similarly, a comparison of the Russian and Yugoslavian systems in terms of the nature and degree of worker participation possible and of the influence of the Communist Party on the operations of the enterprise at all levels, would seem to be another profitable line to pursue for the same purposes.

The reference above to the chiliastic attitudes of those who anticipate the inevitable conversion of voluntary collectivist societies, raises in another form the ideological element in social analysis referred to at the beginning of this book.[1] Because Marx asserted that the outcome of the conflict between the capitalist and the proletarian classes would be a classless society, Communist societies have often been deemed classless because they obviously have no capitalists left within them. By the same reasoning, the Welfare States have often been termed capitalist because they are obviously not classless. As this study has attempted to show, neither of these positions is tenable, or, rather, an explanation of the facts along state and voluntary collectivist lines seems to make better sense than both of these alternatives. Although the obviously tentative nature of all the amendments to the Marxist position, which

[1] See above, pp. 258–63.
[2] See above, p. 14.

306

have been offered here, must be manifestly apparent, an interpretation of the social structure of modern industry which stresses its relatively novel, class character is to be preferred, sociologically speaking, either to blind optimism about the future of Communist democratic centralism, or to a perverse refusal to recognise the difference between capitalism in all its forms and the particular organizations which characterize the productive system in the Welfare State.

Does this mean that they should despair who aspire to see men and women everywhere reach full human status, their 'latent creative powers' no longer 'stifled and repressed under the social conditions of all class societies.'[1] By no means—although certainly the lesson of the previous chapters should enhance the realization that the Arcadian dream of the youthful Marx and Engels is unlikely to be realized by the collectivist organization of manpower in the modern manner. That kind of 'communist society, where nobody has one exclusive sphere of activity, but each can become accomplished in any branch he wishes', where 'society regulates the general production and thus makes it possible for me to do one thing today and another tomorrow, to hunt in the morning, fish in the afternoon, rear cattle in the evening, criticize after dinner, just as I have a mind, without ever becoming hunter, fisherman, shepherd or critic'[2] is incompatible with the massive organization of labour necessary for the regular and ever-increasing flow of consumer goods, and the power, tools and machines required to achieve this flow, which people in all kinds of collectivist societies seem to expect. Nor does it seem to make good sociological sense to assume that the dream could be realised provided that men could be persuaded to liberate a 'technological and productive explosion' to 'underpin' the kind of varied daily routine Marx and Engels deemed ideal.[3]

On the contrary, what the sociologist can reach for at the present time are much more limited objectives. For example, while Blauner was no doubt basing his remarks on sound *moral*

---

[1] Zeitlin, *Ideology*, op. cit., p. 84. Zeitlin's account of Marx's sociology of alienated labour turns on this philosophical criterion for assessing and evaluating social systems.

[2] Marx and Engels, *The German Ideology*, op. cit., p. 22.

[3] Coates and Topham, op. cit., p. 409.

grounds when he issued a plea to social scientists to fuse their 'empirical, realistic approach with the valuable humanistic tradition of alienation theory that views all human beings as potentially capable of exercising freedom and control, achieving meaning, integration, social connection, and self-realization',[1] such a plea can only lead to fruitful programmes of social change, if it is realised that the collectivist ruling class of the present time will be unmoved by humanistic considerations whenever these appear to conflict with the current canons of efficient and productive man management. Thus, to the degree that meaninglessness and social isolation in work are products of technical and organizational processes which make the employee an appendage of the machine, to that degree the introduction of new processes which call for more personal responsibility on the part of the operative and effective co-operation with others, as is the case with some forms of 'automation',[2] is likely to reduce alienation amongst the rank-and-file; but they will not be introduced if they are believed to raise the costs of production above that limit, which directors, on the basis of advice from their senior managers, decide is economically acceptable. This means that the sociologist in his further role of social reformer must show that these new costs are lower in fact than the costs which already accrue to the industrial collectivity from labour turn-over, absenteeism, sickness and strikes which, in part at least, can be demonstrated to result from such alienation. In this respect sociologists may assist rank-and-file workers to take advantage of the self-interest of their collectivist masters to make work rather more bearable. To the extent, too, that the co-ordination of a large and highly specialized work force is impossible without human relations' policies and without some involvement of the rank-and-file employee in the decision-making process, albeit at a very localized level, the demonstration that an increase in the formal opportunity to participate not only reduces a worker's sense of alienation from the industrial power structure but also increases his willingness to co-operate for

---

[1] Blauner, op. cit., p. 187.

[2] E. R. F. W. Crossman, *Automation and Skill*, Department of Scientific and Industrial Research, Problems of Progress in Industry, No. 9, H.M.S.O., 1960, *passim*.

productive purposes,[1] is another way in which the sociologist may take advantage of that same self-interest for more generally humanitarian ends.

All this, it must be admitted, implies that the sociologist accepts the collectivist class system and its exploitation of labour as *social facts*, however much on moral grounds he may abhor them; but this should not be interpreted as meaning that he thinks of them as eternal and immutable facts, or that he thinks of social science as divorced from the concern for human betterment. What it means, indeed, is that in his criticism of the *status quo* the sociologist is unmoved by Utopian assumptions that any kind of change is as good as any other. Because he cannot, *in the present state of knowledge*, put forward proposals which will abolish exploitation altogether and replace the present class system by a genuinely classless society, he prefers to make no proposals on this point at all. Instead, he demands more research, and a greater application of scientific procedures to the problem in hand. In this respect, it may be said, that just as politics is the art of the possible, sociology is its science. Whereas in the past men blundered from one social experiment to another by rule of thumb and rarely, if ever, achieved their objectives, modern man may make use of social scientific techniques; but he will not find an answer to all his problems immediately. The continuous amendment of hypotheses about the nature of social relationships in the light of ever-accumulating knowledge must necessarily underpin all valid proposals for social reform. It is in the light of this conviction that the present attempt to amend the Marxist framework of ideas has been pursued.

[1] See, for example, N. C. Morse and E. Reimer, 'The Experimental Change of a Major Organizational Variable', *The Journal of Abnormal and Social Psychology*, Vol. 52, 1956, pp. 120–9.

SUBJECT INDEX

Subject Index

INDEX OF SOURCES

319

Index of Sources

Index of Sources